IN
NIRMALA'S
KITCHEN

EVERYDAY WORLD CUISINE

LAKE ISLE PRESS

IN
NIRMALA'S
KITCHEN

EVERYDAY WORLD CUISINE

BY NIRMALA NARINE

FOREWORD BY ERIC RIPERT, *LE BERNARDIN*

PHOTOGRAPHY BY TINA RUPP

LAKE ISLE PRESS

Recipes copyright © 2006 by Nirmala Narine

Cover photography copyright © 2006 Tina Rupp

Published by:
Lake Isle Press, Inc.
16 West 32nd Street, Suite 10-B
New York, NY 10001
(212) 273-0796
E-mail: lakeisle@earthlink.net

Distributed to the trade by:
National Book Network, Inc.
4501 Forbes Boulevard, Suite 200
Lanham, MD 20706
1(800) 462-6420
www.nbnbooks.com

Library of Congress Control Number: 2006930192

ISBN-13: 978-1-891105-26-5

ISBN-10: 1-891105-26-4

Food photography © 2006 Tina Rupp
Complete list of photo credits: see page 301

Book and cover design: Ellen Swandiak

Editors: Rowann Gilman, Pimpila Thanaporn, Katherine Trimble

This book is available at special sales discounts for bulk purchases as premiums or special editions, including customized covers. For more information, contact the publisher at (212) 273-0796 or by e-mail, lakeisle@earthlink.net

First edition

Printed in the United States of America

10 9 8 7 6 5 4 3 2 1

DEDICATION

For my grandfather Payo, who enlightened my
soul, who helped me develop a sense of
adventure for exotic foods and cultures, and
who instilled in me compassion and courage
with no bounds.

And for all the homeless children whose paths
I've crossed in my travels—I wish I could
spend eternity cooking for you.

ACKNOWLEDGMENTS

To my mom, daddy, and my three brothers, Kishore, Rudy, and Visho, with deepest gratitude. My sisters-in-law, Lelia and Lolita, for bringing into this world my two gorgeous princesses, Nadine and Nadiya, and my two handsome princes, Shane and the brilliant David and his wife, Nehal. For my Uncle Gopi, who brought me to my new home so I could live the American dream.

To my publisher Hiroko Kiiffner, who believed in me from the start. You embody grace, humor, and entrepreneurship; and to your talented, professional team, my editors Pimpila Thanaporn and the divine Kate Trimble, my gratitude for your diligence and enthusiastic support; and Ellen Swandiak, one artistic book designer. Rowann Gilman, the editor for this book, who tamed my rambling prose.

Tina Rupp, one talented photographer, for seeing me and my food through her gifted third eye. Toni Brogan, the food stylist, and Stephanie Basralian, the prop stylist, for their extraordinary work.

My stylist, Renee Majour, for staying by my side at those never-ending photo shoots.

My sexy diva of recipe testing, Jill Anton, for sharing my vision with patience and hard work, and for giving me your honest opinion, not to mention toning down the hot spices. Thanks to Barry Friedman for being the guinea pig and little Sammy for posing with dishes. Tifphani White, my very own high-maintenance Nubian princess, for always being there, supporting and encouraging me with your kind words. You are priceless and the most loyal girlfriend anyone could ever hope to have.

And to the talented, dynamic team at Nirmala's Kitchen who have talent, big hearts, and creative souls. I thank Ben Gutkin for giving me honest feedback and listening to my sometimes raw, outrageous ideas. Most importantly, I am grateful for our friendship. Barbara Berger, the most expensive chocolate addict I know and graphic designer extraordinaire; Alex Liu for feeding my appetite for the latest tech tools; Jacqueline Duran, Corinne Bernstein, Karen Comerford, Jose Figueroa Martinez, and Yasmine Duran for your diligence. My attorneys, the beautiful Kim Schefler, Hyman Hacker, and Julien Neals for all your sensitivity, experience, and wisdom. My bankers Dwight Genias and Rafael Nisimov. All of you make me feel totally secure.

To my Fancy Food Show family, Gerry Shamdosky and Anthere Motayne, who embraced me from day one, and the other wonderful staff members: Roger Grant, Phyliss Mintz, Marsha Echols, Chris Crocker, Patrick Lynch, Ava Jagarnauth, Stephanie Morris, Tressa Kennedy, Cindy Eisemann, Sareth Neak, Jennifer Maslow, Ron Tanner, and Denise Shoukas, my Greek Goddess.

To all the talented food editors, radio, and television personalities who have interviewed me throughout the years. I thank you for all your kind words and encouragement and give special thanks to the Queen Bee of the *New York Times*, the divine Ms. Florence Fabricant.

With very special thanks to all my friends: Grey Sullivan and Patricia Sullivan, an extraordinary woman of endurance; Laurie Holz, my Tiger Lily, who encouraged me to write (see what happens); Eric Ripert, who has the heart and soul of a sage and is a pioneer, and a gift to our palates, thanks for your friendship and wisdom; talented and adventurous chef, Michelle Lindsay—we are soul sisters; Chris Muller, your diligence is omnipresent, orchestrating the kitchen with grace and panache; Mandy Oser—the goddess with eight arms, Stephane Creiser, for memorable days in Africa; Michael King aka "big and sexy," Jennifer Murray and Emily Patten for always thinking of me; my papi chuelo Felix Villa, I have tremendous respect for you, Jamie Brent, Anne Evanoff, Joanna Rosenberg, Brooke Supernaw, Jaeca Yuzon, Sandy Kortright, Hargit Grewall, Cairo Marsh, Sammy DiGennaro, Lucinia Lugo, Maria Bandel, Ann Richter, Fernado Maneca, Vic Thompson, Angelo and Mario Autiero, Joe Pontevolpe, Jessica Malave, Jorge Manahan, Saori Kawano, Richard Goldberg, Scott Liebowitz, Maya Kaimal, Paul Naraine, Richard Chin, Joan Bussdieker, Donna Enache, Dave Whelan, Pat Vargas, Rob Webber, Paul Romanelli, May Song, Marisa Ghezzi, Savi Virsawmi, Errol Schweizer, Ed Piston, and Scott R. Price (SRP).

All the professors at universities and museums around the world, especially the Cairo Museum, who have indulged me with history and culture.

My auntie Ms. Sylvie Narine-Adhar, the former headmistress of Tagore Memorial High School in Guyana, and to the rest of my family and friends throughout the Caribbean.

And lastly, to the melodious voices of Edith Piaf, Nina Simone, and the ghazals of Jagjit Singh and Abida Parveen, my companions while writing, and to all those I have met on my travels around the world, you are the true inspiration and the heart and soul of *In Nirmala's Kitchen*.

TABLE OF CONTENTS

FOREWORD

Nirmala is unique and while I could create an endless list of words to describe her…passionate, full of life, wise, fearless…no words could ever accurately capture her spirit and the joy that she brings to everyone around her when she enters a room.

A friend first introduced me to Nirmala. I remember her calling to say there was an amazing woman she had just met and that I must meet her and try her spices. Needless to say, once I met Nirmala, I was immediately captivated.

Nirmala travels the world and seeks out the exotic. She then brings it home to share and, in doing so, inspires creativity in those around her. For example, she will return from some far-off locale, stop at *Le Bernardin* and bring me a brand-new spice I have never seen or a new blend that she has created. When she arrives at my kitchen door, she spreads so much positive energy, and everyone is a little bit more excited about their work after her visits.

I believe Nirmala has a special ability to see things a little bit differently than the rest of us, and a true talent for discovering wonderful things that you or I may overlook. We like to refer to her as the Indiana Jones of spices.

When I first had the opportunity to flip through a copy of *In Nirmala's Kitchen*, I completely stopped what I was doing. I love this book. What you'll find in it are wonderful recipes that are exciting and authentic. She has created dishes with unexpected combinations of flavors. You will definitely learn new things…whether it be about technique or the ingredients. Yet the recipes are simple, straightforward, and fun to cook.

But what really brings these recipes alive are the stories and photographs from Nirmala's travels that guide you through the book. Nirmala lives her life like an adventure and in this book she brings you along. It is a real treat, and I guarantee you will want to read every word, from the essays at the beginning of each section to the anecdotes from her childhood and travels that accompany the recipes.

This book will inspire you to get into your kitchen and cook and perhaps it just might move you to embark on your own travels. I know it will inspire you as it's already inspired me.

Eric Ripert
Executive Chef/Co-owner
Le Bernardin

INTRODUCTION

When I was just four years old, my grandfather chopped down all the guava trees in our backyard because I whiled away my days frolicking in them like a happy monkey. Thus began my introduction to domesticity and the cooking life. My culinary lessons started in our Guyanese kitchen, no bigger than a walk-in closet. My grandfather's podium was the hammock, adjacent to the doorway of our wood plank house and secured to sturdy stilts outside. This outdoor set-up was strictly my grandfather's domain; in our family, men never entered the kitchen, not even for a cup of water. Cooking, serving, and cleaning were solely women's work.

With my grandfather's guidance, I survived in our tiny but functional kitchen, which had neither running water nor electricity. My essential cooking tools were always within arm's reach: my dad's old sugarcane machete and my masala brick, which appears on the cover of this book. My masala brick is now more than 150 years old. It belonged to my great-great-grandmother who brought it with her to Guyana when she left India. It had been her dowry gift and was highly treasured. The masala brick was, and still is, my blender, grater, and mixer, and can ably replace the most expensive food processor available on the market today.

As I cooked our family meals, my grandfather swept my imagination away to far-off lands, even though he was just a hammock away. He would read to me from the sutras *Upanishads*, *Mahabharata*, and *Ramayana*—Hindu books that are meant as a kind of guide to metaphysics and the complexities of the human condition. Or he might read histories and stories about ancient civilizations. He taught me about the world's religions and also, not surprisingly, about different foods and ingredients, including the very flowers, herbs, and spices that my ancestors brought with them from India. They found imaginative new ways to fuse them with the mélange of edibles in our new West Indian and South American home.

My arduous gastronomic lessons were based on the principles of ayurvedic cooking, which traditionally were taught only to the men in our family. I was an exception. Ayurveda, which means "knowledge of life" in Sanskrit, is meant to prevent health disorders, maintain a high quality of life through the practice of yoga, increase one's longevity, and create harmony and balance within oneself. Among the basics of ayurvedic beliefs is that the foods we put in our bodies are reflections of who we are, and eventually we become that food. Each ingredient in my repertoire of menus possessed significant benefits for my family's physical well-being. My grandfather keenly perceived that my karma with food would eventually take me to the far-away lands we had read about, and he was right; as an adult I have been able to visit many of them. When I left our tiny village for the shores of America, I landed in the most astonishing place of all: Queens, New York. What better mecca could I have chosen? The Queens I still call home embraces more than 167 nationalities from around the world; and more than 116 different languages are spoken here. Over the years, my neighbors, of diverse backgrounds, have nourished my cultural roots and fed my appetite for exotic cuisines.

As cooks near and far shared their culinary specialties and secrets with me, I felt I should share the excitement of discovery with like-minded adventurers. That thought made me put pen to paper. In this book you'll find chapter introductions providing interesting facts, anecdotes about the country you're about to explore, and a brief history of its culinary influences. You will also find a description of essential ingredients for each cuisine, items you should have on hand. Recipes are presented menu-style, and are intended to be a feast for the eyes and an adventure for the senses. All have been inspired by my extensive travels around the globe, many further away than even my grandfather could have imagined. The far-flung villages, markets, and street food vendors of the world were my main sources for authentic regional cuisines, though many recipes came from the homes of everyday people who invited me to their family tables. I have included an extensive glossary of exotic delights with which you can experiment, most to be found in supermarkets, specialty stores, and online sources. It is my hope the glossary will familiarize you with the key ingredients that determine the signature tastes and textures of foods from regions around the world.

This book is intended for cooks of every kind: the curious, the adventurous, even the beginner. If you have children, why not cook with them and share the information? It's a wonderful way to teach them about the limitless variety of cultures, beliefs, customs, and foods of the world.

I hope you will allow *In Nirmala's Kitchen* to transport your palate and imagination to the many streets and exotic locations I've explored, without leaving the comforts of home. My grandfather would heartily approve.

GUYANA

Guyana, the name alone evokes a never-ending memory of my childhood. • As sparkling as a Maharaja's crown, my night skies are studded with stars as I lay to sleep on my woodsy straw-filled mattress. In the morning, I am serenaded by the symphony of our village—the crowing of cocks, sporadic high notes from braying donkeys, and the chiming of yellow-belly birds as they feast on our guavas. I lie awake in bed, as the branches of our coconut tree lazily poke through my mother's crisp white curtains. Outside, the cool Atlantic wind sweeps up fragrances of citrus, warm spices, and herbs. At midday, the blazing sun fills me with energy and with my leathery bare feet I climb and explore every fruit tree imaginable. Mid-afternoon, I am drenched in equatorial rains. In the evening, my primitive, arduous kitchen duties call. • My beloved Guyana, on the coast of the Atlantic Ocean, is bordered by Venezuela, Brazil, and Suriname, making it a combination of the best of the Caribbean and South America. It is a mosaic of many cultures, beginning with the native Arawak Indians, or Amerindians, who named her (*Guyana* is derived from a word meaning "land of many waters"). In the early 1600s, the Dutch settled in the lower coast along the Essequibo River, where they traded with the Arawak tribe and established sugar

NIRMALA'S GUIDE TO
THE FLAVORS OF GUYANA

Indispensable to the Guyanese pantry are: Rice, chiles, green onions, curry powder, and vegetables such as cabbage, okra, and long beans. Peas, including black-eyed peas, pigeon peas, and yellow split peas, are also common ingredients, usually accompanying a rice dish. Coconut oil is widely used by villagers, but now that corn and vegetable oils are available, they are used as well. Condiments, including hot pepper sauce made with fresh habanero peppers and chutneys made with fresh bilimbi (a cousin of the star fruit) or green mango are also on almost every Guyanese table. These add plenty of heat to every meal.

plantations labored by African slaves. At the same time, the British established their own plantations on the coast of Suriname. The English and the Dutch fought many battles over the territory of both countries, but by 1796, the English had prevailed. Then, in 1834, the British abolished slavery. Seeking another source of labor, they brought indentured servants from China, Germany, Portugal, Ireland, Scotland, and Malta. They also looked to India, and that is when my people entered the picture. My great-great grandparents were among these indentured servants. In 1966 Guyana won its independence from Britain; it remains the only English-speaking country in South America. • Guyanese cuisine has a number of influences, beginning with the native Arawaks. Their staples include: taro root, corn, yams, cassava, and peanuts, along with fresh fish and wild game. The Arawak are also to be credited for their barbecue technique, called "barbacoa," which involved fabricating grills out of sticks. African slaves, particularly from West Africa, introduced staples such as okra, pigeon peas, plantains, callaloo (a leafy, spinach-like vegetable), and breadfruit. As for my great-great grandparents, they brought their aromatic Indian spice blends. You can imagine the limitless ways in which these varied ingredients and cooking techniques have combined to create an entirely new cuisine.

MENU GUYANA

APERITIF
• COCONUT WATER MARTINI (THE "NIRMALA")

APPETIZER
• YELLOW SPLIT PEA FRITTERS with GREEN MANGO CHUTNEY

SOUP
• GUYANESE FISH SOUP with PLANTAINS, YUCCA, AND SWEET POTATOES

SALAD
• FRAGRANT FLOWER SALAD with PASSION FRUIT VINAIGRETTE

ENTREE
• PAN-SEARED GARAM MASALA DUCK with ROTI

DESSERT
• AUNTY DAISY'S GUINNESS STOUT MUFFINS with BROWN SUGAR-RUM SAUCE

" 'Mayo,' my grandmother, perfected her unique elixir of gin smoothed with coconut water in honor of special celebrations, such as having the good fortune to cook a meat dish for dinner. When her gin supply needed topping-up, she'd point me to her shawl drawer where she had tucked away an old, frosted Gilbey's gin bottle. There, I'd secretly tilt my head back to get the last few mouth-puckering drops of liquor—it was a wicked, tingly sensation. Mayo would wrap the bottle as tenderly as she would a dozen eggs and place it in my market basket. Off I'd go to the local rum shop, wobbling into the street, dodging ringing bicycles and braying donkeys, pretending I was the village drunk. Presenting the bottle at the shop, they'd fill it up a quarter of the way with gin. No wonder this cocktail always brings happy memories. These days, I make this cocktail for my three brothers with vodka, who have dubbed it the 'Nirmala.' "

COCONUT WATER MARTINI
(THE "NIRMALA")

SERVES 2

1 cup canned clear coconut water (do not use coconut milk or milk from dried coconut)
2 + 1/2 ounces vodka
4 to 6 ice cubes
2 red Thai chiles, pricked several times with a toothpick
Lime twists or fresh coconut slices for garnish

1. Pour coconut water and vodka into a shaker. Add the ice cubes and shake well. Strain into chilled martini glasses, drop in the chiles, and garnish with lime twists or coconut slices.

Note: To add an extra kick to your vodka, try dropping two or three whole Thai chiles in the bottle and storing it in the freezer.

COCONUT WATER MARTINI

School children throughout Guyana love these round, golden "bara," or snacks—a traditional recipe brought to us from India. In Trinidad and Tobago, where they are called 'doubles,' they are flat, a bit larger, and filled with savory chickpeas. We used to buy these spicy treats from street vendors in the market or during recess in our schoolyard. The sweet-sour Green Mango Chutney complements their heat perfectly. Try serving them as party appetizers, as the Guyanese do at almost any social occasion. Your vegetarian friends will love them too. ""

YELLOW SPLIT PEA FRITTERS
with GREEN MANGO CHUTNEY

MAKES 15 FRITTERS

1 cup yellow split pea flour
1/2 cup self-rising flour
2 teaspoons curry powder
1 teaspoon baking powder
1 teaspoon salt
1/2 cup spinach leaves, julienned
1 teaspoon minced Thai or birdseye chile
1 tablespoon minced shallot
2 teaspoons minced garlic
Vegetable oil for deep-frying
Green Mango Chutney (recipe follows)

1. In a large bowl, sift together the split pea flour, self-rising flour, curry powder, baking powder, and salt. Add the spinach leaves, chile, shallot, and garlic and mix well. Slowly drizzle about 1/2 cup water into the mixture until a soft dough forms and sticks to your fingers. Cover with plastic wrap and let sit at room temperature for 30 minutes.

2. Preheat a small, deep saucepan over medium-high heat. Add oil to a depth of 3 inches; heat oil until a deep-fry thermometer reads 365°.

3. Wet your fingers with water. Take about 1 tablespoon of the batter, shape it into a ball and carefully drop in the oil. Continue to make fritters, frying them in small batches, turning once until golden brown on both sides, about 2 minutes. Remove fritters with a slotted spoon and drain on paper towels. Serve with Green Mango Chutney.

GREEN MANGO CHUTNEY

MAKES 2 CUPS

2 large green (unripe) mangoes, peeled and chopped (about 3 cups)

1 small fresh Thai or Serrano chile, stemmed and roughly chopped

1 large garlic clove, chopped

1/4 cup loosely packed cilantro leaves, coarsely chopped

1 tablespoon freshly squeezed lime juice

3/4 cup freshly squeezed orange juice, plus more if necessary

4 teaspoons sugar

Sea salt

1. Combine all ingredients in a blender or food processor and process to desired thickness. Add more orange juice to thin mixture if necessary.

Make Ahead Tip: Green Mango Chutney can be stored in an airtight plastic container and refrigerated for up to 2 weeks.

Variation: If you cannot find green mangoes, substitute peeled, cored, and chopped green apples.

School children from my village in Guyana.

In Guyana, Saturday is usually the day for preparing one-pot meals or soups. It's a tradition that began with native Guyanese, the Amerindians, whose staple one-dish meal was called 'Pepperpot.' This dish was later adapted by African slaves who relied on whatever ingredients they could scavenge and assemble to create a savory, nourishing meal. Fortunately, we no longer have to depend on leftovers to enjoy this fresh-flavored fish soup.

GUYANESE FISH SOUP
with PLANTAINS, YUCCA, AND SWEET POTATOES

SERVES 4

2 tablespoons all-purpose flour
1 teaspoon curry powder
1 teaspoon salt
1 pound firm-fleshed fish fillets such as red snapper or kingfish, cut into 2-inch squares
1/4 cup vegetable oil
2 cups canned unsweetened coconut milk
5 cups low-sodium chicken stock
1 cup cassava or yucca, peeled and cut into 2-inch cubes
1 medium green plantain, cut in 4-inch lengthwise strips
1 whole fresh habanero chile or 2 birdseye chiles, chopped (optional)
4 garlic cloves, thinly sliced
1 medium onion, chopped
1 teaspoon dried thyme
1 can (12 ounces) black eyed peas, drained
1 sweet potato, peeled and cut into 2-inch cubes
Minced green onions, for garnish

1. In a medium bowl, whisk together the flour, curry powder, and salt. Add the fish, turning to coat with mixture.

2. Heat a deep saucepan over medium-high heat and add the oil. When oil is hot, fry the fish in small batches of about 4 to 5 pieces at a time. Fry until fish is golden and crispy, turning once, about 1 to 2 minutes per side. Remove fish from pan, drain on paper towels, and set aside.

3. In a large stockpot, combine 1 cup of the coconut milk and the chicken stock and bring to a boil over high heat. Add the cassava or yucca, plantain, habanero chile, garlic, onion, and thyme. Reduce heat to medium-low and cook until the vegetables are fork tender, about 30 minutes.

4. Add the remaining 1 cup coconut milk, black eyed peas, sweet potato, and the fried fish. Season with salt to taste, reduce heat to low, and cook for 7 to 8 minutes more, stirring to evenly combine ingredients.

5. Garnish with minced green onions and serve.

Variations: You may substitute the same amount of potatoes or rutabagas for cassava or yucca, if desired.

Note: Habanero (sometimes called Scotch bonnet) is the hottest of all chiles so be careful not to let it break when cooking if you want a milder soup. I prefer a lot of heat, so I boldly break it in my soup.

“ Ever since I was two years old and throughout my childhood, my grandfather, 'Payo,' gave me yoga lessons. One morning, on our way toward the ocean where we were to seek our 'third eyes' and embrace our chakras, Payo and I walked a narrow pathway overrun with dewy blades of grass, fragrant white jasmine, nectar-filled hibiscus blossoms, fresh basil, and passion fruit dangling from the vines above. As Payo chanted his mantras, yoga beads dangling from his fingertips, my own yoga beads became a belly chain and my tiny fingers plucked everything edible in sight. I filled my pockets as if they were little salad bowls. Most of our meals consisted of one course, so salad wasn't something I grew up with. But when I got home from our yoga expedition, I'd empty my pockets of riches, and enjoy a treat that was bursting with colors, aromas, and flavors…the ones that inspired this beautiful salad. ”

FRAGRANT FLOWER SALAD
with PASSION FRUIT VINAIGRETTE

SERVES 4

4 cups butter lettuce or baby salad greens, washed and dried
10 small basil leaves
1/4 cup canned or bottled passion fruit juice
1/4 cup extra virgin olive oil
2 tablespoons balsamic vinegar
1 teaspoon Honey-Dijon mustard
Sea salt and freshly ground pepper
1 cup whole edible flowers

1. In a large salad bowl, combine lettuce and basil leaves; set aside.

2. In a small bowl, combine the passion fruit juice, olive oil, vinegar, mustard, and a pinch of sea salt, whisking vigorously to combine. Season with salt and pepper to taste. To serve, divide lettuce evenly among 4 deep salad bowls and drizzle with vinaigrette. Garnish with edible flowers.

The house I grew up in.

> For a time, wheat flour was contraband in Guyana. We used flour to make roti—a flavorful, flaky flatbread that was indispensable to Guyanese breakfasts and special occasions. Since rice was a staple in Guyana, my mother tried her best to stress the importance of it, emphasizing its strengthening powers for working in the fields. As a child, every meal I cooked was accompanied by rice—I even pounded it on my masala brick to make rice flour roti which my brothers and I detested. Real flour roti was what we yearned for, but in vain...until my youngest brother's fifth birthday. Our mother called my three brothers and me into our tiny kitchen and closed the door. To our amazement, she plopped down a piping hot, puffed-up, real flour roti. We were speechless with joy! We all tore into that one perfectly round roti, speckled brown from the griddle, and all of its thin, flaky layers. All the while, my mother pressed her fair, moon-shaped face against the wooden slats of our kitchen, scanning the road for unwanted visitors as we feasted, whispering to eat quickly before the police came. I never forgot that day. These flaky roti of my childhood are a wonderful contrast to the spiced duck and help tame their chile heat.

PAN-SEARED GARAM MASALA DUCK with ROTI

SERVES 4 TO 6

2 tablespoons chopped shallot
2 garlic cloves, chopped
3 fresh Thai or Serrano chiles, seeded and chopped
2 teaspoons garam masala
2 teaspoons curry powder
1 + 1/2 cups canned unsweetened coconut milk
2 boneless duck breasts (about 2 pounds), cut into 1-inch cubes

1. Make the masala paste: In a food processor or blender, combine the shallot, garlic, chiles, garam masala, curry powder, and 1/4 cup of the coconut milk. Blend until smooth and set aside.

2. Heat a heavy skillet until very hot. Add the duck breasts and sauté over high heat until browned on all sides, about 5 minutes. Remove duck and transfer to a plate lined with paper towels. Cover with aluminum foil to keep warm.

3. Discard all but 2 tablespoons of duck fat from the skillet. Reduce heat to medium and heat remaining fat, adding the masala paste. Sauté for 2 minutes, stirring frequently until mixture is well combined. Whisk in the remaining 1 + 1/4 cups coconut milk until well combined. Bring mixture to a boil, then reduce heat and simmer until the mixture thickens, about 8 to 10 minutes. Add the duck and simmer until the duck is hot and cooked through, about 3 to 5 minutes. Serve with Roti or rice.

ROTI (ROUND FLATBREAD)

MAKES 6 ROTI

3 cups all-purpose flour, plus more for dusting
1/2 teaspoon baking powder
3 tablespoons ghee or vegetable oil, plus more for coating pan

1. In a large bowl, combine the flour and baking powder. Gradually add about 1 + 1/4 cups water until dough is smooth and soft. Knead dough for 3 minutes, then cover with a damp cloth and let rest for 30 minutes.

2. Knead dough a second time for 3 minutes then divide into 6 small balls. Lightly flour a work surface, and working with one ball at a time, roll each out to an 8-inch circle. Brush each circle of dough with about 2 teaspoons of ghee or oil. Using a small, sharp knife, slit the dough from the center of the circle to the edge and loosely roll dough into a cone shape. Press the peak into the center of the cone with the palm of your hand to flatten. (This technique will make the roti flaky, like a croissant.) Repeat with remaining balls of dough. Cover with a damp kitchen towel and allow to rest for 15 minutes.

3. Heat a griddle or 12-inch sauté pan over medium-high heat and lightly coat with ghee or oil. On a lightly floured surface, roll each portion of dough until it is very thin, about 8 to 10 inches in diameter. Carefully pick up the dough and place it on the hot griddle. Cook each roti for about 1 minute. If you lift it slightly you should see specks of brown on the underside. Flip roti over with a spatula and using a pastry brush, coat with additional ghee or oil. Cook until both sides of roti are nicely toasted with specks of brown; remove from griddle and keep warm while making the remaining roti.

Variation: You may substitute whole-wheat flour for all-purpose flour.

❝ It's ironic that Guyana's British occupation brought with it a symbol of Irish pride, Guinness Stout. We made good use of it—in baking and making soups—as well as enjoying it as a drink. My first encounter with Guinness Stout happened when I was eight years old. At the time all of my friends had rubber flip-flops, and I decided that I could no longer walk to school barefoot on the hot pitch road. So I started my own herb patch to raise some rubber flip-flop money. Trying to sell my produce became a dilemma: the men in my family did not want me to leave the village, but the women, especially my grandmother, thought it would be a good experience. Finally, it was agreed that after my Saturday chores were done, I could sell my crop, but was forbidden to go past our village. Some five villages and a half-empty basket later, I came to a house with a huge gray mud oven in the yard, tiny puffs of smoke escaping from a handmade zinc chimney. There was a nutty aroma of toasted coconut, burnt brown sugar, and fresh nutmeg that made me all but forget the hot road under my bare feet. A frail, old Afro-Guyanese woman came out of the house and invited me into her yard. Fears of Hansel and Gretel weren't enough to keep me from these wonderful smells. Her name was Aunty Daisy, and she was the great-great-granddaughter of a slave. We became fast friends, and every Saturday after selling my produce I'd spend hours at her house, where she taught me how to bake in her mud oven. One of my happiest chores was going to buy bottles of Guinness and helping her bake these decadent muffins. I was especially excited to have the job of cutting the empty ghee tins that she used as her "baking pans." You will quickly become addicted to these treats, and you'll find dozens of other ways to use the delicious, rum-rich topping, a favorite of mine on pancakes. ❞

AUNTY DAISY'S GUINNESS STOUT MUFFINS
with BROWN SUGAR-RUM SAUCE

MAKES 6 MUFFINS

8 tablespoons (1 stick) unsalted butter, softened, plus more
  for buttering tins
1/2 cup sugar
1 + 1/2 cups all-purpose flour
1 teaspoon baking powder
1 teaspoon pure vanilla extract
1/2 teaspoon salt
2 large eggs
1/2 cup Guinness Stout or other good quality stout
1/2 cup coarsely chopped pitted dates
Brown Sugar-Rum Sauce (recipe follows)
Confectioners sugar for dusting

1. Position oven rack in the center of the oven and preheat to 350°F. Lightly brush standard 6-muffin tin with melted butter and set aside.

2. In a medium bowl, cream together the butter and sugar until smooth. Add the flour, baking powder, vanilla, salt, and eggs. Mix until batter is smooth and well combined. Add the stout and dates; stir until just combined.

3. Spoon the batter into muffin tins and transfer to oven. Bake until a toothpick inserted into center of a muffin comes out clean, about 20 to 25 minutes. Turn muffins onto a rack and let cool slightly. Drizzle with Brown Sugar-Rum sauce and lightly dust with confectioners sugar. Serve immediately.

BROWN SUGAR-RUM SAUCE

MAKES ABOUT 3/4 CUP

6 tablespoons unsalted butter, softened
6 tablespoons dark brown sugar, loosely packed
6 tablespoons heavy cream
4 tablespoons El Dorado Rum or other good quality dark rum

1. In a heavy saucepan, combine the butter, brown sugar, and cream and slowly bring to a boil over medium heat. When boiling, add the rum and stir briskly to combine.

AUNTY DAISY'S GUINNESS STOUT MUFFINS

CARIBBEAN

"Get yuh straw hat 'cause we goin' island hoppin' in deh Caribbean." • Fine-as-powder sand and turquoise waters are the perfect setting for soaking up sunshine and relaxing to the tunes of carnival—from soothing steel drums to the rhythmic beat of soca, reggae, and rumba. With a glass of good rum by my side and a Trinidad Fundadores cigar in hand, I am truly content. • What we call the Caribbean, often referred to as the West Indies, is a group of islands in the Caribbean Sea, and it includes Cuba, Jamaica, Trinidad and Tobago, the Dominican Republic, Puerto Rico, the Bahamas...and dozens of other magical places. Guyana, my birthplace, maintains not only a major political connection, but cultural and culinary ties to the Caribbean as well. • Caribbean fare is shaped by a melange of influences. Its pantry offers a taste of the world, both old and new, beginning with the indigenous Arawak Indians. Their staple crops, yucca, sweet potato, pumpkin, chiles, tomatoes, and corn, were grown in abundance and continue to be widely cultivated today. • In the 15th century, the Spaniards arrived bringing goats, cattle, chickens, and pigs. Pork fat was—and is—widely used in Cuban, Jamaican, and Puerto Rican kitchens. The Spanish also brought delights such as oranges, cumin, saffron, and exotic fruits. Among the cooking techniques they

THE FLAVORS OF THE CARIBBEAN

Must-haves for preparing the many foods of the Caribbean are thyme, shallots, oregano, parsley, culantro (a cousin of cilantro), green onions, and curry powder. Also necessary are vegetables and tubers such as yams, sweet potatoes, cabbage, okra, and ackee (a native tree fruit). Many beans and peas are used in Caribbean fare, including black-eyed peas, pigeon peas, black beans, and yellow split peas. These usually accompany or are used in combination with rice dishes. Carambola (star fruit) and green mangoes appear on nearly every island table in the form of hot pepper-enhanced chutneys. As the islands are surrounded by the ocean, there is a king's ransom of fresh seafood, and goat, lamb, and pork are also staples.

introduced was ceviche, a method of cooking seafood using citrus juices, which they adapted from the Moors of their homeland. The Portuguese soon followed, introducing *baccalá* (salt cod), sugarcane, cilantro, and parsley. • From the 1500s to the 1800s, the Dutch, French, and British all had a hand in ruling the West Indies. Capitalizing on Caribbean commodities such as sugarcane, cotton, rice, and coffee, these European empires set up numerous plantations. Slaves from West Africa were brought over as labor, and for nearly 400 years they toiled the land. These slaves preserved their heritage and dignity by forming communities that cherished their religion, food, music, and traditions. They planted their home gardens with seeds brought from their homeland—okra, callaloo (a leafy, spinach-like green), millet, and the treasured "grains of paradise," or melegueta peppers. The Africans were known for their one-pot meals, made from scraps discarded by their owners. Some of these dishes, such as coo-coo, a corn meal polenta with okra, are still savored throughout the Caribbean today. Add to this cultural mix the indentured servants who arrived from China and India, and the Jews who fled European persecution in the 18th and 19th centuries, and you have a true "melting pot" cuisine. • Today, each island, whether British, French, Dutch, or Danish carries a bounty of fresh meats and produce. Street food vendors and local markets offer up the best sampling of

Caribbean flavors—fried fish stuffed into breads, fish fritters, fried empanadas, sweet potato and yucca chips, black pudding, spicy roasted nuts—and more, all complemented by habanero chile sauce, sofrito (a flavor base of many dishes that includes culantro, chiles, and sometimes onion and garlic), and a variety of chutneys. As for drinks, ice water is a constant savior, but juice made from fresh fruits such as soursop, guavas, sugarcane, and the beloved coconut water, are all winners as well. A favorite sweet enjoyed by all—rich, poor, young, and old—is shaved ice drizzled with red syrup and evaporated milk. It's how our palates seek refuge from the heat of our always-present, brilliant sun.

MENU **CARIBBEAN**

STREET FOOD STYLE

> I had the best mojito of my life in Cuba. It was made with a dash of fresh-squeezed sugar cane juice and Cuba's Havana Club rum, all of which mingled with the fresh, bright flavor of mint. To make it here at home, I replace the sugar cane juice with brown sugar or demerara sugar (unrefined brown sugar) instead of the regular white version. And I use the best rum I can find, particularly my favorite, El Dorado, from Guyana. Professional bartenders use a "muddler," which can be found at housewares stores, to crush the mint, sugar, and lime right in the glass, but you can also use a wooden pestle or the handle of a wooden spoon.

CUBAN MOJITO

SERVES 2

16 to 20 mint leaves, plus more for garnish
2 teaspoons brown sugar
2 thick lime slices
Ice
4 ounces good-quality dark rum
Lemon-lime soda, such as 7-Up brand

1. In a small pitcher, combine the mint, sugar, and lime. Crush the mixture with a wooden pestle, the back of a wooden spoon, or a muddler. Divide the mixture evenly between 2 highball glasses. Fill each glass with ice. Pour 2 ounces rum in each glass and top with lemon-lime soda. Stir and garnish with fresh mint.

> Any time I'd visit her food stall in Trinidad's San Fernando, Auntie Dolly would greet me happily and murmur 'Gyal tek wan lil ting nah!' as she unearthed a bottle of Fernandes Vat 19 white rum from the depths of her food cart. With that, she'd spike my lemonade and add pieces of star fruit—my own authentic, volatile Trinni-style cocktail. I've left out the alcohol, but it's a real refresher anyway. It's a great treat for kids, who love to see the star fruit 'stars' floating in the glass. "

TRINNI STAR FRUIT LEMONADE

SERVES 4

1/2 cup freshly squeezed lime juice
1/4 cup superfine sugar
About 2 cups ice
1 star fruit (carambola), sliced crosswise into 1/4-inch thick "stars"

1. In a one-quart pitcher, combine 4 cups water, lime juice, and sugar; stir until the sugar is completely dissolved. Add more sugar to taste, if desired. Add ice and star fruit. Stir to combine and serve in tall glasses.

Variation: Turn the lemonade into a cocktail by stirring in 1 cup of light rum.

> This is my friend Rosa's famous smoothie recipe. It is lusciously thick, milky, and thoroughly delicious. (If you've never tried soursop, or guanabana as it is known in the Caribbean and Spanish-speaking countries, it is an unusual-looking tree fruit with a smooth, creamy-sweet interior. It's like eating fruity candy, and is often used for making sweets like ice cream, sherbert, and drinks like this one.) This smoothie is a wonderful way to introduce children to the flavor of spices, in this case, aromatic ground nutmeg. "

PUERTO RICAN SOURSOP SMOOTHIE

SERVES 4

1 package (14 ounces) frozen guanabana (soursop) pulp
1 cup canned sweetened condensed milk, chilled
2 cups ice-cold whole milk
1/2 teaspoon freshly ground nutmeg
Maraschino cherries for garnish

1. In a blender, combine the soursop pulp, condensed milk, whole milk, and nutmeg; blend until smooth and frothy. Pour into chilled glasses, garnish with cherries, and serve.

Almost every home garden in the Caribbean grows ginger, so ginger beer is a sensible and efficient drink throughout the islands. When a guest enters your home, he or she is always offered something to drink, and when there is no one home to climb the coconut tree for fresh coconuts, you simply uproot some fresh ginger from the garden and prepare a pitcher of ginger beer. My uncle Ramesh, who lives on Abaco Island in the Bahamas, has several gingerroots growing in his garden, and my grandfather, Payo, taught him how to make great ginger beer with them. This is my grandfather's original recipe, complete with bits of whole spice and sweetened with rich brown sugar.

BAHAMIAN GINGER BEER

SERVES 6 TO 8

1/2 pound peeled, fresh ginger
6 allspice berries
2 whole star anise
1/2 cup freshly squeezed lime juice
1 cup brown sugar
Mint sprigs for garnish

1. Grate the ginger on the widest holes of a box grater. In a large saucepan, combine 8 cups cold water with the ginger, allspice berries, and star anise. Bring to a boil over medium-high heat. Cover, reduce heat, and simmer for 15 minutes. Remove from heat, stir in lime juice and sugar; let cool completely.

2. Pour the mixture through a fine sieve into a pitcher and refrigerate until well chilled. To serve, pour ginger beer into tall glasses filled with ice and garnish with fresh mint.

Variation: This refreshing drink can also be enjoyed warm. Simply pour into mugs while still warm after straining the mixture.

“ A visit to Mrs. Reynolds' house in Barbados is never complete without downing some of her excellent Guava Rum Punch. In her house, though, the punch is the topic of much controversy. There is always the arduous choice of either the Cockspur Rum of her native Barbados, or the El Dorado rum of my native Guyana, which is her husband's country as well. I make it a point never to get in the middle of the family rum dispute, but no matter which one ends up winning the day's contest, her drink is always fabulous. The juice of the guavas is deceptively sweet, so you really don't taste the alcohol. It doesn't really hit you until you try to stand up. ”

“ This is a very popular street drink in Jamaica—it really helps cool you down after eating spicy 'jerk' dishes and other hot foods. It's so simple to make, and my niece Nadine absolutely adores it: it's like having a peanut butter milk shake. ”

BAJAN GUAVA RUM PUNCH

SERVES 4

2 cups canned or bottled guava juice or nectar
2 cups dark rum
1 cup pineapple juice
1/4 cup freshly squeezed lime juice
1/4 cup superfine sugar
A few dashes of Angostura bitters
2 cups crushed ice cubes
Maraschino cherries and pineapple wedges for garnish

1. In a one-quart pitcher, stir together all ingredients except the cherries and pineapple. Pour punch into four tumblers and garnish each with a wedge of fresh pineapple and a maraschino cherry.

JAMAICAN PEANUT PUNCH

SERVES 2

3 cups milk
6 tablespoons creamy-style peanut butter
3 tablespoons sugar
2 maraschino cherries for garnish

1. Combine the milk, peanut butter, and sugar in a blender and blend on low speed for 10 seconds. Increase speed to high and blend for 30 seconds more, or until frothy. Add additional sugar to taste and blend until it's dissolved. Pour punch into a pitcher and refrigerate until well chilled. When ready to serve, stir the punch and serve in tall glasses, garnished with maraschino cherries.

Variation: You can also make this punch with chunky-style peanut butter or Nutella (chocolate-hazelnut butter).

CUBAN VACA FRITA WITH YUCCA PANCAKES

> Vaca frita sounds more romantic than 'fried cow,' which is what it means. But this delicious shredded flank steak is juicy, crispy, and bursting with the flavor of lime. When I was in Cuba, I lived on this dish for days on end. I ordered it in *paladares*, which are private dining rooms that are set up in private homes. It's a unique way to dine, and an adventurous way to savor true Cuban home-cooked cuisine. Here is one of my favorite recipes for this Cuban classic. To balance the flavors and texture, I serve vaca frita with yucca pancakes instead of the plain boiled yucca that usually accompanies it in Cuba. "

CUBAN VACA FRITA
WITH YUCCA PANCAKES

SERVES 6 TO 8

3 pounds flank steak, excess fat removed
1 tablespoon salt
2 bay leaves
6 tablespoons freshly squeezed lime juice
6 garlic cloves, minced
Sea salt and freshly ground pepper
Scant 1/4 cup vegetable oil
Yucca Pancakes (recipe follows)
Finely chopped chives for garnish

1. Place the steak in a large pot and cover with 2 inches of cold water. Add salt and bay leaves. Cover and bring to a boil over high heat. Reduce heat to medium and cook until the meat is quite tender, about 1 + 1/2 hours, adding more water if necessary for the meat to remain covered.

2. Remove the steak and transfer it to a plate to cool. Discard the cooking liquid and bay leaves. Once the meat is cool enough to handle, cut it into 4-inch squares, then shred the squares into small pieces and set aside.

3. In a large non-reactive bowl, combine the lime juice, garlic, and shredded meat; toss to combine. Season with salt and pepper to taste. Cover with plastic wrap and refrigerate for 2 hours or overnight.

4. In a large, heavy skillet, heat the oil over medium-high heat until very hot. Remove beef from the bowl and using your hands or a clean kitchen towel, squeeze out excess marinade. Shape the beef into 2-inch patties, pressing firmly to hold their shape. Cook patties for 2 to 3 minutes on each side, or until crisp and golden. Transfer patties to a plate lined with paper towels and cover with aluminum foil while you continue to fry the remaining patties. Add more oil if necessary.

5. To serve, place each patty on a Yucca Pancake and sprinkle with chopped chives.

Variations: Vaca Frita can be served on top of a salad, alongside beans and rice or boiled potatoes, or stuffed into a baguette or other crusty bread.

YUCCA PANCAKES

MAKES 20 PANCAKES

1 cup all-purpose flour
1 + 1/2 cups yucca flour (do not substitute all-purpose flour)
1 teaspoon salt
2 large eggs, lightly beaten
1 + 1/2 cups milk

1. In a medium bowl, sift together the all-purpose flour, yucca flour, and salt. Add the eggs and milk and whisk until the batter is smooth. The mixture should resemble a thin pancake batter. If the batter seems too thick, add a little water until it reaches the right consistency.

2. Heat a large nonstick griddle or frying pan over medium-high heat. Pour about 2 tablespoons of the batter onto the griddle to form a pancake with a 3- to 4-inch diameter. Cook pancake until very lightly brown, about 1 to 2 minutes, turning it over when bubbles appear on the top. Cook about 1 minute on the second side, then transfer to a plate and cover with a warm towel. Keep warm. Repeat with remaining batter.

Even the chickens have it good in the Caribbean.

❝ Any time I visit Jamaica, I make my culinary pilgrimage to Clifford's food shack in Kingston. Unlike any other food shack, Clifford's boasts a full kitchen with lots of pots, some containing his famous 'Mannish Water' soup; others keep oil for frying at a boil. The shack is just a couple of sheets of old zinc and a few dried coconut branches, and his grill is an empty barrel that's been cut in half, blackened and gleaming from years of use. Hanging on a nail is his basket overflowing with fresh ingredients. There is always a jar of peanut butter on hand for making Peanut Punch. An old Sanyo tape deck is secured to a coconut branch, so that the soft tunes of Jimmy Cliff waft among the fragrant smoke and warm island breezes. It is completely romantic. To look at Clifford's shack, you'd never imagine the incredibly delicious foods that come out of it. One such dish is his Buttermilk Jerk Fried Chicken: exotic herbs and spices saturate the tender chicken, which is cooked until the meat falls off the bones. When in Jamaica, I like to wash it down with a few gulps of Mannish Water— it's made with a goat's head and its...well...what we call 'prairie oysters' up here. This version, which isn't as messy to prepare as Clifford's version, is nevertheless a truly Jamaican specialty. ❞

CLIFFORD'S
BUTTERMILK JERK FRIED CHICKEN

SERVES 4

1 chicken (about 3 pounds) cut into 10 pieces, each breast split in half
3 cups buttermilk
1 tablespoon plus 1 teaspoon kosher salt
6 tablespoons Jerk Paste (recipe follows)
1 tablespoon light rum
2 cups all-purpose flour
1 tablespoon curry powder
Vegetable oil for deep-frying
Sea salt

1. Rinse the chicken pieces and pat dry with paper towels. Make several 1/2-inch slits in each piece with a small paring knife.

2. Place buttermilk in a large bowl. Whisk in the 1 tablespoon salt, Jerk Paste, and rum. Add the chicken and rub the buttermilk mixture into each piece. Cover the bowl with plastic wrap and refrigerate for at least 3 hours or overnight, turning once so the chicken marinates evenly. Before frying, allow chicken to come to room temperature.

3. In a large shallow dish or pie plate, mix together the flour, curry powder, and remaining 1 teaspoon salt.

4. Line a baking sheet with parchment paper and set aside. Remove chicken from marinade and place on a wire rack to drain. Dip each piece of chicken in the flour mixture and tap to remove excess flour, then dip each in buttermilk mixture again, letting excess marinade drip off. Immediately coat with flour mixture again. Tap to remove excess flour and place on prepared baking sheet.

5. In a deep, heavy pot, heat enough vegetable oil for deep-frying (about 3 inches) over medium-high heat until a deep-fry thermometer reads 365°.

6. Fry the chicken in small batches until each piece is browned, about 15 to 18 minutes. An instant-read thermometer inserted into a piece should read 170°. Transfer chicken pieces to a wire rack and allow to drain. Season with salt to taste and serve immediately.

JERK PASTE

MAKES ABOUT 3/4 CUP

- 2 Scotch bonnet or habanero chiles, stems removed and cut in half
- 8 green onions, coarsely chopped
- 3 shallots, coarsely chopped
- 8 garlic cloves, coarsely chopped
- 3 tablespoons dried thyme leaves, or 2 tablespoons fresh thyme leaves
- 1 tablespoon ground allspice
- 1/4 cup extra virgin olive oil
- 1/4 cup freshly squeezed lime juice
- 1 teaspoon sea salt

1. Combine all ingredients in a food processor and process mixture into a smooth paste.

Note: When working with habanero chiles, use a pair of rubber or plastic gloves, as oils in the pepper will burn.

Make Ahead Tip: Jerk Paste can be made a week ahead. Cover and refrigerate.

" Trinidad and Tobago, the almost-joined twin islands in the Caribbean, share the same culinary influences as Guyana. The people are just wonderful, and my favorite Trinni, as the locals fondly refer to each other, is a woman I call Auntie Dolly. Dolly runs a small food stall in Trinidad's San Fernando. She serves up the best Shark and Bake, which are sandwiches made with fried shark steaks, although they can also be made with tuna, kingfish, mullet, or catfish. Auntie Dolly sometimes even makes her Shark and Bake with canned sardines or salmon. In Guyana, we used a fish called 'high water,' similar to catfish. They're all great substitutes, but no matter what kind of fish is used, the name of the dish never changes. "

TRINNI SHARK AND BAKE SANDWICHES

"SHARK"

MAKES 4 SANDWICHES

2 tablespoons extra virgin olive oil
1 medium red onion, finely diced
2 small red Thai or Serrano chiles, finely chopped
2 tablespoons tomato paste
2 cans (6 ounces each) salmon, drained and flaked
3 tablespoons freshly squeezed lime juice
Sea salt
3 tablespoons chopped parsley

1. Heat the oil in a small frying pan over medium-high heat. Add the onion and chiles and sauté until soft, about 3 minutes. Add the tomato paste and mix well until the paste is evenly distributed.

2. Add the salmon and lime juice; season with salt to taste. Continue to cook until all the liquid has evaporated, stirring frequently, about 5 minutes. Remove from heat, stir in the parsley and set aside to cool. Cover with plastic wrap and refrigerate until ready to use.

"BAKE"

MAKES 8 FRIED DOUGH RECTANGLES

2 + 1/4 cups all-purpose flour, plus more for rolling dough
1 tablespoon baking powder
1 teaspoon salt
8 tablespoons (1 stick) butter, melted
2 teaspoons sugar
Vegetable oil for frying

1. In a large bowl, sift together the flour, baking powder, and salt. Add the butter and sugar and mix with a fork until the butter is evenly distributed.

2. Slowly add about 1/2 cup water, then gently knead the dough until it forms a ball. Do not add too much water at a time or the dough will become too sticky. Continue to knead for 3 minutes more until the ball of dough becomes slightly elastic.

3. Pat the dough into a rectangle on a lightly floured surface. Roll out to 1/4-inch thickness, adding more flour if necessary. Cover with a damp towel and let rest for 10 minutes.

4. In a heavy skillet over medium heat, slowly heat enough oil for deep-frying (about 3 inches) until a deep-fry thermometer reads 365°.

5. Cut the dough into four 6-inch by 3-inch rectangles. Drop the dough into the oil and fry in small batches, turning them when they are just golden, about 2 minutes. When both sides are golden brown, remove fried "bakes" with a slotted spoon and transfer to a plate lined with paper towels. Allow to cool.

6. Assemble the sandwiches by carefully slicing the "bakes" in half lengthwise. Divide the salmon mixture into 4 equal portions; place one portion between each sliced "bake."

Variation: This fried dough recipe also makes great beignets. When dough is golden brown, drain and sprinkle with confectioners sugar while piping hot. Serve immediately.

" Abaco Island is a hop and a skip from the island of Nassau, and it's home to my Uncle Ramesh, an English teacher at one of the local primary schools. Visiting him is always a treat because he never lets me forget how mischievous I was as a child. Of course it's pure torture for me to hear these stories, like the one about the time I climbed a villager's fence to steal guavas, and his three hungry dogs bit my butt. My grandmother dragged me, butt-naked, to the owner's home, demanding to know why the dogs were not tied up. Uncle Ramesh always has to hold his belly when he tells it because he laughs so hard. Uncle Ramesh and I hopped over to Nassau's Junkanoo Festival, a huge annual Bahamian cultural celebration during which the streets come alive with music, food, and colorful costumes. That's where Uncle Ramesh first introduced me to conch fritters, a festive, native street food. Unfortunately, I can't abide the smell of conch, so I've developed my own recipe using codfish, which I've often had in other parts of the Bahamas. These are called 'Accras' in Trinidad, and 'Stamp and Go' in Jamaica, and they're famous throughout the Caribbean. "

BAHAMIAN CODFISH FRITTERS
with GREEN MANGO CHUTNEY

MAKES ABOUT 16 FRITTERS

1/2 pound salt cod
1/2 cup mashed russet potato
1 teaspoon baking powder
2 to 4 tablespoons warm milk
1 large egg, lightly beaten
1 teaspoon minced garlic
1 tablespoon finely chopped chives
1 tablespoon chopped parsley
1 teaspoon chopped fresh thyme
1 tablespoon seeded and finely chopped Thai or Serrano chile
Vegetable oil for frying
Green Mango Chutney (page 23)

1. Place salt cod in a medium bowl and cover with 2 inches of cold water. Cover with plastic wrap and refrigerate for 3 hours or overnight. In a colander, drain fish; discard water, and rinse fish under cold running water for 1 minute.

2. Place fish in a medium saucepan and cover with 1 inch cold water. Bring to a boil over medium-high heat and simmer for 12 minutes. Remove saucepan from heat, drain, and set aside to cool. When fish is cool enough to handle, remove any bones or skin. Squeeze out excess water, then shred the codfish into small pieces and set aside.

3. In a heavy pot or Dutch oven over medium heat, slowly heat enough vegetable oil for deep-frying (about 3 inches) until a deep-fry thermometer reads 365°.

4. Prepare the fritters: In a medium bowl, mix together the potato, baking powder, 2 tablespoons milk, and the egg. Add the garlic, chives, parsley, thyme, chile, and shredded codfish; stir to combine. The mixture should be fluffy yet just thick enough to roll into balls. If the batter is too thick, add up to 2 more tablespoons milk, gently mixing to incorporate it. Be sure not to let the batter become too thin.

5. Lightly dampen your hands with water and form the fritters into 1-inch balls. Carefully drop them, a few at a time, into the hot oil and cook until light golden brown, about 3 minutes, turning once or twice so the fritters brown evenly. Remove with a slotted spoon and transfer to a plate lined with paper towels. Serve warm with Green Mango Chutney.

BAHAMIAN CODFISH FRITTERS

PUERTO RICAN SEAFOOD AND STAR FRUIT CEVICHE

Late one morning I decided to go for a swim in the El Yunque rainforest. The fact that I do not know how to swim didn't prevent me from forging ahead with a life jacket, but first I had to pick up a little something to eat.

One of my new friends, Gonzales, runs a *cuchifrito*, and he's perfected the best fried pork skin accompanied by a killer sofrito. (Cuchifrito has two meanings: one refers to deep-fried pork rinds and other parts of the pig; the other refers to the actual stall that sells the cuchifritos 'to-go.') Gonzales also happens to make the best ceviche in Puerto Rico—it's bursting with unbelievable flavors, and packs a kick of culantro and lots of fresh, hot habaneros. It will waken the sleepiest of palates. Many people question the use of raw fish in ceviche. The trick to this delectable dish is that the natural acids from the citrus juices in which the fish marinate 'cooks' it (it destroys any harmful bacteria that the fish may harbor), yet the seafood flavors come through beautifully, sweet and delicate. If you serve the ceviche with fried plantain chips, you have an instant chip-and-dip arrangement with definite panache. **"**

PUERTO RICAN
SEAFOOD AND STAR FRUIT CEVICHE

SERVES 4 TO 6

1/2 pound sea scallops, membranes trimmed, cut into quarters
1/2 pound large shrimp, shelled, deveined, and cut into thirds
1 cup freshly squeezed lime juice
1/2 cup freshly squeezed orange juice
1/3 cup tomato juice
1/3 cup extra virgin olive oil
1 teaspoon sugar
2 ripe star fruit, thinly sliced (reserve a few slices for garnish)
4 tablespoons finely chopped red onion
2 tablespoons chopped cilantro or culantro
1 tablespoon chopped parsley
1/2 habanero chile, seeded, veins removed and finely chopped
Sea salt and freshly ground pepper

1. In a medium non-reactive bowl, combine the scallops and shrimp then add the lime juice and orange juice, stir to combine. Cover the bowl with plastic wrap and let marinate at room temperature, stirring occasionally, for 3 hours.

2. Strain the seafood mixture and discard marinade. In a large bowl, combine the tomato juice, olive oil, and sugar; stir until the sugar is dissolved. Add the seafood, star fruit, onion, cilantro, parsley, and chile; gently toss to combine. Cover with plastic wrap and refrigerate for 1 hour.

3. Just before serving, season with salt and pepper to taste. Divide the ceviche among chilled martini glasses and garnish with reserved star fruit slices. Serve with plantain chips (page 92).

Variation: For even more intense seafood flavor, top each serving with a dollop of caviar.

" As I watched Abuelita Josephina make these flans in the tiny town of Baracoa, I recaptured so many memories of my childhood days in Guyana. For baking pans, she recycled empty, oval-shaped sardine tins. My Auntie Daisy and I baked in empty ghee tins. There aren't many ovens in the islands, so this dessert was actually baked over hot coals. Yet in the end, the decadent creation turned out soft and velvety, and came bathed in luscious Cuban brown sugar syrup. Here the flans can also be baked in ramekins that have first been swirled with creamy caramel. Today I still bake in washed ghee or tuna tins—some old habits are hard to break. "

CUBAN COCONUT FLAN

MAKES ONE 9-INCH FLAN

1 + 1/2 cups sugar
2 tablespoons freshly squeezed lemon juice
1 vanilla bean or 1 tablespoon pure vanilla extract
1-inch piece lime peel
1 cup canned unsweetened coconut milk
1 cup heavy cream
6 whole eggs
3 egg yolks
1/8 teaspoon salt

1. Stir 1 cup of the sugar and 1/4 cup water together in a 12-inch, heavy, light-colored skillet set over medium heat. It's best to use a light-colored skillet so that you can easily monitor the color of the caramel. After this point, do not stir, but swirl the pan occasionally to keep the caramel cooking evenly (stirring can cause sugar to crystallize).

2. Continue to cook and swirl the caramel mixture; swirl more frequently as the caramel begins to darken. Cook until the sugar is dark amber in color, about 15 to 20 minutes depending on the size and weight of the pan. If the sugar appears to be cooking too quickly, reduce heat to medium-low to prevent it from burning.

3. As soon as the caramel has reached the desired color, add the lemon juice and swirl to combine (the caramel may harden a bit but keep swirling and it will soften). Working quickly, pour the caramel into an ungreased 9-inch round pan and swirl to coat the bottom of the pan before it hardens.

4. Preheat the oven to 325°. Split the vanilla bean in half lengthwise, if using, and scrape out the seeds. In a medium saucepan combine the vanilla seeds or extract, lime peel, coconut milk, and cream. Bring the mixture to a brief simmer over medium-high heat, stirring frequently. Remove from heat and let cool for 15 minutes.

5. In a large bowl, combine the eggs, egg yolks, and salt with the remaining 1/2 cup sugar. Whisk until the mixture is thick and pale yellow in color. Gradually whisk in the cream mixture, being careful not to add it too quickly to prevent eggs from scrambling.

6. Pour the mixture through a fine sieve into a large measuring cup and discard the lime peel. Pour the custard into the caramel-coated pan. Place the pan in a roasting pan and pour in enough warm water to come halfway up the sides. Very carefully transfer the roasting pan to the oven and bake until the custard is just set, about 35 minutes. Carefully remove from oven and let the custard rest for 1 hour in the water bath. Remove flan from the bath, cover with plastic wrap and refrigerate overnight.

7. Immediately before serving, run a sharp knife around the edge of the pan to loosen the custard. Cover the pan with a flat serving dish and, holding securely, invert the pan and plate together. Slowly lift one edge of the pan and then gently lift the pan off completely.

Variation: This mixture can also be made in six 6-ounce ramekins. If using ramekins, evenly divide the cooked caramel among them, swirling to coat bottoms. Work quickly so that caramel does not harden. Proceed as above.

Ripe cocoa pods and a machete, from a plantation in Trinidad.

PLANTAIN AND PUMPKIN SPICED DUKANOO

SERVES 6

1/2 cup canned pumpkin
1/2 cup canned mashed sweet potato
1/2 cup superfine cornmeal
1/2 cup dark brown sugar, loosely packed
1/2 cup grated unsweetened coconut
1/4 cup dried sweetened cranberries
4 tablespoons (1/2 stick) butter, melted
1/4 cup all-purpose flour
1 tablespoon blackstrap molasses
1 teaspoon freshly grated nutmeg
1 teaspoon ground cinnamon
1 teaspoon salt
2 teaspoons pure vanilla extract or almond extract
1/2 to 3/4 cup whole milk
Banana leaves, corn husks, or aluminum foil, cut into six
  12-inch squares
About 6 tablespoons crème fraîche
Mint leaves for garnish

1. In a large bowl, combine the pumpkin, sweet potato, cornmeal, brown sugar, coconut, cranberries, butter, flour, molasses, nutmeg, cinnamon, salt, and vanilla extract. Stir until mixture is well combined. Slowly incorporate the milk into the mixture a few tablespoons at a time. It should become quite thick.

2. Place a banana leaf or square of aluminum foil on a work surface and spoon about 1/3 cup of the pudding mixture in the center of the square. Fold the top edge over the filling (toward you); then fold the bottom half up and over filling (away from you). Now fold both remaining sides under to form a small packet and set aside. Continue to make remaining packets using the remaining pudding mixture.

3. Arrange the filled packets in a single layer in a large bamboo steamer and cover. If you don't have a bamboo steamer, a colander works just as well. Place steamer or colander over several inches of boiling water and simmer packets over low heat until they feel firm to the touch, about 40 to 45 minutes. Using tongs, carefully remove the packets from the steamer or colander and let cool slightly. Serve warm or at room temperature by unwrapping the packet, topping the filling with a dollop of crème fraîche, and adding a sprig of mint.

" I discovered dukanoo as a child when I became fascinated by the African slave laborers in the Caribbean Islands. Our Social Studies teacher, Mr. Reynolds, whose mother was from Barbados and whose father was Guyanese, led our imaginations through the lives of the African diaspora—the slaves who were forcibly brought from Africa to island after Caribbean island. The rigors of life on the sugarcane plantations, the mystical beats of African drums, the lore of the West African Fanti, Ashanti, and Yoruba tribes, were all mesmerizing to me. But it was their struggle for food and its preparation that were the most fascinating, like pigs' feet boiled in coconut milk, and the extraordinary "tie-a-leaf," or dukanoo, a pumpkin pudding made with scintillating spices stuffed into plantain leaves and steamed. Any time Mr. Reynolds talked about dukanoo, my mouth watered. He liked to tell us about his mother's recipe which, by his account, was the most authentic. Several years ago I had the pleasure of visiting Mr. Reynolds' mother in Barbados, where she showed me how to make her special dukanoos. Each neatly tied parcel was wrapped in glistening plantain leaves, secured by plantain twine ties. The filling contained precise handful measures of sweet potatoes and pinches of spices to balance the flavors. She said that the flavor of each dukanoo is unique, and that as with many native foods, each family has its own recipe, passed along all the way from Africa in the time of slavery to the island kitchens of today. The delicious dukanoo mixture can be steamed in cornhusks or even aluminum foil if you can't locate plantain leaves. I've added my own touch by including cranberries in the filling. When you think about it, the combination of sweet potatoes, pumpkin, and cranberries make this an ideal and unusual Thanksgiving or Kwanzaa treat. "

MEXICO

When I think of Mexico, I see a colorful tapestry, densely woven with images. There are the sophisticated art galleries of Mexico City, lyrical Zapotec dances of Oaxaca, traditional meals from Puebla's street vendors, and the surreal festivals celebrating Day of the Dead. Always in the background are Mexico's emerald jungles, and fascinating glimpses of the once-thriving Aztec and Mayan civilizations of the Yucatán peninsula. • According to legend, the Aztecs journeyed south from their northern home of Aztlán, guided by their gods to an island with a lake. The gods said they would know that they had reached their new home when they saw an eagle perched on a cactus, eating a snake (which is today a symbol on the Mexican flag). See it they did, and called their new home Tenochtitlán. We now know it as bustling Mexico City. • Surrounded by water, the Aztecs found inventive ways to survive. They created floating plots of land consisting of soil placed atop layers of thick water vegetation. On these they planted crops such as amaranth, squashes, beans, corn, chiles, and cocoa. They also conceived and built a brilliant empire that thrived until the arrival of Spanish conquistadors in 1519. In just a few years the Spaniards demolished all that had been cultivated for hundreds of years. Since then, the Spanish influence, along with that

THE FLAVORS OF MEXICO

Dozens of varieties of chiles are used fresh, smoked, or charred and peeled, with seeds and without. Tomatillos, chorizo (sausage), olives, cornhusks, fresh-made tortillas, avocados, pepitas (pumpkin seeds), cilantro, and cocoa are always at hand. Allspice, cumin, oregano, and black peppercorns are on the spice shelf. Limes and oranges are used quite a bit in Mexican cooking. Rice and various beans are pantry essentials, as well as dried corn and hominy. There is always plenty of coffee, which is savored throughout the day with milk, sugar, and cinnamon. Pork, chicken, turkey, and beef are protein mainstays, and lard is used for much of Mexican sautéing, browning, and baking. Mexico also produces several soft cheeses, such as Queso Blanco and Queso Fresco, which are used extensively for stuffings and fillings. Not a food item, yet a must-have in every Mexican home, is the *molcajete*, a three-legged mortar and pestle made of lava stone. It is used for grinding and mashing spices, herbs, and seeds, and for blending foods like the well-known guacamole.

of other countries who have peopled Mexico over the years, have all played a role in creating a unique cuisine—one that reaches far beyond tacos and burritos. • Mexico boasts many unique regional cuisines. Veracruz, for instance, is bursting with seafood—stuffed, broiled, fried, topped with capers, chiles, and tomatoes—prepared in nearly every style imaginable. This is also where you'll find one of the world's largest vanilla producers, exotic fruits galore, fine aromatic coffees, and terrific guanabana margaritas—which are not to be missed. • In the Yucatán peninsula, ports greatly affect the region's cuisine, bringing influences from Cuba, New Orleans, and Europe, particularly France. The Yucatán is famous for dishes like *Pollo Pibil*, chicken marinated in achiote, black pepper, chiles, Seville orange juice, cumin, garlic, and salt. • Puebla, a four-hour bus ride from Mexico City, boasts the famous *mole* (officially known as *mole Poblano*), a thick, rich, extremely complex sauce that combines many flavors, simmered together for hours. *Mole* commonly includes different kinds of chiles, cinnamon, nuts, epazote (a pungent herb), and cocoa. It is served with turkey, chicken, and pork. Every villager has a different story about how *mole* originated, but most agree that sometime in the 17th century, nuns in the town of Puebla wanted to create a special meal for visiting church officials. They pulled every ingredient from the cupboard shelves and emptied them into the *olla*

(pot). Today, each family has its own unique version, handed down from generation to generation. • Oaxaca borrowed the *mole* idea from Puebla, and today the region is known for its seven varieties, some sweet and some savory. They are distinguished by their different colors, which include red, green, and yellow. Oaxaca is also renowned for *Mezcal*—the brazen beverage with the worm in the bottle—that is a seriously potent cousin of tequila. • Mexico's culinary heritage— native Aztec and Mayan staples fused with newer influences—has developed into one of the most popular cuisines in the world.

MENU MEXICO

APERITIF
• MEXICAN MANGO MARGARITA

APPETIZER
• VERACRUZ CRAB QUESADILLA WITH GUACAMOLE

SOUP
• YUCATAN LIME SOUP WITH LOBSTER AND TEQUILA

SALAD
• DRAGON FRUIT AND PUMPKIN SEED SALAD

ENTREE
• PUEBLA PORK LOIN WITH GUAVA MOLE POBLANO

DESSERT
• OAXACAN CHIPOTLE CHOCOLATE CUPS

My very first trip to Mexico introduced me to this drink. Every time I revisit Mexico I look for it—it's not particularly exotic, but I truly enjoy the blended flavors of mangoes and tequila. Mexico grows many varieties of mangoes, each with its own unique hint of sweetness. Silver, or aged, tequila is the top choice for this cocktail. If you can't find fresh mangoes in season, by all means used sliced, canned, or bottled mangoes, or substitute peaches, which are just as delicious in this drink.

MEXICAN MANGO MARGARITA

SERVES 2

2 cups peeled and diced ripe mango (about 1 large mango)
    reserve 2 slices with skin for garnish
1/4 cup freshly squeezed lime juice
4 ounces silver tequila or any fine-quality aged tequila
1 ounce Cointreau
2 tablespoons sugar
About 1 + 1/2 cups ice cubes

1. In a blender, combine the mango and lime juice and blend until smooth. Add the tequila, Cointreau, and sugar and blend until combined. Add the ice and blend until smooth and very thick (it should have the consistency of a milkshake). Blend with additional ice if the mixture is not thick enough. Serve in chilled margarita glasses and garnish each with a slice of mango.

VERACRUZ CRAB QUESADILLA
with GUACAMOLE

SERVES 4

1 + 1/2 cups lump crabmeat, picked over for any pieces of cartilage
2 tablespoons finely chopped green onions (green parts only)
1 tablespoon chopped cilantro
1 + 1/2 tablespoons finely chopped shallot
2 jalapeño chiles, seeded and chopped
2 teaspoons freshly squeezed lime juice
Sea salt and freshly ground pepper
8 round flour tortillas, 7 to 8 inches in diameter
2 cups (about 5 ounces) shredded Queso Chihuahua cheese
About 1/4 cup extra virgin olive oil
2 tablespoons chopped chives for garnish
Guacamole (recipe follows)

1. In a medium bowl, combine the crabmeat, green onions, cilantro, shallot, chiles, and lime juice. Gently toss until well combined, then season with salt and pepper to taste. Cover and refrigerate until ready to use.

2. Place 4 of the flour tortillas on a work surface. Spread one quarter of the crab mixture evenly over each tortilla to within 1/2-inch of the edges all around.

3. Spread one half cup of the cheese evenly over the crab mixture. Press remaining four tortillas over each of the filled tortillas and press to seal. Heat a large skillet over medium-high heat. Add just enough oil to coat the bottom of the pan.

4. Fry one quesadilla at a time until golden brown on both sides, about 2 minutes on each side, adding more oil when necessary. Let cool for 2 minutes, then cut each quesadilla into 4 triangles, sprinkle with chives, and serve with guacamole.

VERACRUZ CRAB QUESADILLA

GUACAMOLE

SERVES 4

3 small ripe avocados, halved, pitted, and pulp scooped from skins

1/2 teaspoon sea salt

1 tablespoon diced onion

1 small red Serrano chile or green jalapeño chile, seeded and finely chopped

1 tablespoon chopped cilantro

1 tablespoon freshly squeezed lime juice

1 teaspoon sour cream

3 tablespoons diced tomato

1. In a small bowl, combine the avocado pulp and salt and mash coarsely with a fork. Add the onion, chile, cilantro, lime juice, and sour cream; mix well. Gently fold in the tomatoes. Serve immediately, or cover with plastic wrap and keep refrigerated until ready to use.

Cooking Tip: To easily remove the seed of an avocado, cut lengthwise all the way around, twist to separate. Firmly hit the seed with a knife, gently twist, remove the seed, and scoop with a spoon.

Before the Spanish conquistadors decimated the ancient Mayan culture, its province extended from the Yucatán peninsula to western Honduras, El Salvador, most of Guatemala, and northern Belize. The Mayans created awe-inspiring architecture that can still be glimpsed in the ruins at Chichen Itza in Cancun, including pyramid temples and observatories, all built without metal tools. Their food was quite different from that of the rest of Mexico: Mayan farmers cultivated beans, squash, avocados, sweet potatoes, guava, chiles, cacao, vanilla, papaya, and of course, maize, or corn. Mayan women ground the corn into flour to make a paste that was baked over an open fire—these became the ubiquitous tortillas. Today, all of these ingredients remain staples of the Mexican diet, along with a few foreign influences absorbed along the way. When I visited Cancun to see the ruins, I was served this robust soup made with tequila, lime, lobster, and tortilla chips. In honor of the Mayan culture, I reproduced it here at home. The flavor is unique and addictive.

YUCATAN LIME SOUP
with LOBSTER AND TEQUILA

SERVES 4

4 corn tortillas cut into 3-inch strips
1 tablespoon extra virgin olive oil
1/2 cup finely chopped onion
1 tablespoon minced garlic
1/2 cup seeded and chopped tomatoes
1 tablespoon minced jalapeño chile or 1 teaspoon minced Serrano chile
1/2 teaspoon ground cumin
1 teaspoon smoked paprika
4 cups low-sodium fish or vegetable stock
1/4 cup sliver tequila, or any fine-quality aged tequila
3 tablespoons freshly squeezed lime juice
2 cups (about 14 ounces) lobster meat, cut into 2-inch pieces
Sea salt
1/4 cup chopped fresh cilantro
1 lime, cut into thin slices for garnish
Crème fraiche

1. Preheat oven to 375°. Place the tortilla strips on a baking sheet and bake until lightly golden, about 8 minutes. Set aside until ready to use.

2. Heat the oil in a medium stock pot over medium-high heat. Add the onion and garlic and sauté until soft, about 3 minutes. Add the tomatoes, chile, cumin, and paprika and sauté for 3 minutes, stirring frequently. Add the stock, tequila, and lime juice; simmer over medium heat for 5 minutes.

3. Add the lobster meat and cook for 1 minute. Season to taste with salt, remove from heat and stir in the cilantro. Ladle soup into 4 warm soup bowls and top each serving with a slice of lime and a small dollop of crème fraiche. Serve with the toasted tortilla chips on the side.

YUCATAN LIME SOUP

Jorge, my driver in Mexico, and I stopped for lunch in Puerto Escondido, which means 'hidden port.' And so it is: it's a quaint beach town tucked away in southern Oaxaca. From one of the many food vendors, Jorge selected a salad piled high with the bountiful produce of Mexico, topped by several crunchy, fried grasshoppers. Many cultures still eat all sorts of insects—they're not only considered a tasty treat, but stand in for the lack of protein in an otherwise mostly meatless diet. As for me, the grasshoppers definitely made the salad crunchy, but they were fibrous and their blandness didn't engage my palate. For this version of an otherwise zesty salad, I added *pepitas*—pumpkin seeds—instead. They're just as crunchy, protein-rich, and much more delicious than grasshoppers. They're also a wonderful contrast to the juicy, sweet dragon fruit, a member of the cactus family whose skin resembles a dragon's scales. If you can't find exotic dragon fruit, you can substitute honeydew melon for the same sweet and juicy results.

DRAGON FRUIT AND PUMPKIN SEED SALAD

SERVES 4

1 cup shelled, unsalted pumpkin seeds (pepitas)
2 cups peeled, diced dragon fruit (from 1 large dragon fruit)
2 tablespoons freshly squeezed lime juice
1/4 cup extra virgin olive oil
1 tablespoon chopped cilantro
1 tablespoon finely chopped red onion
1 small jalapeño chile, seeded and cut into strips
1/3 cup pitted black Kalamata olives, sliced
1 teaspoon capers, drained
Baby spinach or a mixture of salad greens, washed and dried
Sea salt

1. In a small skillet over medium-low heat, toast the shelled pumpkin seeds until they begin to pop, about 5 to 6 minutes. Remove from heat and set aside.

2. In a large salad bowl, toss in the remaining ingredients with the toasted pumpkin seeds. Divide among 4 salad bowls and sprinkle with sea salt.

PUEBLA PORK LOIN WITH GUAVA MOLE POBLANO

SERVES 6 TO 8

1 corn tortilla, finely chopped
1/3 cup shelled, unsalted pumpkin seeds (pepitas)
1/4 teaspoon cumin seeds
3 whole dried pasilla chiles
4 whole dried ancho chiles
3 whole dried poblano chiles
4 cups low-sodium vegetable or chicken stock
Vegetable oil for coating pan
1 boneless pork loin (about 4 to 6 pounds) trussed with
    kitchen twine
4 tomatillos, diced
1 cup peeled, seeded, diced tomato
4 tablespoons guava paste
2 tablespoons toasted sesame seeds,
1 garlic clove, crushed
1 teaspoon ground allspice
1/2 teaspoon freshly ground pepper
1/4 teaspoon salt
1/2 ounce finely chopped dark or bittersweet chocolate

1. In a large, ovenproof skillet, toast the tortilla pieces over medium-high heat until golden, tossing frequently for about 3 to 4 minutes, then set aside. Toast the pumpkin seeds in the same skillet, tossing frequently, until most of the seeds have popped and are lightly golden, about 5 to 6 minutes; set aside. Toast the cumin seeds in the same skillet, stirring constantly for 30 seconds; set aside. Add the chiles to the pan and with the heat on medium-high, toast them, turning occasionally for 6 minutes. Transfer chiles to a plate and allow to cool.

2. When cool enough to handle, remove the stems, seeds, and membranes from the chiles. Wear disposable rubber gloves or put a sandwich bag over your fingers when doing this so the seeds do not burn you.

3. In a medium saucepan, bring the stock to a boil over medium-high heat. Add chiles, reduce heat, and simmer for 30 minutes. Strain liquid through a fine sieve, reserving both the liquid and chiles. Preheat oven to 350°.

4. Heat the same skillet used for toasting chiles over high heat until very hot and lightly coat the pan with oil. Sear the pork loin on all sides. Transfer skillet to the oven and cook until an instant-read thermometer inserted into the center of the roast reaches 150°, about 1 hour.

I searched long and hard throughout Puebla and Oaxaca for a mole recipe I thought my readers would enjoy. This mole poblano, which I was introduced to in Puebla, has incredible finesse, balancing the hot and smoky flavors of the chipotle and other chiles with a hint of musky bitterness from the chocolate and spices. I've added a touch of guava paste, a sweet, yet tangy element. I prefer not to saturate meat with the mole; instead, I serve it on the side so that my palate can adjust to the riot of flavors. This mole is also delicious with chicken or turkey.

5. Meanwhile, continue to make the mole: In a food processor, combine the tortilla pieces, reserved chiles, reserved stock, pumpkin seeds, cumin seeds, tomatillos, tomato, guava paste, sesame seeds, garlic, allspice, pepper, salt, and chocolate, and process until very smooth, about 1 minute. If necessary, blend in batches and set aside.

6. When the pork loin is done, transfer it to a carving board, cover with aluminum foil and let rest for 10 minutes. Add the mole mixture to the skillet along with any juices left from the pork. Cook the sauce over high heat, stirring constantly for 5 minutes. The sauce should not be too thick (add additional stock if necessary to thin it). Strain mole through a sieve, pressing out as much of the liquid as possible. Slice the pork to desired thickness and arrange the slices on a serving platter. Pour some of the mole over the pork and serve the remaining sauce on the side. Serve with white rice.

Make Ahead Tip: The mole can be made a week ahead and stored in an airtight container in the refrigerator. Leftover mole can be frozen.

Prickly pear cactus, mangoes, corn, and honey at a market stall in Tlaquepaque, Mexico.

In Mexico, The Day of the Dead is a festive occasion—for Mexicans, death is simply an extension of life. Every November 1st, in homage to departed loved ones, cemeteries are strewn with the riotous colors of marigolds, papier-mâché sculptures, brightly lit candles and black and white 'skulls' made out of sugar. The living make altars in their homes or at the graves of the deceased, and each altar or grave is laden with fruit, the traditional bread called *Pan de Muertos,* and favorite things of the spirits—certain foods, cigarettes, alcohol, toys, and photographs. I had returned to Oaxaca from the jungles of Palenque to revisit one of the local home bakeries there. The one I wanted to see in particular was run by a woman named Gloria, who makes the best *Pan de Muertos.* When I met Gloria on my previous visit, she described a special chocolate recipe that she prepares in individual ramekins, but I felt that I had to see it being made in person. Although she agreed, Gloria stressed that she would prepare it only on the Day of the Dead. That early November morning, Gloria showed me how to make this sweet from start to finish, grinding the cocoa beans by hand on a *molcajete*—a mortar made of lava stone—and told me that these were her father's favorite. Gloria's decadent chocolate 'cups' are rich with the luscious flavors of Mexican chocolate, vanilla, coffee, and ground chile. With each spoonful, you'll be glad you're alive to enjoy it.

OAXACAN CHIPOTLE CHOCOLATE CUPS

SERVES 6

2 teaspoons unflavored gelatin (from 1 package)
2 cups heavy cream
2 cups whole milk
2 teaspoons prepared instant coffee
1/4 teaspoon ground chipotle chile or paprika
3/4 cup confectioners sugar
2 teaspoons vanilla extract
8 ounces dark or bittersweet chocolate, finely chopped
Crème fraiche
Edible violets or lavender flowers for garnish

1. In a small bowl, soften the gelatin in 1/4 cup water and set aside.

2. Combine the cream, milk, coffee, chipotle chile, sugar, and vanilla in a medium saucepan. Bring to a simmer over medium heat and cook for about 10 minutes, stirring frequently so the cream does not stick to the pan.

3. Add the chocolate, whisking until it has completely melted and the mixture is smooth. Remove from heat and pour the gelatin mixture into the chocolate mixture. Whisk until the gelatin is completely dissolved.

4. Evenly divide the chocolate mixture among six 8-ounce ramekins, filling them three-quarters full. Refrigerate until chocolate cups are set, about 8 hours or overnight. Serve with 1 teaspoon of crème fraiche and a violet or lavender flower perched on top.

SOUTH AMERICA

As a little girl growing up in Guyana, South America, I took the first of many trips with my Uncle Buck to a "nameless village" that he called the gateway to the Amazon. It would be the first time I was to meet the natives of my country. My grandmother allowed me to go because she said the Arawak Indians would show me how to make the best *casreep*, a sweet-peppery condiment made from yucca juice that we used to season pepperpot soups and chicken stews. Uncle Buck and I ventured through the rainforest on boat, gliding on calm, mysterious brown water. The area around us was dense with trees competing for a glimpse of sunshine. The chatter of excited monkeys sent waves of brilliantly-colored birds through a clearing in the canopy. We finally arrived at a small village with several brown, cone-shaped huts. Immediately, I smelled barbecue. In the center of the village sat a large, shallow open pit glowing with red embers and topped by an iron spit. That evening, the village chief fed me roasted guinea pig wrapped in plantain leaves, a great delicacy. I sipped a cloudy drink from a calabash that I later found out was fermented yucca juice. The chief drank El Dorado rum, no doubt rations my Uncle had brought for him. After dinner, as I lay in my hammock pondering the stars, I began to dream about what lay beyond the dark, steaming jungle around me...I

NIRMALA'S GUIDE TO
THE FLAVORS OF SOUTH AMERICA

These ingredients aren't limited to the countries discussed in this chapter, but are common to almost every other South American country as well. Grains such as quinoa, amaranth, and corn are, of course, native to the continent. There are dozens of varieties of beans including chickpeas, fava, black, and lima beans. Tomatoes, squashes, and native chiles are cultivated and used extensively, as are fresh herbs including cilantro, parsley, oregano, and thyme, which heighten the flavors of soups and stews. Beef, of course, is a mainstay, as are pork and chicken, and an abundance of seafood, thanks to its vast coastlines.

longed to see my South America. • It took 15 years of longing and wondering before I once again ventured into the continent that had cradled me. This time I wanted to explore its backbone: the snowy Andes mountains. The Andes run through seven countries—almost the entire length of South America—from the humid tropics of Colombia to the barren ice fields of Patagonia. The brilliant Incan empire once ruled this entire mountain range, until it fell at the hands of Spanish conquistadors in the 1500s. The Incas had been great hunter-gatherers, but they were also an agricultural society, raising such crops as corn, yucca, potatoes, beans, squash, and chiles. These remain typical ingredients in South America today. • Of all the regions of the Andes, the ones that hold me in their sway are Argentina, Chile, and Peru. Besides the fauna and the flora, I had of course traveled there for the food. In Peru, typical dishes vary regionally. Seafood is widely available in the coastal areas, while wild game such as guinea pigs and duck are a staple among locals in the highlands. A popular Peruvian corn drink, one of my favorites, is Chicha Morada, made with purple corn, spices, and pineapple. Another favorite is Aji de Gallina, a chicken dish with milk, cashews, purple potatoes, and *aji*, the Incan name for chiles. • Chile, a slender landscape along the western coast, quickly engulfs one's spirit of adventure. With the Andes as a backdrop, its lush forests and numerous volcanoes, the climate is as

diverse as its topography. In Chile's midst is the food basket of the country—here there are flourishing farms, and vineyards producing some of today's finest wines. In Santiago, its cosmopolitan capital, you'll find European influences that have trickled down to today's Chilean cuisine. Still, it manages to keep its authentic identity in delicacies such as empanadas filled with meat, vegetables, or seafood, and the world-renowned, enormous grilled South American steaks. This is no place for vegetarians. • Argentina will seduce you with its sexy tango moves and its steaks drizzled with garlicky chimichurri, but it is also the largest wine-producing country on the continent. The vast green pastures feed some of the world's leanest beef, tended to by *gauchos* (cowboys) who can cook up a mean steak in their special *parrillas*, or barbecue pits. Argentina's culinary map has also been greatly shaped by influences from Italy and Spain. Early Italian settlers missed their Parmigiano, and so began to make their own, including a version made from sheep's milk called *capilla*. Small Buenos Aires cafes are frothing with cappuccino, and they serve terrific pizza with chorizo. • If you crave a truly eclectic culinary destination and a culture that manages to be both sophisticated and primitive at the same time, book a trip to my own South America.

MENU SOUTH AMERICA

- MIGUEL'S PERUVIAN CHICHA MORADA
- SOUTH AMERICAN PASSION FRUIT SMOOTHIE

APPETIZERS
- ROSALITA'S AREPAS CON QUESO
- ANDEAN GRILLED SWEET CORN
- CHILEAN SPICY CHICKPEAS with CHORIZO

SOUPS
- FELIX'S CHILEAN PORK SOUP with BLACK AND WHITE BEANS
- ANDEAN GAZPACHO SOUP

SALADS
- INCA QUINOA SALAD with SUNDRIED TOMATOES
- PERUVIAN PURPLE POTATO SALAD

ENTREES
- ARGENTINE GAUCHO GRILLED STEAK WITH CHIMICHURRI SAUCE AND PLANTAIN CHIPS
- PERUVIAN AJI DE GALLENA (CHICKEN IN CHILE SAUCE WITH CASHEWS)

DESSERT
- ANDEAN MORA BERRY CHEESECAKE

" I learned how to make this very popular Peruvian drink from Miguel, a street vendor in Arequipa, a city that rests on the skirts of the western range of the Andes. Chicha Morada is made with dried purple corn kernels, fresh pineapple, and spices— it tastes like a combination of just-picked cherries with subtle hints of tartness from the star anise and lime. I've leisurely sipped many glasses of this chilled drink during my strolls through the streets of Peru. This is not the same as fermented Chicha—an alcoholic beverage. Whole ears of purple corn can be found in Latin American grocery stores, in plastic bags. If I want to make this drink into a cocktail, I just add Japanese plum wine or red wine. "

MIGUEL'S PERUVIAN CHICHA MORADA

SERVES 6 TO 8

3 small ears (about 8 ounces) purple corn, broken in half
2 cups diced fresh pineapple
3 whole star anise
3 tablespoons freshly squeezed lime juice
1/3 cup sugar
Mint sprigs or strips of lime peel for garnish

1. In a large pot, bring 1 gallon cold water to a boil over medium-high heat. Add the ears of corn, pineapple, and star anise. Boil uncovered for 1 hour or until the liquid is deep purple in color and reduced by half.

2. Strain mixture through a fine sieve and discard corn, pineapple, and star anise. Add lime juice and sugar; stir until the sugar is dissolved. Let cool completely. Add additional sugar to taste, if desired. Let mixture rest for 30 minutes at room temperature until all flavors are blended, then chill in the refrigerator. Serve in tall glasses filled with a few crushed mint leaves or lime peel.

A beautiful salt lake in Salar de Altiplano, Chile in the Atacama Desert region.

Passion fruit is native to the Amazon and is a childhood favorite throughout the continent, almost the way apples are here. It's used for making aromatic cakes, flans, and drinks. There are several varieties of the fruit: the most common are yellow and purple in color. They're about the size and shape of an egg, with a tough skin. Inside, though, there's a juicy, yellow-orange, sweet-tart pulp filled with edible seeds. It's amazing to me that you can now find passion fruit juice and frozen passion fruit pulp in American supermarkets, a long way from the Amazon. Here is a full-flavored, nutritious breakfast smoothie featuring the unique flavor of passion fruit. The banana contributes potassium, the orange juice, vitamin C, and the yogurt, calcium. It's almost a meal in a glass.

SOUTH AMERICAN PASSION FRUIT SMOOTHIE

SERVES 2

1/2 cup canned or bottled passion fruit juice
1 large ripe banana, peeled and sliced
1/2 cup plain yogurt
1/4 cup freshly squeezed orange juice
1/2 cup ice cubes
Sugar or honey to taste
Mint sprigs for garnish

1. Combine passion fruit juice, banana, yogurt, orange juice, ice cubes, and sugar in a blender. Blend until smooth. Pour into 2 tall glasses and garnish with springs of fresh mint.

Arepas are usually the first street food to greet me in every country of South America. These corn cakes are said to have originated in Venezuela or Colombia, but every country in the continent claims its own version of them. Some arepas are savory and stuffed with meat or cheese; others are like this sweet version from Rosalita. I met Rosalita in the bustling, noisy streets of Lima. She looked like an Incan goddess as she emerged from the dark gray smoke surrounding a group of food vendors. She wore a white dress, embroidered with two stems of red and green roses, and spattered with oil stains. Her eyes were wide and bright, her hair was jet black, and resting on one hip she held an orange plastic bowl where her arepas nestled in a warm white towel. She was no more than seven years old. Our eyes met, and her moon-shaped face revealed the stains of dry tears.

Instead of bringing her home, as I wanted to do with the hundreds of poor young children I've met on my travels, I bought all of her arepas. We sat on an old tree trunk and ate them, washing them down with cans of ice-cold Inca cola. We even shared our bounty with a stray dog. At that moment, the world stood silent, as if only Rosalita, the dog, and I existed. These sweetened cheese-filled delights will surely hold time in suspended animation for you too.

ROSALITA'S AREPAS CON QUESO

MAKES 6 AREPAS

3/4 cup whole milk

3 tablespoons unsalted butter, plus more for pan

1/4 cup buttermilk

1 cup frozen corn kernels, thawed

1 cup finely ground yellow cornmeal

1/4 cup sugar

1/4 teaspoon salt

1 cup (about 2 + 1/2 ounces) grated Monterey Jack cheese

About 1 tablespoon of butter for grilling

6 slices (about 1 ounce each) mozzarella cheese

1. In a medium saucepan, bring the milk to a boil over high heat. Remove from heat and let sit for a minute or two. Stir in the 3 tablespoons of butter and buttermilk. Stir until the butter has completely melted, then let sit for 2 minutes.

2. Pulse the corn kernels in a food processor until just coarse. In a large bowl, combine the corn, cornmeal, sugar, salt, and Monterey Jack cheese and stir to combine. Gradually add enough of the warm milk mixture to make a very thick batter.

3. Heat a griddle or large skillet over medium-high heat and melt about 1 tablespoon butter. When foam subsides, drop about 2 tablespoons of the batter onto the skillet for each arepa (they should be about 3 inches in diameter). Cook until underside is golden brown, about 4 minutes, then turn arepas and brown the other side.

4. When the arepas are brown on both sides and batter is cooked through, sandwich one slice of mozzarella cheese between two of the arepas. Reduce heat to low and continue cooking until the cheese melts, turning once or twice. Continue filling and cooking the remaining arepas and serve hot.

ROSALITA'S AREPAS CON QUESO

As you've probably guessed by now, my favorite food is street food. I will devour anything in sight from a food stall or vendor—I've even snacked on fried insects in the jungle markets of Papua New Guinea. I've had grilled corn from street stalls in every country I've visited in South America, so I've assembled all the different flavors from the vendors whose corn pleased my palate to create these perfect, grilled specimens.

ANDEAN GRILLED SWEET CORN

SERVES 4 TO 6

4 tablespoons unsalted butter
1 teaspoon minced garlic
1 tablespoon minced shallot
1/2 teaspoon ground cumin
1 teaspoon paprika
6 ears fresh corn, husks intact
Sea salt

1. Heat the butter in a small saucepan over medium heat until melted. Add the garlic and shallot and sauté until soft, about 3 minutes. Add the cumin and paprika, stir to combine, then remove from heat.

2. Heat a charcoal or gas grill until hot. Place the corn on the grill and cover. Grill for 6 minutes, turning every two minutes. Remove corn and let rest for 5 minutes.

3. Pull back the husks on each ear of corn almost to the bottom, being careful not to break them off the cob. Remove and discard as much excess silk as possible. Return the corn to the grill and cook until the kernels are tender and nicely charred, turning occasionally, about 7 minutes.

4. Drizzle or brush the corn with the butter mixture, sprinkle with sea salt and serve immediately.

"I was in the beautiful city of Santiago, on Chile's west coast. My driver, Juan Carlos, was ready to call it a day, but I was anxious to see more of the city, and especially experience it at night. I insisted on tagging along with him. He led me to a small café located in an alleyway—these cafes are notorious in Chile and are called 'cafés con piernas'—cafés with legs. It was smoky, and filled with men sipping café con leche served by young women in hot pink bikinis and skimpy lingerie. Clearly, I was out of place. Everyone stared at me, and I became bored and uncomfortable. I spotted the kitchen and since there was no other way to escape, I walked through its doors. There were three male cooks in the kitchen, and one of them, Pedro, had a cousin in Jackson Heights, Queens. I was hailed as family on the spot! That night Pedro, his two brothers-in-law, and I cooked up this dish, which we enjoyed with blood sausages. We sat on empty tomato crates, playing cards and downing these spicy gems by the spoonful and washing them down with Cerveza Escundo. I've replaced blood sausage with spicy chorizos, which are readily available. Make sure to have really good, ice-cold beer on hand."

CHILEAN SPICY CHICKPEAS WITH CHORIZO

SERVES 4

1/4 cup extra virgin olive oil
1 small onion, chopped
2 teaspoons ground cumin
1 tablespoon minced garlic
1 cup diced chorizo (about 4 sausages)
2 cans (15 ounce) chickpeas, drained
2 teaspoons red pepper flakes
1/4 cup packed chopped cilantro and parsley leaves
Sea salt and freshly ground pepper

1. Heat the oil in a large skillet over medium-high heat. Add the onion, cumin, and garlic and sauté until soft, about 5 minutes. Add the sausage and cook for two minutes more, stirring occasionally. Add the chickpeas and cook for another three minutes, stirring occasionally. Add the red pepper flakes, cilantro, and parsley. Stir well to combine and remove pan from heat. Season to taste with salt and pepper; serve warm.

Variation: You can add a spicier flair to this dish by adding up to 1 teaspoon curry powder along with the other herbs and spices.

FELIX'S CHILEAN PORK SOUP
with BLACK AND WHITE BEANS

SERVES 4 TO 6

1 can (15 ounces) whole tomatoes
3 tablespoons vegetable oil
1 pound lean pork, such as pork tenderloin, cut into 1/2-inch cubes
3 garlic cloves, minced
1 large onion, coarsely chopped
2 teaspoons chipotle flakes or red pepper flakes, plus more to taste
1 tablespoon fresh thyme leaves, chopped
6 cups vegetable or beef stock
1 can (15 ounces) black beans, drained and rinsed
1 can (15 ounces) white beans, drained and rinsed
1 large carrot, diced
3 stalks celery, diced
Sea salt and freshly ground pepper
1 can (2.8 ounces) fried onions
1/4 cup finely chopped cilantro for garnish

1. Drain tomatoes and reserve liquid. Coarsley chop tomatoes and set aside.

2. In a large pot, heat oil over high heat. Add the pork and brown well on all sides, about 8 to 10 minutes. Remove pork with a slotted spoon and set aside.

3. Reduce heat to medium-high and add the garlic and onion. Sauté until soft, about 5 minutes. Add the chipotle flakes or the red pepper flakes, thyme, and tomatoes. Cover and cook for 3 minutes.

4. Add the stock and reserved tomato juice, and bring mixture to a boil over high heat. Reduce the heat to low, add the beans, carrot, and celery; cover and let simmer for 15 minutes. Season with salt and pepper to taste. Ladle the soup into four warm bowls and garnish with fried onions and cilantro.

Make Ahead Tip: This soup can be made up to two days ahead, but add the fried onions and cilantro garnish just before serving.

" Throughout the Andes, I sampled gazpacho from many different street vendors. Some sold it in plastic cups, some provided Styrofoam bowls, and some even offered plastic bags to use as containers. When I make it here at home, I serve it in chilled martini glasses rimmed with sea salt—it's a stunning presentation. If I want to add a protein boost, I put in one-half cup of cooked quinoa, which has a slightly nutty taste and unique texture. While this soup shares several of the ingredients with the gazpacho we're more familiar with here, the cumin, chiles, lime juice, and cilantro make this version unlike any other you've ever had. "

ANDEAN GAZPACHO SOUP

SERVES 4 TO 6

1 pound (about 3 medium) ripe tomatoes, peeled, seeded, and chopped
1 medium cucumber, peeled, seeded, and chopped
1 medium green bell pepper, stemmed, seeded, and chopped
1 small shallot, chopped
1/2 cup chopped onion
2 garlic cloves, coarsely chopped
2 green jalapeño chiles, stemmed, seeded, and chopped
2 tablespoons red wine vinegar
2 tablespoons extra virgin olive oil
2 teaspoons ground cumin
1/4 cup chopped fresh cilantro leaves, plus more for garnish
2 tablespoons freshly squeezed lime juice
1/2 cup tomato juice
Sea salt and freshly ground pepper
Lime wedge for rimming glasses
2 tablespoons sea salt for rimming glasses
Red chili oil (optional)

1. In a food processor, combine the tomatoes, cucumber, bell pepper, shallot, onion, garlic, jalapeño, vinegar, oil, cumin, cilantro, and lime juice. Pulse to combine. Slowly add tomato juice until soup reaches the desired consistency.

2. Pour gazpacho into a large bowl and cover with plastic wrap. Chill for at least 1 hour. When ready to serve, season to taste with salt and pepper. Rim 4 to 6 martini glasses by rubbing the lime wedge around the rims and dipping them into sea salt. Carefully ladle the gazpacho into the glasses. Drizzle with red chili oil if desired, garnish with cilantro and serve immediately.

Pronounced 'keen-wa,' quinoa is a delicate grain indigenous to the Andes. It has a pleasant, nutty taste that people quickly take to once they've tried it. It is a complete grain that contains all the essential amino acids, and because it is high in protein, there is little need to add meat or fish to quinoa preparations. It's a vegetarian staple, and can be used in place of almost any grain in any recipe (my mother, a strict vegetarian, thrives on it). In addition, quinoa is gluten-free, making it an ideal food for children and adults with gluten allergies. Most quinoa available in stores is already washed, but you should still rinse it before cooking until the water runs clear. This recipe is a vegetarian delight.

INCA QUINOA SALAD
with SUNDRIED TOMATOES

SERVES 4

1/4 cup extra virgin olive oil
1 teaspoon minced garlic
1 small shallot, finely chopped
1 small jalapeño or Serrano chile, seeded and finely chopped
4 sundried tomatoes, julienned
1 teaspoon curry powder
1 + 1/2 cups cooked quinoa (see Note)
1 small cucumber peeled, seeded, and diced
2 tablespoons finely chopped cilantro
1 tablespoon freshly squeezed lime juice
About 12 Belgian endive leaves (from 2 Belgian endives)
Sea salt

1. Heat the olive oil in a small skillet over medium-high heat. Sauté the garlic, shallot, and chile for 1 minute, or until soft. Add the sundried tomatoes and curry powder; cook for 2 minutes more, stirring frequently. Remove from heat and let cool.

2. Combine the cooked quinoa, sundried tomato mixture, cucumber, cilantro, and lime juice in a large bowl and lightly toss. Spoon the quinoa mixture into the endive leaves and transfer to a platter. Season with sea salt and serve.

Note: To cook quinoa, place 1/2 cup quinoa in a fine-mesh sieve; rinse and drain well. In a medium saucepan, combine 1/2 cup quinoa and 1 cup water and bring to a boil over high heat. Reduce heat to a simmer, cover, and cook until all of the water is absorbed, about 15 minutes. The quinoa is done when all the grains have turned from white to transparent, and the spiral-like germ of the grain is visible. This proportion will yield 1 + 1/2 cups cooked quinoa.

Make Ahead Tip: Quinoa can be cooked a day ahead and stored, covered, in the refrigerator until ready to use.

❝ Take your favorite potato salad recipe to a more colorful level: make it with the purple potatoes that are native to Peru (but easily found here in specialty food markets). These spuds are seriously purple yet taste just the same as white potatoes, and your family will love them in this multicolored, tasty side dish. In Peru, I had this salad topped with yellow tomatoes, which are not as acidic as red tomatoes. Cool, diced cucumber balances the flavors nicely. ❞

PERUVIAN PURPLE POTATO SALAD

SERVES 6 TO 8

2 pounds purple potatoes, unpeeled, and cut into 1/2-inch cubes
1 teaspoon salt
4 hard-boiled eggs, coarsely chopped
2 tablespoons finely chopped shallot
1 tablespoon chopped fresh dill
1 celery stalk, finely chopped
1/2 cup mayonnaise
1 tablespoon grainy mustard
1 teaspoon ground cumin
Sea salt and freshly ground pepper
1 small yellow or red tomato, peeled, seeded, and diced
1 medium cucumber, peeled, seeded, and diced

1. Place potatoes in a large saucepan. Add 1 teaspoon salt and cover them with cold water by 1 inch. Bring to a boil over medium heat, cover, and cook until potatoes are just tender but still firm, about 8 minutes. Immediately drain and set aside to cool.

2. In a large bowl, combine the potatoes, eggs, shallot, dill, celery, mayonnaise, mustard, and cumin. Gently toss to combine and season to taste with sea salt and pepper. Transfer potato salad to a serving bowl and garnish with diced tomatoes and cucumber. Serve immediately or cover with plastic wrap and refrigerate until ready to serve.

Gauchos are the cowboys of Argentina. I had heard so much about them—and how well they cook—that I wanted to see how they live. After a three-hour drive from Buenos Aires, I arrived at a local ranch where I was greeted by Pablo, an incredibly handsome, raven-haired, blue-eyed native. Pablo led me to his *parrilla*, or barbecue pit, which is made of mud bricks that have been painted white and adorned with stripes of blue and yellow. Inside the pit was a large iron grill supporting enormous steaks and sausages basking in the high heat. Trying not to gaze too long at Pablo, I watched him quietly prepare his chimichurri sauce. We were both completely silent. About half an hour later, sipping a bottle of red wine from Argentina's wine country, Pablo served me the biggest piece of beef I've ever seen, still bubbling with hot brown juices. I dunked it into the astonishing chimichurri sauce, where the flavors of the velvety, tender steak and the hints of garlic, parsley, fruity olive oil and chiles in the sauce besieged my senses. My mother, religiously vegetarian, would have been appalled at the sight of me—we are Hindu, and cows are sacred—yet the riot of flavors in my mouth was overwhelming and I kept taking bite after bite. I think I now know my status on the reincarnation list. "

ARGENTINE GAUCHO GRILLED STEAK with CHIMICHURRI SAUCE AND PLANTAIN CHIPS

SERVES 4

2 sirloin steaks (about 1 + 1/2 pounds each), cut about 1 + 1/4-inches thick
Sea salt and freshly ground pepper
Chimichurri Sauce (recipe follows)
Plantain Chips (recipe follows)

1. Rinse steak with cold water and pat dry with a paper towel. Season both sides well with salt and pepper.

2. Heat a charcoal or gas grill to hot. You can also cook the steaks in a preheated broiler. Grill steaks about 6 minutes on each side for medium-rare. Let steak rest for 5 minutes. Carve steaks into thick slices and transfer to a heated serving platter. Spoon about half of the Chimichurri sauce over the steak and serve the remaining sauce on the side. Serve with Plantain Chips.

CHIMICHURRI SAUCE

MAKES ABOUT 3/4 CUP

1 cup loosely packed parsley leaves
4 garlic cloves, coarsely chopped
1 small shallot, coarsely chopped
1/4 cup loosely packed fresh oregano leaves
1 tablespoon freshly squeezed lemon juice
2 tablespoons apple juice or red wine
2 teaspoons sweet paprika
1 teaspoon chipotle flakes or red pepper flakes
1 teaspoon ground cumin
1/4 cup extra virgin olive oil
Sea salt and freshly ground pepper

1. In a food processor, combine all the ingredients except the oil, salt, and pepper; pulse until mixture is coarsely chopped. Slowly drizzle in the oil and process until all ingredients are well combined, about 15 to 30 seconds.

2. Transfer sauce to a small bowl and season to taste with salt and pepper. Cover with plastic wrap and refrigerate until ready to use.

ARGENTINE GAUCHO GRILLED STEAK

PLANTAIN CHIPS

MAKES ABOUT 20 CHIPS

Vegetable oil for frying
2 large green plantains
Sea salt

1. Slowly heat enough vegetable oil for deep-frying (about 3 inches) in a deep pot over medium-high heat until a deep-fry thermometer reads 365°.

2. Peel the plantains (see Note) and cut in half crosswise then slice plantains into thin strips lengthwise no thicker than 1/8-inch thick. Carefully drop the plantains into the hot oil, about 6 at a time, until they are golden brown on both sides, about 3 to 4 minutes. Drain on paper towels, and immediately sprinkle with sea salt. Serve hot.

Note: To peel a plantain, use a sharp knife to score the skin down the entire length of the fruit. Lightly oil your hands so the sap does not stain them, and use your fingers to peel off the skin.

Selling peanuts on the road to Machu Picchu.

This is a terrific summer picnic dish when served cold. At its heart is a special seasoning that the Incas called uchu, which was used mostly to flavor wild game. Today, the spice blend uses the yellow chile called 'aji.' These yellow chiles are grown by small farmers in the foothills of the Andes, where I discovered this dish at the home of a local grower. If your local Latino market doesn't have an aji blend available, use ground cayenne instead. "

PERUVIAN AJI DE GALLINA
(CHICKEN IN CHILE SAUCE WITH CASHEWS)

SERVES 6 TO 8

2 pounds boneless, skinless chicken breasts
1 teaspoon salt, plus more to taste
2 slices white bread, crusts removed
2 tablespoons extra virgin olive oil
1 medium onion, finely chopped
2 garlic cloves, minced
1 teaspoon smoked paprika
1 tablespoon ground aji chile or cayenne pepper
1/2 cup unsalted cashew nuts, finely chopped
3/4 cup evaporated milk
5 tablespoons grated Parmesan cheese
8 small Peruvian blue or red bliss potatoes, boiled and cut in half
3 hard-boiled eggs, cut in half lengthwise
1/2 cup pitted black Kalamata olives
Finely chopped fresh chives, for garnish

1. Cover chicken breasts with 1 inch cold water in a medium saucepan. Add 1 teaspoon salt and bring to a boil. Boil until tender and cooked through, 10 to 15 minutes depending on the thickness of the breast.

2. Remove the chicken breasts and set aside to cool. Discard all but 1/2 cup of the cooking liquid. In a small bowl, soak the bread in the reserved liquid and set aside. When chicken is cool enough to handle, shred it into small pieces and set aside.

3. Heat the oil in a large skillet over medium heat. Add the onion, garlic, paprika, and aji chile and cook until the onions are soft, about 5 to 7 minutes. Reduce heat to low and add the soaked bread. Stir continuously with a wooden spoon breaking up the bread, about 3 minutes.

4. Add the cashews, evaporated milk, grated cheese, and shredded chicken; continue cooking for about 5 minutes more or until heated through. Transfer chicken mixture to the center of a large serving platter. Arrange potatoes around the outer edge of the platter. Top the chicken with hard-boiled egg halves and olives, and garnish with chopped chives.

> Andean mora berries are blackberries with a rich tart-sweet flavor that will delight your senses. There are plenty of desserts one can cook up using these unique berries, but I wanted to create a recipe we're already familiar with as an introduction to this new fruit treasure. Mora berries can be found in pulp form in the frozen food section of Latino markets, but you can also substitute pureed regular blackberries. I've only used them as a garnish here, as the mora berry flavor shouldn't be missed. "

ANDEAN MORA BERRY CHEESECAKE

SERVES 8

Cheesecake piecrust
2 cups graham cracker crumbs
3 to 4 tablespoons unsalted butter, melted
2 tablespoons light brown sugar
1 teaspoon ground allspice

Cheesecake filling
1 package (8 ounces) cream cheese at room temperature
1 can (14 ounces) sweetened condensed milk
1 teaspoon vanilla extract
1 egg

Mora berry topping
1/2 cup frozen mora berry pulp, thawed
1 teaspoon grated orange zest
4 tablespoons sugar
2 teaspoons cornstarch, dissolved in 1 tablespoon cold water
1 cup fresh blackberries

1. Make the piecrust: Lightly butter the bottom of a 9-inch pie plate. In a mixing bowl, add the graham cracker crumbs, butter, brown sugar, and allspice; mix well. Press crust mixture onto bottom and sides of the pie plate. Be sure to make the top edge a bit thicker than the sides. Cover and chill for about 30 minutes.

2. Preheat the oven to 350°.

3. Remove piecrust from the refrigerator and bake for about 10 to 12 minutes. Remove and let cool completely.

4. Make the filling: In a medium bowl, beat the cream cheese with an electric mixer until fluffy. Slowly add the condensed milk, vanilla, and egg; continue to beat until fluffy.

5. Pour the mixture into the cooled piecrust and bake until filling is just set, about 20 to 25 minutes.

6. Remove cheesecake from oven and let cool completely on a wire rack, then chill in the refrigerator for at least 2 hours.

7. Make the topping: In a small saucepan combine the mora berry pulp or blackberry puree, orange zest, and sugar. Bring to a slow simmer, add the dissolved cornstarch and cook until mixture begins to thicken. Remove from heat and let cool. When completely cool add the whole blackberries and stir to coat.

8. Evenly spread the mora berry topping over the top of the cheesecake. Serve at room temperature.

Variation: Fresh blueberries or raspberries can be substituted for the blackberries and a store-bought 9-inch crust can be used.

Make Ahead Tip: The cheesecake can be made up to two days ahead and kept refrigerated. When ready to serve, allow cheesecake to come to room temperature.

A variety of handmade dolls at a Peruvian marketplace

NORTH AFRICA

Perched at the top of Africa, overlooking the Mediterranean, are three countries known as the Maghreb: Algeria, Tunisia, and Morocco. I traveled there to learn more about this region's cuisine and the intricate art of their exotic spice blends, particularly those of the Berber tribesmen. • Of all the cooking styles throughout the enormous continent of Africa, the food of the Maghreb is considered to be the most inventive, flavorful, romantic, and ingenious. Just hearing the word "Maghreb" conjures up memories of my visit. I am enveloped by the scent of warm spices, orange blossoms, and honey—all perfuming its souks (markets) and winding alleyways—as I think back on my time in this sensuous land. • Each of the three countries has a distinct style of cooking, but together they share the same staples: couscous, lamb, paper-thin pastry, and sweetmeats. Tunisians love their spices, so be prepared to encounter the fiercely hot paste blend they are known for: *harissa*, made with hot chiles and other spices. In Algeria, meals are not quite as spicy, while Moroccans treasure the rich, bold flavors of their famous *tagines*, a reference to both the food and the pot in which it is cooked. • Because of its location, for hundreds of years North Africa has traded with many different peoples. Some came to visit; some invaded, but each left a legacy. In the 1st century, Phoenician traders introduced

NIRMALA'S GUIDE TO

THE FLAVORS
OF NORTH AFRICA

These ingredients are not limited to North Africa but are indispensable throughout the Middle East: Couscous, pita bread, rice, lentils, and beans are basics found either as ingredients or as accompaniments to almost every meal. There are spices galore: cumin, cinnamon, cloves, black pepper, coriander, cayenne pepper, turmeric, allspice, ginger, saffron, paprika, and five-alarm chiles are musts for the various spice blends. Some of these spices are frequently toasted to intensify their flavors. Fresh vegetables such as eggplant, tomatoes, okra, and cabbage are partnered by fresh herbs including cilantro, parsley, mint, oregano, and thyme. North African cooking also frequently uses preserved lemons—quartered lemons steeped in salt—which yield a slightly tart, acidic accent to tagines and other dishes, as are raisins and almonds.

dried sausages to Algeria, which today are called *merguez*. Thereafter, the Carthaginians brought semolina, a derivative of durum wheat, which the Berbers adapted to make the well-loved staple, couscous. The Arabs invaded in the 7th century and, as the reigning merchants of the spice world, brought exotic treasures such as cloves, cinnamon, and black pepper from the Spice Islands, known today as Indonesia. The Moors, who had been expelled from Andalusia, brought with them the recipe for delectable *B'stilla,* or pigeon pie, encased in layers of tissue-thin pastry, as well as olives, olive oil, and citrus fruits. In the 14th century, the Ottoman Turks introduced a variety of delicate, sweet pastries (the region continues to have a serious sweet tooth to this day). And during the Crimean War, tea arrived in Tangiers by way of the Europeans. • As early as the 1830s, the French ruled all of the Maghreb, occupying Algeria the longest. Today, French is fluently spoken in each country, and North Africa's cuisine has absorbed a touch of French sophistication. In Algeria, housewives today often buy French baguettes, instead of the traditional Arabic *kesra,* one of my favorite flat breads, which I use to make pizza. • The Maghreb remains a complex area combining multiple cultures (Morocco also hosts an enormous Jewish community), and in it, Berbers, Arabs, Bedouins, and Jews alike share the same ingredients to create subtle variations on their individual culinary themes.

MENU **NORTH AFRICA**

APERITIF
- MOROCCAN MINT TEA

APPETIZERS
- ALGERIAN ROASTED GARLIC-CHILE BABAGANOUSH
- TUNISIAN TUNA BRIK

SOUP
- TANGIER HARIRA SOUP (RAMADAN SOUP)

SALAD
- TUNISIAN CARROT SALAD

ENTREES
- NORTH AFRICAN SPICED LAMB BURGERS
- MOROCCAN CHICKEN TAGINE with CRANBERRY-CURRY COUSCOUS

DESSERT
- ALGERIAN SEMOLINA CAKE with SAFFRON HONEY AND PISTACHIO NUTS

“ Despite the heat of the daytime, nights are very cool in the harsh but sublime Sahara Desert, and this mint tea warmed me on many such nights. Abdul, my personal 'Indiana Jones' made it for me, and while I savored every drop he would play his *Rahab*—a kind of primitive-looking violin. It is made from goatskin, but has only one string, so let's just say that this tea tastes better when sipped to the melodious strains of Itzhak Perlman. ”

MOROCCAN MINT TEA

SERVES 2

Handful of fresh mint sprigs
2 tablespoons loose black tea or 2 tea bags (Darjeeling or
    Pekoe)
Sugar or honey

1. Tear the mint with your fingers and divide between 2 tall glasses and set aside.

2. In a small saucepan, bring 2 cups of water to a boil. Add the tea, remove saucepan from heat, and let steep, covered, for 3 minutes. Sweeten with sugar or honey to taste and stir well.

3. Pour tea through a sieve into the mint-filled glasses. Cover each glass with a saucer and let the tea steep for 2 minutes more. Remove saucers and serve.

I've had babaganoush on just about every continent. Each time I've had it, this classic spread has come with its own unique flavors and was prepared in its own particular cooking style. In Guyana, we have a version called *baigan choka,* which we eat with roti for breakfast. Our version, which is Indian, has tomatoes and the heat of hot peppers, but no parsley. The Middle Eastern version incorporates tahini, while the Maghreb version doesn't. They're all delicious, and good for you too. This recipe is my favorite and I hope will become yours as well: I created it to include all of the ingredients that I think make the perfect version. Roasting the garlic gives the mixture a nutty flavor that's braced with hot chiles, while the lemon juice and tomato give it a slightly acidic edge.

ALGERIAN ROASTED GARLIC-CHILE BABAGANOUSH

MAKES ABOUT 2 CUPS

2 large eggplants (Black Beauty variety)
6 garlic cloves
1 small Serrano or Thai chile, seeded and cut in half
1/4 cup loosely packed parsley leaves, finely chopped
1 tablespoon freshly squeezed lemon juice
3 tablespoons extra virgin olive oil
2 tablespoons tahini (optional)
1 small tomato, seeded and diced (optional)
Sea salt

1. Preheat the oven to 375°. Make four 1-inch incisions around each eggplant with a paring knife. Insert 3 garlic cloves and 1/2 of a chile into the slits of each eggplant. Wrap each eggplant tightly in 2 layers of foil. Place eggplants in a roasting pan and bake for 45 minutes. The foil packages will become quite soft and the eggplant should reduce in volume by about half.

2. Remove pan from oven and let eggplant rest until completely cool. Slice the packages open lengthwise with a sharp knife. Scoop out the insides of the roasted eggplants, including the garlic cloves and chiles, and place in a food processor. Add the parsley, lemon juice, and oil, and pulse to desired thickness. Transfer to a mixing bowl. Add the tahini and tomato, if using, and gently fold to combine. Season with salt to taste. Transfer the babaganoush to a serving bowl and serve with pita chips or roti (page 27).

TUNISIAN TUNA BRIK

MAKES ABOUT 20 BRIK

1 tablespoon extra virgin olive oil
1 small red onion, finely chopped
1/4 cup finely chopped celery
1 garlic clove, crushed
1 can (6 ounces) tuna packed in oil, drained
3 tablespoons chopped parsley leaves
1 teaspoon freshly squeezed lime juice
Sea salt and freshly ground pepper
5 sheets phyllo dough, thawed if frozen
1 large egg white, lightly beaten
Vegetable oil for frying

1. In a large skillet, heat olive oil over medium-high heat. Add the onion, celery, and garlic and cook until soft, about 5 to 7 minutes. Transfer to a medium bowl. Add the tuna, parsley, lime juice, and salt and pepper to taste; mix well and set aside until completely cooled.

2. Cut each phyllo dough sheet into 4 long strips about 4 inches wide. Cover phyllo dough with a damp kitchen towel as you work so that it does not dry out. Working quickly, take one strip of phyllo and place 1 tablespoon of the tuna mixture on the bottom of the strip, about 1/2 inch from the bottom. Lightly brush all the edges with egg wash. Diagonally fold the bottom by lifting the phyllo and filling over to form a triangle shape. Press edges together. Fold again in the opposite direction and repeat until you have a small package in the shape of a triangle. Press firmly around all edges making sure they are sealed. Transfer to a large plate and cover with damp towel as you make the remaining brik. Repeat until the filling is used up.

3. In a medium saucepan set over medium-high heat, slowly heat enough vegetable oil for deep-frying (about 3 inches) until a deep-fry thermometer reads 365°.

4. Fry the brik, a few at a time, for about 30 seconds, turning once or twice until they are lightly golden on both sides. Remove with a slotted spoon and transfer to a plate lined with paper towels. Fry remaining brik and serve immediately with a salad or Tamarind Chutney (page 151).

TUNISIAN TUNA BRIK

During the holy month of Ramadan, Muslims around the world fast from sunup to sundown, when they break their fast with this soup. When Sarhan, my driver, invited me to dinner at his home, his mother, and indeed the entire village, became very excited—they thought he was bringing home his bride. After enjoying this hearty, multi-spiced soup rich with lamb, lentils, and tomatoes, we drank a glass of milk and had some dates, which I had seen Sarhan bargain for in the market several days before. I've only found this particular custom of having sweets right after the fast in Tangier—a city in the north of Morocco.

TANGIER HARIRA SOUP
(RAMADAN SOUP)

SERVES 4 TO 6

1 pound veal or lamb loin, cut into 1-inch cubes
Sea salt and freshly ground pepper
2 tablespoons unsalted butter
2 tablespoons extra virgin olive oil
1 teaspoon ground cumin
1 teaspoon ground allspice
1/2 teaspoon ground ginger
1/2 teaspoon ground turmeric
Pinch of saffron threads
2 medium onions, chopped
3 garlic cloves, minced
3/4 cup loosely packed parsley leaves, chopped
1 + 1/2 pounds tomatoes, peeled, seeded, and chopped
2 tablespoons tomato paste
8 cups low-sodium vegetable or chicken stock
1 cup dried red lentils, rinsed
Cilantro leaves and lemon wedges for garnish

1. Season the meat with salt and pepper. In a large pot, heat butter and oil over medium-high heat. Add the meat and cook until lightly browned on all sides, about 5 minutes. Remove meat and set aside, leaving oil in the pot.

2. Reduce heat to medium-low and add the cumin, allspice, ginger, turmeric, saffron, onions, garlic, parsley, and 1/4 teaspoon salt. Sauté for 3 minutes. Add the tomatoes, tomato paste, and browned meat; cook for 10 minutes, stirring occasionally.

3. Add the stock and lentils, and bring to a boil over high heat. Reduce heat and simmer, partially covered, for 1 hour or until the soup reaches desired consistency and the lentils are tender. Add more stock if needed, and season with salt and pepper to taste. Serve very hot, garnished with cilantro leaves and lemon wedges.

Make Ahead Tip: This delicious soup can be made a day in advance. Allow it to cool, then transfer it to an airtight container and refrigerate. Reheat gently over low heat, stirring occasionally.

" While I was in El Jem, right across from the enormous ruins of the amphitheatre, I found Aziz, a very shy food vendor who serves this salad made with rounds of carrot, rather than the shredded carrot salad we're more familiar with in the U.S., wrapped in warm pita bread. I think it's the touch of sugar combined with the garlic and spices that works the magic in this particular recipe. It was the ideal accompaniment for roaming the amphitheatre, the largest building ever erected by the Romans on the African continent, and the sole cultural attraction in the city. "

TUNISIAN CARROT SALAD

SERVES 4

1 pound carrots, peeled and cut into 1/4-inch rounds
1/4 cup extra virgin olive oil
2 garlic cloves, crushed
1 teaspoon ground cumin
1 teaspoon curry powder
1/4 teaspoon cayenne, plus more to taste
1 teaspoon sugar
1 tablespoon freshly squeezed lemon juice
Sea salt and freshly ground pepper
3 tablespoons chopped cilantro

1. Place the carrots in a medium saucepan and cover with cold water. Bring to a boil over high heat and cook for 5 minutes, or until carrots are tender but still slightly crisp.

2. Drain carrots and set aside. Add the oil, garlic, cumin, curry powder, cayenne, sugar, and lemon juice to the saucepan and cook over medium heat until fragrant, about 1 minute. Add the carrots, stir, and continue cooking for 2 minutes more. Season with salt and pepper to taste. Remove carrots from heat and add the cilantro. Let cool before serving.

A night market in Marrakesh.

> I've always liked my burgers nestled into pita breads instead of buns, so in this recipe, I've shared my preference. No ordinary burger, the ground lamb is mixed with spices and a dash of barbecue sauce, then partnered with fresh warmed pitas and lettuce and onion fillings. When I was in North Africa, I was fortunate to have visited pita kitchens—it was fascinating to watch as the pita dough was kneaded and tossed into the ovens where they puffed up in seconds.

NORTH AFRICAN SPICED LAMB BURGERS

SERVES 4

1 pound ground lamb
1/3 cup seasoned breadcrumbs
1 egg yolk, lightly beaten
1/3 cup finely grated onion
1/2 teaspoon minced garlic
1 teaspoon extra virgin olive oil
1 tablespoon chopped fresh parsley
1 tablespoon chopped fresh cilantro
1 teaspoon ground cumin
1/4 teaspoon ground cayenne, plus more to taste
1 tablespoon barbecue sauce
Sea salt and freshly ground pepper
4 (7-inch) pita breads
1 cup shredded romaine lettuce
1 small red onion, thinly sliced
1/3 cup plain Greek yogurt or Tzatziki (page 118)

1. Preheat the broiler or a gas grill to 400°.

2. In a large bowl, combine the lamb, breadcrumbs, egg yolk, onion, garlic, olive oil, parsley, cilantro, cumin, cayenne, and barbecue sauce; mix well until thoroughly combined. Season with salt and pepper.

3. Shape the mixture into 4 burgers, each about 1 inch thick.

4. Broil or grill the burgers for 5 to 7 minutes on each side until browned, turning once. Remove burgers from heat and allow to rest for 2 minutes.

5. Warm the pita breads in a pan or on the grill; make a slit on the side of each pita. Place some of the lettuce and sliced onion in each pita, then place a burger inside each one. Spread with yogurt or Tzatziki and season with salt and pepper to taste.

MOROCCAN CHICKEN TAGINE
with CRANBERRY-CURRY COUSCOUS

SERVES 6 TO 8

3 tablespoons extra virgin olive oil
3 tablespoons unsalted butter
1 chicken (about 3 pounds), cut into 8 pieces
1 tablespoon ground ginger
2 teaspoons ground turmeric
1 teaspoon ground allspice
1 tablespoon smoked paprika
1/8 teaspoon saffron threads
1 large onion, chopped
2 tablespoons minced garlic
3 cups low-sodium chicken stock
2 tablespoons finely diced preserved lemon
1 cup pitted black Kalamata olives
Sea salt and freshly ground pepper
1/4 cup loosely packed cilantro leaves, finely chopped
Cranberry-Curry Couscous (recipe follows)

1. In a Dutch oven or large skillet with a tight-fitting lid, heat oil and butter over high heat. Add the chicken pieces and lightly brown on both sides, about 3 minutes per side. Transfer chicken to a plate and reduce heat to medium-low.

2. Add the ginger, turmeric, allspice, paprika, and saffron to the skillet and cook for 30 seconds stirring constantly. Add the onion and garlic and cook for 3 minutes more, stirring occasionally.

3. Return the chicken to the skillet. Add the stock and preserved lemon; stir well. Cover and cook over medium-low heat for about 30 minutes, or until chicken is cooked through.

4. Turn off heat, add the olives, and season with salt and pepper to taste. Stir, replace cover and let rest for 5 minutes.

5. To serve, place Cranberry-Curry Couscous on a platter or a tagine serving bowl and spoon the chicken and sauce over the couscous. Sprinkle with cilantro and serve immediately.

CRANBERRY-CURRY COUSCOUS

SERVES 4 TO 6

2 cups couscous
2 cups boiling chicken stock
1 teaspoon curry powder
1 teaspoon finely diced preserved lemon
1 shallot, finely diced
3 tablespoons extra virgin olive oil
1/2 cup dried cranberries
Sea salt and freshly ground pepper

1. Place couscous in a large bowl. Mix the hot stock with curry powder, preserved lemon, shallot, and olive oil. Stir and pour over couscous, add the cranberries and immediately cover. Let rest 10 minutes. Uncover and fluff with a fork. Season with salt and pepper to taste, and add more olive oil if necessary.

Variation: Barberries can be substituted for cranberries

Making pita bread in Algiers.

ALGERIAN SEMOLINA CAKE

Algeria boasts some truly great bakeries that produce warm, crusty baguettes and other French specialties, but this elegant semolina cake, flavored with orange zest and drizzled with a fragrant saffron honey, is clearly Arab in origin.

ALGERIAN SEMOLINA CAKE
with SAFFRON HONEY AND PISTACHIO NUTS

SERVES 6

1 cup semolina flour
2 + 1/3 cups hot milk
6 tablespoons unsalted butter, melted, plus additional softened butter for preparing ramekins
1 large egg, lightly beaten
1 teaspoon orange zest
1/4 teaspoon kosher salt
Saffron Honey (recipe follows)
About 1/2 cup finely chopped unsalted pistachio nuts

1. Place the semolina in a medium bowl, pour in the milk and stir until well combined. Cover the bowl with plastic wrap and let rest 10 minutes, or until the milk is completely absorbed.

2. Preheat the oven to 375°. Generously butter 6 individual 8-ounce ramekins and set aside. Add the melted butter, egg, orange zest, and salt to the semolina mixture and stir until well combined. Divide the mixture evenly among the molds, placing approximately 1/2 cup of the mixture into each one. Press down firmly so the mixture is packed well and flat on top. Place the ramekins on a baking sheet and transfer to oven. Bake until the tops just begin to brown and the cake is firm to the touch, about 15 minutes. Transfer to a cooling rack and allow to cool slightly.

3. To serve, spoon a small amount of the Saffron Honey onto 6 dessert plates. Invert the ramekins to release the cakes and place one on each plate. Prick each cake several times with a wooden skewer almost to the bottom, then evenly pour the remaining Saffron Honey evenly over the cakes. Sprinkle with pistachio nuts for garnish.

SAFFRON HONEY

1 cup honey
2 large pinches saffron threads
2 whole star anise
1/4 teaspoon rose water or orange water

1. In a small saucepan, combine the honey, 1/2 cup water, saffron, star anise, and rose water. Bring the mixture to a boil over medium-high heat, stirring occasionally. Reduce heat to medium-low and simmer until the mixture thickens, about 5 minutes.

MEDITERRANEAN

Out of the many islands and countries that comprise the Mediterranean, the three that intrigue me the most are Greece, Cyprus, and Turkey. This region bears the indelible marks of the many civilizations that have ruled, namely, the ancient Hittites, the Romans, and the mighty Ottoman Empire. Their cities are embedded with magnificent architecture, sky-blue domes, mosaic-tiled walkways, and intricate minarets and mosques. Surrounded by blue skies and azure seas, you can wander scarlet bougainvillea-laden alleyways and ancient roads once traversed by the gods and goddesses of myth. The sun warms whitewashed homes and vast vineyards, citrus, and olive groves alike. To escape the heat, take a dip in the sea, where the great Poseidon once ruled. • The culinary map of this region is unique in that each country shares the same ingredients, yet each has developed its own singular style, rooted in antiquity. • Turkey, with one foot in Asia and the other in Europe, has a cuisine that goes far beyond *shish kebabs*. The powerful sultans of the once-flourishing Ottoman Empire had imaginative, if erotic, sensibilities, as evidenced by the names of some dishes: "Ladies' Navels" and "Sweet Lips" were dessert cakes laden with sugar syrup; "Women's Thighs" were long,

THE FLAVORS OF THE MEDITERRANEAN

Lemons, garlic, and yogurt are prime ingredients for prepared dishes and in marinades. There are dozens of fruity, aromatic olive oils and sweet honeys. Cheeses, such as kefalotyri, Manouri, and feta, are enjoyed on their own and serve as ingredients in traditional meals, too. Spice shelves of the region house coriander, allspice, cinnamon, cumin, bay leaves, and cloves. In the fresh herb department, rosemary, oregano, thyme, mint, and dill are essential. Olives of all kinds are used in cooking, and eggplants, okra, capers, dates, and figs are also plentiful. Grape leaves are brined and used for enclosing a variety of fillings. Commonly used grains include brown lentils, black-eyed peas, and broad beans, all of which are used in soups. Lamb and seafood are abundant, versatile sources of protein. And of course, extra virgin olive oil and a good loaf of bread are givens.

shapely mounds of rice and minced meat. Contemporary Turkish dishes include *borek,* a layered pastry dish filled with cheese, meats, and fish, and *pilav,* a cracked-wheat pilaf made with tomatoes, onions, and peppers, all sautéed in butter. • Greece, home to more than 2,000 islands, is a haven for some of the freshest seafood in the world. Much of its culinary heritage reflects its nearly 400 years of Turkish rule. Today, popular Greek dishes include my all-time favorite seafood soup, *soupa tou psara* (page 124), and *kotopita,* a phyllo-encased chicken pie. • In Cyprus are world-renowned vineyards, said to have borne fruit for the wines of the gods. In fact, the Old Testament's Song of Solomon compares the sweetness of a woman's kiss to the sweetness of Cyprus's grapes. This was the home of Aphrodite, the goddess of love, and even Marc Anthony felt its passion so strongly that he gave the island to Cleopatra in 36 BC as a gift. • Many of the region's foods were introduced by its neighbors: dates, okra, and onions came from Persia and the African continent. Alexander the Great brought rice from India, and in the 16th century, chiles and tomatoes arrived from the Americas. • Mediterranean cuisine, sumptuous enough to appease the gods, more than satisfies the epicurean tastes of those of us here on earth.

MENU MEDITERRANEAN

APERITIF
- MEDITERRANEAN SPICED LEMONADE

MEZE
- YOGURT DIP (TZATZIKI) WITH SPICED PITA CHIPS
- CYPRUS SPICED OLIVES
- SULTAN'S STUFFED DOLMADES
- TURKISH LAMB KEBABS
- ZUCCHINI PANCAKES

SOUP
- GREEK FISHERMAN'S SOUP (SOUPA TOU PSARA)

SALAD
- JOHN'S GREEK VILLAGE SALAD

ENTREES
- TUNA IN GRAPE LEAVES with SHALLOT AND CAPER SAUCE
- AUNT ROSALIE'S ROAST LEG OF LAMB, CYPRIOT-STYLE

DESSERT
- APHRODITE'S FIGS with HONEY

❝ Be warned:
Mediterranean lemons are
fragrant, plump and powerful,
packing such an intense
lemon tartness that your
mouth will water like never
before. But add a little spice
and a touch of honey, and
that wild fruit will be
enchantingly tamed. If you've
never tamed a lemon before,
this recipe works just as well
with our own supermarket
variety. ❞

MEDITERRANEAN SPICED LEMONADE

SERVES 4

1/2 cup freshly squeezed lemon juice
2 cinnamon sticks (about 3 inches long)
8 whole cloves
6 tablespoons honey
Lemon slices and fresh mint sprigs for garnish

1. In a medium saucepan, combine 4 cups cold water, lemon juice, cinnamon, and cloves; bring to a boil over medium-high heat. As soon as the mixture boils, turn off heat and pour it through a sieve into a large pitcher. Discard spices. Stir in honey until dissolved. Serve warm in mugs, or chill and serve over ice. Garnish with lemon slices and mint sprigs.

❝ Meze is the heart of Mediterranean life—they bring people together much the way backyard barbecues do here. Enjoyed outdoors on a beautiful day, these "tasty morsels" (translated from the Greek) are meant to be the gateway to lavish main meals. Usually finger foods, meze are presented as an assortment of small plates offering a variety of tastes and textures. Of course, they all showcase the wealth of the region's wonderful herbs and spices. My Turkish friend, Mithin, shared some meze etiquette: olive oil is a must—almost everything is drizzled with it. Meze can be served warm, cold, or even at room temperature but all of the dishes should be served at once so that guests can delight in the variety of foods. I've hosted many meze and wine parties here at home because they're so simple to put together, making it an easy way to gather with friends. I get to spend more time with them instead of being stuck in the kitchen. These are some of my favorite meze, which can be assembled in a flash. When I make them, my guests leave feeling satisfied and happy. ❞

" In Greece, tzatziki is the classic dinner party dip. You know it as the yogurt-cucumber-garlic-and-dill mixture that's placed on your table in a Greek restaurant before you place your order. In Turkey they call it *cacik;* in Cyprus, it's *talattouri,* but they all share the same ingredients. I like to serve it with fresh-baked, spiced pita chips for dipping. "

YOGURT DIP (TZATZIKI)
WITH SPICED PITA CHIPS

SERVES 4 TO 6

2 medium cucumbers, peeled and coarsely grated
2 + 1/4 cups Greek yogurt or plain whole milk yogurt
1 tablespoon chopped fresh dill or mint, plus more for garnish
1 tablespoon extra virgin olive oil
2 garlic cloves, coarsely chopped
Sea salt and freshly ground pepper
Pitted black olives for garnish
Spiced Pita Chips

1. Place grated cucumber in cheesecloth or a clean kitchen towel and squeeze to release as much water as possible. In a food processor, combine the cucumber, yogurt, dill, oil, and garlic and pulse until smooth.

2. Transfer mixture to a large bowl and season with salt and pepper to taste. Cover with plastic wrap and chill until ready to serve. Just before serving, garnish with dill and black olives.

SPICED PITA CHIPS

3 tablespoons extra virgin olive oil
1 teaspoon ground cumin
1 teaspoon minced garlic
3 whole wheat or white pita breads, each cut into 6 triangles
Sea salt and freshly ground pepper

1. Preheat oven to 350°. In a medium bowl, stir together the oil, cumin, and garlic. Add the pita triangles and gently toss until the bread is evenly coated, then place on a large baking sheet in a single layer. Sprinkle with salt and pepper.

2. Bake until crisp, shaking the pan halfway through, about 8 to 10 minutes. Serve warm with Yogurt Dip.

There's one thing you will always find in my kitchen: homemade spiced olives. Marinating your own olives is quite easy, and they'll stay fresh-tasting for weeks. In my case, they only last a few days because I love them so much.

CYPRUS SPICED OLIVES

MAKES 3 CUPS

3 cups fresh Greek or Kalamata olives
2 tablespoons diced lemon zest
1 tablespoon coriander seeds, lightly crushed (see Note)
4 garlic cloves, lightly crushed
1 sprig fresh thyme
3 large or 6 small Thai chiles
2 Turkish bay leaves
1 tablespoon whole peppercorns, lightly crushed (see Note)
Extra virgin olive oil

1. Rinse the olives and pat them dry with paper towels. Score or crack each olive and place in a large bowl. Add the lemon zest, coriander, garlic, thyme, chiles, bay leaves, and peppercorns and toss until well combined.

2. Place the olive mixture in a large glass jar with a tight-fitting lid. Tightly pack the ingredients into the jar and pour enough olive oil to cover the olives by 1/2 inch. Close the jar tightly and let the olives stand at room temperature for 1 + 1/2 to 2 weeks before serving. Gently stir the olives every few days.

3. Scoop olives from marinade using a slotted spoon and place in a medium bowl. Serve as part of your meze.

Tip: The remaining marinade can be used as a salad dressing or an excellent dipping oil for crusty bread.

Note: To crush peppercorns and coriander seeds, place in a self-sealing plastic bag and pound with a small, heavy saucepan, rolling pin, or mallet.

In Turkey, these stuffed, rolled-up grape leaves are called *zeytingyalgi yaprak;* in Cyprus, they're *koupepia,* but I like to stick to the easy-to-pronounce Greek word— dolmades. Generally, the grape leaves encase a filling of minced meat or vegetables. My recipe, a vegetarian delight, is stuffed with rice and a hint of the sweet, fresh figs and pine nuts that grow in abundance in this part of the world. "

SULTAN'S STUFFED DOLMADES

MAKES ABOUT 35 DOLMADES

3/4 cup extra virgin olive oil
2 medium onions, finely chopped
2 garlic cloves, minced
1/2 cup pine nuts
1/2 teaspoon ground allspice
1 cup long-grain rice
1 + 1/2 cups low-sodium vegetable stock
1 jar (8 ounces) grape leaves
2 fresh ripe figs, diced
2 tablespoons finely chopped fresh dill
1/4 cup finely chopped parsley
Sea salt and freshly ground pepper
2 tablespoons freshly squeezed lemon juice

1. Prepare the rice stuffing: Pour 1/2 cup of the olive oil into a large skillet and heat over medium-high heat. Add the onion and garlic and cook until soft, stirring frequently, 5 to 7 minutes. Add the pine nuts, allspice and rice, and stir so that the rice is evenly coated with the oil. Sauté for 3 minutes, stirring occasionally.

2. Add 1 cup of the stock and bring to a boil. Reduce heat and simmer until all the liquid has been absorbed and the rice is still firm on the inside, about 10 minutes. Transfer the rice mixture to a large bowl and let cool.

3. Meanwhile, soak the grape leaves in a large bowl of warm water until the leaves are loose and pliable, about 10 minutes. Drain, and trim away any hard stems with scissors. Pat leaves dry with paper towels.

4. Add the figs, dill, and parsley to the rice mixture and toss to combine. Season with salt and pepper to taste.

5. To assemble the dolmades, lay one grape leaf on a work surface with the shinier side facing down. Place about 1 + 1/2 tablespoons of the rice filling near the stem end of the leaf. Fold the stem end over the filling, then fold both sides toward the middle, and roll up like a cigar. (The leaf should be snug but not overly tight, as the rice will swell once it is fully cooked.)

6. Place any torn or extra grape leaves on the bottom of a large round skillet large enough to hold the stuffed grape leaves in a single layer. Lay the stuffed grape leaves over them, seam sides down, in a single layer.

7. Pour the remaining 1/2 cup stock, remaining 1/4 cup olive oil, and lemon juice over the grape leaves. The liquid should reach about halfway up the rolls; add water if necessary. Cover the skillet and simmer over low heat for 35 minutes, or until the grape leaves are tender when pierced with a knife or fork. Allow to cool in the pan and serve at room temperature.

Variation: 1/2 cup of raisins, dried cranberries, or diced apricots can be substituted for the figs.

TURKISH LAMB KEBABS

SERVES 4 TO 6

2 pounds lamb shoulder, cut into 1-inch cubes
1 medium zucchini, cut into 1/2-inch pieces
18 fresh bay leaves
2 garlic cloves, crushed
1 tablespoon dried oregano
1/2 cup extra virgin olive oil
1/3 cup freshly squeezed lemon juice
Sea salt and freshly ground pepper
Chopped parsley and lemon wedges for garnish
Yogurt Dip (page 118)
Pita Bread

1. Assemble the kebabs: Alternately thread the lamb cubes, zucchini, and bay leaves onto six 12- to 14-inch metal skewers, placing 3 bay leaves on each skewer.

2. Place the kebabs in a large baking pan. In a small bowl, whisk together the garlic, oregano, oil, and lemon juice. Pour the marinade over the kebabs, cover with plastic wrap, and refrigerate for at least 45 minutes or up to 2 hours, turning occasionally so they marinate evenly.

3. Heat a charcoal or gas grill until very hot. Grill the kebabs for 3 to 5 minutes on each side until medium-rare, or longer for well done. The kebabs can also be cooked in a preheated broiler.

4. Transfer kebabs to a heated serving platter and sprinkle with salt, pepper, and parsley. Serve warm with lemon wedges, Yogurt Dip, and pita bread. Discard the bay leaves as meat and vegetables are removed from the skewers while eating.

❝ I fell in love with lamb kebabs in the town now called Kapikiri, the same place that the moon goddess, Selena, fell in love with the handsome shepherd, Endymion of Greek myth. The kebabs of my dreams were made with fresh Turkish bay leaves, which lend a slightly sweet yet complex flavor that is quite different from the dried bay leaves we're used to using. They also emit a lovely floral aroma that perfumes the air while grilling. When my brothers and I were growing up in Astoria, Queens, we treasured the *souvlaki* sold by the food vendors in our Greek neighborhood, but these Turkish kebabs quickly turned my taste buds around. ❞

ZUCCHINI PANCAKES

ZUCCHINI PANCAKES

MAKES ABOUT 10 PANCAKES

2 medium zucchini, grated (about 2 cups)
1 medium onion, grated
1 teaspoon minced garlic
1/4 cup breadcrumbs
1/4 cup self-rising flour
1 tablespoon chopped parsley
1 egg, lightly beaten
1/3 cup grated Greek Kefalotyri cheese or grated Parmesan cheese
Sea salt and freshly ground pepper
Vegetable oil for frying
Yogurt Dip (page 118)

1. Place grated zucchini in cheesecloth or a clean kitchen towel and squeeze to release as much water as possible; set aside. Repeat with grated onion.

2. In a large bowl, combine the zucchini, onion, garlic, breadcrumbs, flour, parsley, egg, and cheese; season with salt and pepper to taste. Mix until the mixture is well combined and holds together.

3. Lightly coat a large nonstick skillet with oil and heat over medium-high heat until hot but not smoking. Drop zucchini mixture, 2 tablespoons at a time, into skillet and flatten into 1/4-inch thick pancakes with an offset spatula. Cook 2 to 3 minutes on each side or until pancakes are golden and cooked through. Drain on a plate lined with paper towels and serve hot with Yogurt Dip.

Almost every coastal fishing village in Greece boasts its own seafood soup featuring the local catch of the day. This recipe is the traditional base for a simple yet authentic version. You can add more shellfish, if you prefer, and tweak the ingredients to your taste. Try to use fish stock, which is available frozen in some specialty markets, as it adds a deeper layer of seafood flavor. The usual Greek companion to this soup is a cool glass of Retsina, a strong-flavored Greek white wine.

GREEK FISHERMAN'S SOUP
(SOUPA TOU PSARA)

SERVES 4

1 can (28 ounces) whole peeled tomatoes in juice
2 tablespoons extra virgin olive oil
2 medium onions, finely chopped
4 garlic cloves, minced
2 carrots, diced
3 celery stalks, diced
2 teaspoons ground cumin
2 teaspoons paprika
2 bay leaves
1 teaspoon chopped fresh thyme leaves
2 tablespoons chopped parsley
8 cups low-sodium fish stock or vegetable stock
1/2 pound boneless halibut, cod or other white firm-fleshed fish, cut into 1-inch cubes
10 mussels, debearded and scrubbed
10 littleneck clams, debearded and scrubbed
1/2 pound large shrimp, peeled and deveined
1 pound sea scallops, membranes trimmed
Sea salt and freshly ground pepper
Chopped parsley and lemon wedges for garnish

1. Drain tomatoes and reserve liquid. Coarsely chop tomatoes and set aside.

2. Heat oil in a large pot over medium-high heat. Sauté the onions and garlic for 2 minutes, stirring occasionally. Add the carrots, celery, cumin, paprika, and tomatoes; cook for 5 minutes, stirring frequently. Add the bay leaves, thyme, parsley, stock, and reserved tomato juice. Raise heat to high and bring soup to a boil, then reduce heat to a simmer and cook for 10 minutes more.

3. Add the halibut, mussels, clams, shrimp, and scallops. Increase heat and bring back to a boil. Season soup with salt and pepper to taste, cover, and reduce heat to low and simmer until the seafood is tender and cooked through, about 8 to 10 minutes. Divide soup among 4 warm soup bowls, sprinkle each serving with parsley and serve with lemon wedges.

Variations: Monkfish, swordfish, and red snapper are also good choices for this soup.

❝ I really didn't have to travel to Greece to find out how to make this wonderful salad—I've known how it is made since I was twelve years old, at home in Astoria, Queens. To the left of our neighborhood, it seemed that all of Greece had moved in, and it's where I developed my curiosity about Greek food. John and his wife, who were among our gracious neighbors, made this salad for my mother, the vegetarian in our family. It is bursting with zesty, savory ingredients like capers and feta cheese, but cooled by cucumber and sweet red and yellow bell peppers. It's the real thing. ❞

JOHN'S GREEK VILLAGE SALAD

SERVES 4

4 medium tomatoes cored and cut into 1-inch wedges
1 cup pitted Kalamata olives
2 medium cucumbers, unpeeled, cut into 1/2-inch rounds
1 medium red onion, thinly sliced
1 tablespoon capers, rinsed and drained
1 tablespoon fresh oregano leaves
1 cup shredded romaine lettuce
1 cup diced red and yellow bell peppers, seeds and membranes removed
1/4 cup extra virgin olive oil
2 tablespoons freshly squeezed lemon juice
1 tablespoon red wine vinegar
6 ounces feta cheese, cubed
Sea salt and freshly ground pepper

1. In a large bowl, toss together the tomatoes, olives, cucumber, onion, capers, oregano, lettuce, and peppers. Drizzle the salad with olive oil, lemon juice, and vinegar, and toss until all ingredients are evenly coated. Sprinkle with feta cheese and season with salt and pepper to taste.

TUNA IN GRAPE LEAVES

When you love fish as much as I do, you want to go directly to the source. There's nothing more exhilarating than catching a fish you're going to cook yourself. To get the best fish, it's a good idea to befriend a fisherman, and since I was in the quaint fishing village of Perdika in the island-dotted Saronic Gulf, this wasn't a difficult task. Yet even in this small fishing village, I had to prove to Captain Zale and his crew of two that I had adequate knowledge of Greek food, just to get them to take me out to sea. I dutifully named some Greek ingredients and rattled off some recipes, but instead the crew plopped down a red mullet for me to clean. I cleaned and scaled the mullet, but left the tail fins on because I knew that fishermen liked to see their fish in their natural state. That was my ticket! I got on board and later that evening after sharing a bottle of good Greek table wine, the fishermen caught two tuna with which they made this fabulous meal wrapped in grape leaves. Before wrapping the tuna steaks, the crew dipped each grape leaf into seawater. Talk about intense flavor!

TUNA IN GRAPE LEAVES
WITH SHALLOT AND CAPER SAUCE

SERVES 4

16 to 20 grape leaves in brine
2 tablespoons freshly squeezed lemon juice
4 garlic cloves, minced
1/4 cup extra virgin olive oil
1/4 teaspoon sea salt
Pinch of freshly ground pepper
4 tuna steaks, 7 to 8 ounces each
Shallot and Caper Sauce (recipe follows)
Fresh mint leaves for garnish
Seeds of 1/2 medium pomegranate (optional)

1. In a medium bowl filled with hot water, soak the grape leaves until pliable, 10 to 15 minutes. Preheat the oven to 375°.

2. Whisk together the lemon juice, garlic, oil, salt, and pepper in a medium bowl. Add the tuna fillets and turn to coat. Marinate for 20 minutes, turning several times so the tuna marinates evenly.

3. Drain the grape leaves and trim away any hard stems with scissors; pat dry with paper towels. Place 4 to 5 grape leaves on a work surface, slightly overlapping each other. Place one tuna steak in the center of the leaves, along with some of the marinade. Fold leaves over the tuna steak so that it is completely enveloped. Use additional leaves if necessary. Transfer the wrapped tuna package to a shallow baking dish and continue to wrap remaining steaks.

4. Transfer baking dish to oven and bake 8 to 10 minutes for rare, or 10 to 12 minutes for medium-rare, depending on the thickness of the fish. To serve, place tuna parcel at the center of a large plate with Shallot and Caper Sauce on the side. Garnish with mint leaves and sprinkle with pomegranate seeds, if using.

SHALLOT AND CAPER SAUCE

MAKES ABOUT 3/4 CUP

1 tablespoon capers, chopped
1/4 cup Greek yogurt or plain whole-milk yogurt
1 tablespoon finely minced shallot
1 tablespoon finely chopped parsley
2 teaspoons grainy mustard
1 teaspoon freshly squeezed lemon juice
Sea salt and freshly ground pepper

1. In a small bowl, whisk together all ingredients. Season with salt and pepper to taste.

AUNT ROSALIE'S ROAST LEG OF LAMB, CYPRIOT-STYLE

SERVES 10

1 teaspoon ground cumin
1 teaspoon ground coriander
1 teaspoon paprika
1 teaspoon kosher salt
1/2 teaspoon freshly ground pepper
1 leg of lamb, bone in, about 6 to 7 + 1/2 pounds
2 lemons, cut in half crosswise, seeds removed
7 garlic cloves, peeled and sliced in half lengthwise
3 tablespoons chopped fresh rosemary leaves
1 cup low-sodium vegetable or beef stock

1. Make a rub for the lamb by combining the cumin, coriander, paprika, salt, and pepper in a small bowl. Stir to combine and set aside. Position an oven rack as low as possible and preheat the oven to 450°. Trim excess fat from the lamb, rinse with cold water, and pat dry with a paper towel.

2. Place the lamb in a large roasting pan. Make fourteen 1-inch deep incisions all around the lamb and squeeze the lemons over the meat. Sprinkle the rub over the lamb on all sides, massaging it well into the meat and incisions.

3. Insert a pinch of chopped rosemary and a slice of garlic in each of the 14 incisions pushing them down beneath the surface.

4. Pour the stock into the roasting pan, taking care not to pour it over the lamb. Tightly cover pan with aluminum foil and place in oven. After 30 minutes, remove foil and reduce the oven temperature to 350°. Continue to cook until an instant-read thermometer inserted in the thickest part of the lamb registers 140° for rare, or 145° for medium-rare, about 1 + 1/2 hours more. Remove pan from oven, transfer meat to a serving platter, and let meat rest 15 minutes before carving.

"All week long, George, my taxi driver, had been bragging about his Aunt Rosalie's lamb, and with a note of patriotic pride in his voice declared that the way she made it was much better than the way the Turks or Greeks did. I wanted to experience Cypriot-style lamb, so one Saturday, George took me to meet his Aunt Rosalie. She immediately hugged me so tightly that she nearly squeezed the breath out of me, pinched my cheeks, then squeezed my hands and shoulders to see if I was plump enough...just like my grandmother! Without being able to speak a word of English, George's vivacious aunt prepared the best lamb I have ever tasted. She made it in a terra-cotta cooking vessel with a tight-fitting lid called a *tava*. The meat was so tender that it was falling off the bone. Aunt Rosalie had spiced the lamb with pinches and dashes of coriander, cumin, and paprika, and she did it the way I do—by eye—which is the way I've cooked since I was a child. Of course, if you want to go head to head with George and make this dish in the Turkish or Greek style, simply omit the trio of spices. "

" Fresh figs are like the fruits of the gods, with their warm color and sensual, exotic, sweet flavor. So in honor of Aphrodite, the Greek goddess of love, beauty, and not to mention sexual pleasure, I've created a simple yet decadent dessert. Do try to find the light, sweet, semi-soft Greek Manouri cheese and real Greek yogurt, which is thicker, richer, and slightly more tart than the supermarket yogurt usually found here. Drizzled with honey and heavenly orange blossom water, this dessert would drive Aphrodite wild. "

APHRODITE'S FIGS WITH HONEY

SERVES 4

8 fresh ripe figs, stems trimmed
1 cup Greek Manouri cheese
1 cup Greek yogurt
1/4 cup honey
1/4 teaspoon orange blossom water or rose water
Fresh mint sprigs for garnish

1. Cut the figs into 1/2-inch cubes, reserving about 12 of the pieces. Evenly divide the remaining figs among 4 stemmed wine glasses; set aside.

2. In a medium bowl, combine the cheese, yogurt, honey, and orange blossom water. Using a hand-held electric mixer, blend until mixture is very smooth.

3. Spoon about 1/2 cup of the cheese mixture over each serving of chopped figs. Sprinkle the reserved figs over the cheese topping, garnish with mint sprigs and serve immediately.

Variations: Fresh peaches can be substituted for the figs, and you can use ricotta or cottage cheese in place of Greek Manouri cheese.

ISRAEL

I went to Israel in search of a date, the kind that melts in your mouth like a cube of brown sugar. I was looking for one in particular, called Deglet Nour, Arabic for "finger of light." • Israel, the tiny land perched in the Middle East, is a country of magnificent beauty, replete with a wealth of fresh ingredients. Olive trees flourish on local Kibbutzim, providing fruity, flavorful oil for cooking and the vineyards that weave through the rolling hills of the Golan Heights produce some of the best dessert wines I've ever tasted. As a finishing touch to any meal, try a drizzle of delectable honey from the Jordan valley. • Centuries ago, the Jewish people were banished from their land by the Romans, and were forced to migrate throughout the world. This diaspora (literally, dispersal), however, could not break the rituals and connection of their own people. They zealously preserved their culture, traditions, and most important, their foods. Wherever the Jewish people found themselves, they adapted traditional foods by integrating the local ingredients of their new-found homes. • In 1948, Israel was established as a Jewish state and hundreds of thousands of Jews returned "home," bringing with them the flavors of their journeys. In general, Jewish cooking falls into two categories: Ashkenazi and Sephardic. The Ashkenazi Jews, who returned from central and

NIRMALA'S GUIDE TO
THE FLAVORS OF ISRAEL

A little bit of everything goes into Israeli cooking. Consider couscous, nuts, honey, lentils, and beans such as fava beans, chickpeas, and black-eyed peas. Israeli food features lots of vegetables, such as eggplant, artichokes, and peppers, and most-used on the spice shelf are cumin, caraway seed, paprika, and cardamom. Parsley, cilantro, and dill are indispensable fresh herbs. For decadent desserts, there is a bounty of fresh fruit: dates, quinces, cherries, and plums.

eastern Europe, tend to use slow-cooking methods such as stewing and roasting, which create juices for flavor, but call for few herbs. They also used ingredients that natives discarded, including innards and organ meats. Fiery horseradish is served with meat and fish dishes, and *always* accompanies the love-it-or-hate-it dish, gefilte fish. Ashkenazi Jews, particularly those of Austrian and Hungarian descent, were also known for being great bakers, perfecting delicacies such as strudel, challah (the braided egg bread that makes the best French toast in the world), and my favorite, the bagel. • The Jews of Spain, Morocco and North Africa, known as Sephardim, have contributed the flavors of their native regions. Sephardic dishes, along with Arab, Druze and Bedouin fare, are imbued with the warm overtones of fresh and preserved lemons, fruits, olives, exotic spices, and flavorful herbs. This cuisine has a long tradition of mouth-watering dishes to sate the most adventurous palate. In Israel, I was fortunate enough to be able to feast on both cuisines in several private homes (I've also sampled Sephardic-style cooking in Morocco, Tunisia, Lebanon, Italy, Ethiopia, and southern India.) Today, Israeli fare has blossomed into a unique, sophisticated cuisine. At its roots, it retains the ancestral heritage of a people from many walks of life and is a celebration of life around the dinner table.

MENU **ISRAEL**

APERITIF
- SPICED HIBISCUS FLOWER TEA

APPETIZER
- ISRAELI HUMMUS

SOUP
- ISRAELI COUSCOUS SOUP

SALAD
- FATTOUSH SALAD with SUMAC

ENTREE
- MATZOH-CRUSTED TILAPIA with ZHOUG

DESSERT
- CARDAMOM COCONUT MACAROONS

SPICED HIBISCUS FLOWER TEA

SERVES 4

1 cup dried hibiscus flower petals
2 whole cloves
1 cinnamon stick (about 3 inches long)
2 tablespoons freshly squeezed lime juice
1/4 cup sugar
Lime wedges for garnish

1. Rinse and drain the hibiscus flowers in a colander. In a medium saucepan, combine 5 cups water, hibiscus, cloves, and cinnamon; cover and bring to a boil over high heat. Reduce heat and let simmer for 15 minutes.

2. Strain the tea through a fine sieve and discard the flower petals and spices. Add lime juice and sugar to taste, stirring until sugar is dissolved. Pour into a pitcher and refrigerate until well-chilled. Serve in glasses over ice and garnish each drink with a slice of lime.

Before departing for my journey into the Judean desert, my driver, David, and I stopped by Tel Aviv's Yemenite quarter to stock up on rations for our trip. A sweet aroma wafting from one of the shops lured me inside where I met Farees, a Bedouin merchant and a friend of David's. Farees offered us glasses of bright red hibiscus tea, Arab style—laced with spice. David tutored me in how to sip the warm elixir with a cube of sugar between my teeth, as both the Sephardic and Ashkenazi Jews still do, but here I've added the sugar directly into the brew. This tea, made with whole dried hibiscus flowers has a cranberry-like taste with overtones of citrus and spice. Traditionally, it is served warm, but I prefer it ice-cold—it's both pretty and refreshing.

SPICED HIBISCUS FLOWER TEA

ISRAELI HUMMUS

SERVES 4 TO 6

2 cups plus 2 tablespoons cooked or canned chickpeas, rinsed
1/4 cup tahini (sesame seed paste)
4 tablespoons freshly squeezed lemon juice
2 garlic cloves, coarsely chopped
About 1/2 cup plus 2 tablespoons extra virgin olive oil
3/4 teaspoon sea salt
Cayenne and chopped parsley for garnish
Pita bread or store-bought or homemade spiced Pita Chips (Page 118) for serving

1. In a food processor, combine 2 cups chickpeas, tahini, lemon juice, garlic, 1/2 cup olive oil, and 3/4 teaspoon salt; blend until smooth. Drizzle additional olive oil into mixture to obtain the desired consistency (it should be thick enough to spoon onto pita bread or chips). Season to taste with additional lemon juice and salt.

2. Transfer hummus to serving bowl. Garnish with remaining 2 tablespoons chickpeas, cayenne, and parsley; drizzle with remaining 2 tablespoons olive oil. Serve with pita bread or Spiced Pita Chips.

❝ One hot day, I decided to immerse myself in the Old City of Jerusalem. Its 3,000 year-old, still-thriving history is written in its densely packed streets, and colorful open markets and bazaars. I came across a food stall tucked into an alleyway, where a man stood behind his makeshift kitchen. Without exchanging a word, he gestured for me to sit on his plastic chair. As I rested my tired feet, a much-needed breeze scented with jasmine and bougainvillea brushed across my face. A few Arabs down the alleyway sat cross-legged, smoking their hookahs. From an apartment window above, a beautiful young woman offered me a shy smile as she reeled in her clothesline, dangling with wet baby clothes. It was a joy to take in these simple sensations. My food merchant returned with a bowl of hummus, glistening with olive oil, sprinkled with whole chickpeas and drenched in hot sauce. This is one of the best versions of hummus I've ever had. When I reproduced the recipe at home, I substituted cayenne for the hot sauce, although you can mix in hot chile sauce if you wish. Try to make fresh-baked pita chips for scooping up the hummus—they make a big difference. ❞

> ❝ I enjoyed this unusual, couscous-based soup while camping in the Negev desert, where I spent several nights in the elaborately decorated tents of the Bedouins. Israeli couscous grains are deliciously plump and tender when cooked and look like mother-of-pearl. Packed with vegetables, potato, and couscous, simmered with homemade stock and garnished with hard-boiled eggs, this soup is immensely satisfying and sustaining. ❞

ISRAELI COUSCOUS SOUP

SERVES 4

3 tablespoons extra virgin olive oil
1 medium onion, finely chopped
4 garlic cloves, minced
2 teaspoons ground cumin
1/8 teaspoon salt
2 medium carrots, peeled and diced
1 large celery stalk, diced
1 small russet potato, peeled and diced
1 cup Israeli couscous
8 cups chicken stock
Sea salt and freshly ground pepper
2 cups loosely packed baby spinach, washed
1 cup loosely packed cilantro leaves, chopped
2 hard boiled eggs, halved

1. Heat oil in a large saucepan over medium-high heat. Add the onion, garlic, cumin, and salt and sauté until onions are soft, stirring occasionally, about 5 minutes.

2. Add the carrots, celery, potato, and couscous and continue to cook, stirring frequently, for 1 minute. Add stock and increase heat to high. Bring soup to a boil, then reduce heat to a steady simmer. Cook until the vegetables are just tender and couscous is still firm, about 5 minutes. Season with salt and pepper to taste.

3. Just before serving, add the spinach. Divide the soup evenly among 4 large soup bowls and garnish with cilantro and eggs.

Mostly a Syrian and Lebanese dish, fattoush seems to have originated as a good way to use up leftover bread, in this case, pita bread. Some believe fattoush must be adorned with pomegranate seeds, some insist upon green bell pepper and onions among the ingredients, and many make it with purslane—a tasty, lemony-tangy salad green. However you make it, though, it is mouth-watering. I had come to meet a Lebanese Jew named Azday, who came to Galilee from Beirut in the 1960s. His home overlooks the calm ripples of the great Sea of Galilee. Azday told me that as he had not caught any fish that day, he would prepare a salad for me. As he was assembling it, I saw that he was adding sumac, a ground red berry widely used in Arabic cooking. He was thrilled to learn that I knew about sumac which, with its burst of slightly sour yet fruity lemon-like flavor, is essential to this salad. If you can't find purslane, try using a slightly peppery green such as arugula or watercress. Fattoush is exotic yet extra-easy to make, and is a perfect dish to enjoy in hot weather.

FATTOUSH SALAD WITH SUMAC

SERVES 2

1 plain pita bread
1 tablespoon ground sumac
2 tablespoons freshly squeezed lemon juice
1/4 cup extra virgin olive oil
Sea salt and freshly ground pepper
1 medium cucumber, peeled and chopped
1 large or 2 small tomatoes, chopped
2 radishes, washed, trimmed, and thinly sliced
1/4 cup chopped parsley
1 small head Boston lettuce, chopped
1/2 cup whole purslane leaves (optional)

1. Cut the pita bread in half and toast in the toaster until well browned. Tear into large pieces and set aside.

2. In a small bowl, whisk together the sumac, lemon juice, olive oil, salt, and pepper to make the dressing.

3. In a large salad bowl, combine the cucumber, tomatoes, radishes, parsley, lettuce, and purslane, if using. Pour the dressing over the salad and toss well. Add the pita bread immediately before serving and lightly toss (the bread should be lightly coated with the dressing).

"Azday, my Galilean friend who had prepared the zesty fattoush salad for me, took me on a day trip to a Druze village in the Carmel Mountains to seek Saint Peter's Fish. I had heard so much about this fish but had never seen one, nor could I begin to imagine what kind of fish it could be. I was surprised to find that the famous fish was tilapia—available at almost any fish market in America—so named because St. Peter and his companions had fished for it in the Sea of Galilee. Arriving at the Druze village (the Druze are a Muslim religious sect primarily settled in the mountains of Lebanon and Syria) was like taking a trip into antiquity: the souks, or markets, were vibrantly colored with heaps of fragrant spices, aromatic fruits, vegetables, and herbs. The Druze are among the most hospitable people I've met, and that day Azday, my Saint Peter's Fish, and I trekked to the home of a friend where, along with a family of six, we prepared this unique, spicy dish. While the recipe calls for three separate mixtures, the dish comes together very quickly. If you can't find tilapia, you can substitute trout, salmon, or red snapper for delicious results. It's a perfect entrée to serve on Rosh Hashanah—the Jewish New Year. L'shana tova!"

MATZOH-CRUSTED TILAPIA
WITH ZHOUG

SERVES 4 TO 6

Olive oil for coating pan
Four boneless tilapia fillets (about 6 ounces each)
Sea salt and freshly ground pepper
Zhoug (recipe follows)
Matzoh Crust (recipe follows)

Zhoug
2 garlic cloves, coarsely chopped
1/2 Thai or jalapeño chile, coarsely chopped
1 large tomato, peeled and coarsely chopped
1 cup loosely packed cilantro leaves
1 cup loosely packed parsley leaves
1 teaspoon curry powder
1/4 teaspoon kosher salt

Matzoh Crust
1 matzoh, broken into fine pieces no larger than 1/4 inch
1 small carrot, grated
1 small zucchini, grated
1 small onion, grated
1 large egg, lightly beaten
1 garlic clove, minced
1 tablespoon chopped parsley
1 tablespoon extra virgin olive oil
Pinch of Kosher salt

1. Preheat oven to 375°. Coat a glass baking dish large enough to hold the fish in a single layer with oil. Season fish with salt and pepper on both sides and arrange in prepared baking dish; set aside.

2. Make the Zhoug: Combine all of the ingredients in a food processor and blend until the mixture resembles a chunky-style sauce. Evenly spread the zhoug over the top of each fillet.

3. Make the Matzoh Crust: In a large bowl, combine all of the ingredients and mix well with your hands. The mixture will form a thick batter. Carefully coat each fillet with 1/4 of the matzoh mixture, spreading it over the zhoug. Place baking dish in oven and bake until the fillets are cooked through and topping is lightly browned, about 15 to 20 minutes, depending on the thickness of the fish. Do not overcook. Serve warm with Lemon Basmati Rice (page 156).

On my last day in Israel, David, my driver and friend, took me to Ein Gedi where his family lives in a *kibbutz*—a collective community of families and enterprises. When his mother asked me if I knew how to cook, I raised my eyebrows, thinking that my karma was about to be written. I had told her earlier that Guyana's first and only female Prime Minister had been Jewish, and that in the 17th century, many Jews fled persecution in Brazil and settled in Guyana's old Dutch colony. Even though David's family and I may have been continents apart, I wanted to make something that was common to our shared heritage. I decided on coconut macaroons. As a child in Guyana, I often made these for dessert, simply calling them coconut sugar cakes. I pinched a couple of fragrant cardamom seeds from David's coffee to flavor the coconut mixture. Later that night, with the crickets serenading us, David's family and I filled the air with laughter as we enjoyed my cardamom-scented coconut macaroons...and I felt just as if I were at home in Guyana with my own family. Even the view was the same: the dark sky a canvas of twinkling stars, scattered in the heavens like tiny diamonds.

CARDAMOM COCONUT MACAROONS

MAKES ABOUT 30 MACAROONS

2 + 1/2 cups unsweetened grated coconut
1/4 cup canned sweetened condensed milk
2 teaspoons ground cardamom
2 large pinches salt
2 large egg whites

1. Position a rack in the center of the oven and preheat oven to 375°. Line a baking sheet with parchment paper or a silicone baking mat.

2. In a medium bowl, combine the coconut, condensed milk, cardamom, and one pinch of salt; mix well with a wooden spoon so that all the coconut is evenly coated with milk. Set aside.

3. In a small bowl, beat egg whites with the other large pinch of salt until stiff peaks form. Fold into the coconut mixture until just combined.

4. For each macaroon, drop about 1 tablespoon of dough onto prepared cookie sheet leaving 1 inch between them. Wet your hands with water and shape dough into rough mounds. Bake macaroons until edges are lightly browned, about 8 to 10 minutes. Let cool for 5 minutes on cookie sheet, then transfer to wire racks and let cool completely.

CARDAMOM COCONUT MACAROONS

INDIA

The seeds of my traditional Indian cooking were sown a continent away in Guyana, South America, where I was born. My grandfather, a Hindu priest, would often read to me from the Vedas, or sacred texts, in Sanskrit. It was also mandatory that I converse with him in this ancient language. Our family practiced the *ayurvedic* way of life. Ayurveda, meaning "science of life," is a holistic system that aims to balance certain energies in the body for optimum health. Much of this is accomplished by eating certain foods. From an early age, I was taught that the foods we consumed were not merely necessary for sustenance, but also had to harmonize our cosmic energies with our spiritual well-being. To this day, I have to be in a happy state of mind whenever I prepare meals. If I rush or am in a bad mood, that negative energy transcends the food and is passed along to all who partake of it. • I distinctly remember the day I asked my grandfather where we came from. He filled my mind with faraway thoughts of Persia, Mesopotamia, and the Indus Valley, and told me that I was a descendant of an ancient Indo-Aryan tribe. As a child, I felt on top of the world knowing that I belonged to a tribe, and this discovery helped to crystallize my identity. • In 1500 BC, my Indo-Aryan tribe invaded the northern part of India from the west, collapsing the Indus civilization. The Indo-Aryans were the fathers of ayurvedic medicine

THE FLAVORS OF INDIA

The soul of every Indian pantry is its spices: saffron, cumin, cayenne, allspice, cardamom pods, mustard seeds, turmeric, nutmeg, fennel, fenugreek, asafoetida, coriander seeds, and cinnamon. Curry powder is usually homemade according to individual recipes using different measurements and varieties of spices. Basmati rice, lentils, and beans are eaten with curries and made into wonderful soups and desserts. Potatoes play a large part in India's vegetarian cuisine, as do cauliflower, carrots, spinach and dozens of other vegetables. Paneer, a homemade cheese, and yogurt are often-used ingredients, with yogurt frequently acting as a marinade for lamb and poultry. Chiles abound: they are savored fresh, dried, or ground into pastes and are indispensable for making delicious sweet-tart chutneys, and both sweet and savory curries.

and its food harmony techniques. When the Muslims invaded India from the Middle East in the 8th century AD, they began to establish their own culture. The first Muslim Mughal emperor was Babar, who was followed by many others for three centuries. These royal rulers were connoisseurs of fine food, and their kitchens prepared daily feasts of hundreds of dishes, all to satisfy the appetites of their guests and the women of their harems. When their empire began to collapse in the 18th century, European traders seized their chance to establish power. Slowly, the British gained control and in 1868, India fell to the British monarchy. The period known as the Raj, when India was completely occupied and ruled by Britain, had begun. India's full independence in 1947 was guided in part by a few grains of salt, when Mohandas Gandhi set out on a march in defiance of Britain's salt monopoly. With each invasion and occupation, India's kitchens were transformed by trade and most importantly, by religion. The latter played a major role in the introduction of vegetarianism. • Each of India's states has its own rich and complex cuisine, and the Indian people are renowned artisans when it comes to spices, blending them in unique combinations tailored to each meal. In the north you'll find Kashmir, with its snowcapped Himalayas and valleys, dominated by wheat fields. Here the people are known for their rich, savory curries and yogurt marinades that are especially good with lamb. • Kerala,

near the coastal waters of the south, is the heart of the spice trade. You'll also find a wealth of fresh seafood, exotic fruits, and vegetables. Of course, no meal here is complete without the local rice that is grown in abundance. The Indian foods most Americans are familiar with are those prepared "Vindaloo"—cooked with a fiery hot, spicy paste inspired by the Portuguese—which originated in the state of Goa, on the Arabian Sea. Tandoori, another favorite, is a method of cooking in large earthen, coal-fired ovens. A variety of foods from breads to meats are cooked inside, giving them a distinctive flavor and sealing in their natural aromas. • It is no wonder that India, brimming with exotic tales, myths, deities, beliefs, and traditions, has created one of the world's most varied, satisfying cuisines.

MENU INDIA

• LUSCIOUS MANGO LASSI with BERRIES AND ROSE WATER

• TOFU SAMOSAS with TAMARIND CHUTNEY

• MULLIGATAWNY SOUP

• AYURVEDIC PAPAYA AND BLOOD ORANGE SALAD

• GOAN VINDALOO FISH CURRY with LEMON BASMATI RICE

• KASHMIRI APRICOT AND SAFFRON PUDDING

Lassi, the nutritious, yogurt-based Indian drink, came to me on a searing hot day. I had vowed to visit the temples of Khajuraho, set in the steamy hot jungle of Madhya Pradesh, a state in Central India. The magnificent temples are known for their depictions of erotica, and I wanted to see more of what I had glimpsed as a young girl in my aunt's book of the Kama Sutra. The day was long, and the temperature reached 108 degrees. All I wanted to do was go back to my air-conditioned hotel room, but I didn't get much further than the lobby, where I surrendered into the arms of a wicker chair. I think I fainted. When I opened my eyes, Baharat, the waiter, held out a cool glass of Mango Lassi with perfect balls of juicy watermelon floating in the glass. What a welcome, chilled hot-weather treat it was. I've added my favorite summer berries, which is exactly the way I like it. ""

LUSCIOUS MANGO LASSI
WITH BERRIES AND ROSE WATER

SERVES 4

30 ounces (5 containers, 6 ounces each) plain yogurt
2 cups ripe mango pulp (fresh or canned), about 1 large mango
1/2 cup sugar
1 teaspoon freshly squeezed lemon juice
1/4 teaspoon rose water (optional)
1/2 cup each fresh raspberries and blueberries
Fresh mint sprigs for garnish (optional)

1. In a blender, process all of the ingredients except the berries and mint with 1 cup water until mixture is thick and smooth.

2. Refrigerate for several hours. Add the fresh berries just before serving and garnish with mint sprigs, if using.

LUSCIOUS MANGO LASSI

TOFU SAMOSAS
WITH TAMARIND CHUTNEY

MAKES 28 SAMOSAS

2 tablespoons ghee or extra virgin olive oil
2 tablespoons minced shallot
1 tablespoon peeled, minced fresh ginger
1/3 cup fresh, shelled green peas
1 tablespoon curry powder
2 teaspoons ground cumin
1/4 teaspoon cayenne, plus more to taste
2 cups firm tofu, (about two 14-ounce packages) cut into 1/4-inch cubes
1/2 cup loosely packed cilantro leaves, chopped
Sea salt
14 (6-inch square) spring roll wrappers
Vegetable oil for deep-frying
Tamarind Chutney (recipe follows)

1. In a large skillet, heat the ghee or oil over medium heat and add the shallots, ginger, and peas. Sauté for 2 minutes, stirring occasionally. Add the curry powder, cumin, and cayenne and cook for 1 minute more, stirring frequently.

2. Add the tofu and toss until all the cubes are well coated. Cook for 3 minutes, stirring occasionally. Turn off heat, add cilantro and toss to combine. Season with salt and cayenne to taste, then transfer to a bowl and let cool completely.

3. Cut the spring roll wrappers in half. Assemble samosas by taking 1 strip and lightly brushing the edges with water. Place 1 tablespoon of the filling about 1/2 inch from the bottom of the strip. Diagonally fold the bottom by lifting the wrapper and filling over to form a triangle shape and press edges together. Fold again in the opposite direction and repeat until you have a small package in the shape of a triangle. Press firmly around all edges, making sure they are sealed. Transfer samosas to a large plate and cover with a damp towel as you assemble the remaining samosas.

4. In a medium skillet set over medium-high heat, heat enough vegetable oil for deep frying (about 3 inches) until a deep-fry thermometer reads 365°. Fry the samosas, a few at a time, until golden, about 1 to 2 minutes, turning once or twice so they brown evenly on both sides. Remove and transfer to a plate lined with paper towels. Serve with Tamarind Chutney.

TAMARIND CHUTNEY

MAKES ABOUT 1/2 CUP

1/4 cup tamarind pulp
1/4 cup dark brown sugar, firmly packed
1 teaspoon ground cumin
1 teaspoon minced garlic
2 teaspoons cayenne

1. In a small bowl, combine all of the ingredients with about 2 tablespoons boiling water and whisk until the sugar is complete dissolved. Serve warm or let cool and store in an airtight container; refrigerate until ready to use. Stir well before serving.

Ringing the bell at a Hindu temple.

I didn't really have to look for this soup in India, where it originated. It's a favorite holdover from my childhood in Guyana, where both Indian and British influences are part of our culture. Mulligatawny means 'pepper water,' and it was introduced to England in the late 18th century courtesy of British government members returning home from India. My father made this soup every Boxing Day—the day after Christmas when it is customary for the British to exchange gifts. He'd add the bony parts of the sheep that had been slaughtered for the holidays, and it took hours and hours to make the soup. It was worth it: in the end, this rich, thick, sweet-sour soup afloat with pieces of tender, shredded meat was always sumptuous...and it still is. These days I use chicken and serve it with steamed rice or a loaf of crusty bread. This simple dish is a one-pot family meal.

MULLIGATAWNY SOUP

SERVES 6

About 2 pounds bone-in, skinless chicken thighs and breasts
Kosher salt
1/4 cup extra virgin olive oil
1 large onion, chopped
1 teaspoon peeled, grated fresh ginger
1 tablespoon curry powder
1 + 1/2 teaspoons cayenne, plus more to taste
6 cups low-sodium chicken stock
2 bay leaves
2 tablespoons tamarind pulp
1 teaspoon ground allspice
1 can (15 ounces) red lentils, rinsed
1 large carrot, coarsely chopped

1. Rinse the chicken and pat dry with paper towels. Season with salt on both sides. In a large saucepan, heat oil over high heat; add chicken pieces, a few at a time, and brown well on both sides, about 10 minutes per side. Remove the chicken and set aside.

2. Reduce heat to medium-high. Add the onion and ginger to the oil remaining in pan and cook until onions begin to soften, about 5 to 7 minutes. Stir in the curry powder and cayenne and cook for 2 minutes more, stirring frequently.

3. Increase heat to high. Stir in the stock and bring to a boil. Add bay leaves, tamarind pulp, and allspice; stir to combine. Reduce heat, return the browned chicken pieces to the saucepan, and simmer for 1 hour, stirring occasionally.

4. Remove chicken from the saucepan. When cool enough to handle, tear large pieces of chicken meat off the bones, and return them to the saucepan. Discard the bones and any pieces of cartilage.

5. Add the lentils and carrots. Adjust the seasoning with salt and cayenne, adding more cayenne to taste, if desired. Continue to simmer soup until carrots are tender, about 15 minutes more. Remove bay leaves and discard. Serve very hot.

Note: This hearty soup can be ladled over steamed white rice or pasta to create a simple one-dish meal.

> The ancient Indian method of Ayurveda is a holistic approach to learning a more healthy way of living. It shows you how to balance your mental and emotional states and deepen your connection to your inner self. The foods one eats are very important in this practice. This simple yet exotic salad is one that I made using ayurvedic techniques: the papayas and papaya seeds are used to restore balance and help ease aches and pains. Papaya is among the plants renowned for the essential enzyme, papain, which has a soothing effect on the stomach and aids digestion. In fact, you will often see papain tablets in health food stores where it is sold as a dietary supplement. I assure you, though, eating this exquisite salad is far and away more enjoyable and healthful than swallowing a pill. "

AYURVEDIC PAPAYA AND BLOOD ORANGE SALAD

SERVES 4

1 small ripe papaya (about 1/2 pound)
1/3 cup blood orange juice (see Note)
2 teaspoons peeled, minced fresh ginger
1 teaspoon minced garlic
2 teaspoons minced shallot
1 teaspoon honey mustard
1/4 cup extra virgin olive oil
1 head Boston lettuce, leaves washed and dried
Sea salt and freshly ground pepper

1. Slice the papaya in half lengthwise. Scrape out the seeds, discarding all but 1 tablespoon. Coarsely chop the reserved seeds and set aside. Peel the papaya, cut it into thin 2-inch long strips, and set aside.

2. Make the dressing: In a small bowl, whisk together the blood orange juice, ginger, garlic, shallot, mustard, and chopped papaya seeds. Slowly drizzle in the olive oil in a steady stream, while continuously whisking until the dressing is emulsified.

3. Evenly divide the lettuce leaves among 4 salad plates. Then evenly divide the papaya strips over the greens. Drizzle the dressing over the salad and season with salt and pepper to taste. Serve the extra dressing on the side.

Note: If you cannot obtain blood oranges, regular orange juice can be substituted. Blood orange juice is also available in canned and bottled form.

Indian ladies going up to Mehrangarh Fort, Jodhpur.

GOAN VINDALOO FISH CURRY

This recipe hails from the region of Goa, a western coastal state on the Arabian Sea where fish abound. Goa's distinctive cuisine was greatly influenced by the Portuguese, whose rule prevailed for more than 400 years. This classic Goan dish takes its name from the Portuguese word meaning vinegar and garlic. Created by excellent Goan cook Vanessa Hernandez, this version of the fish-based dish filled with fragrant spices and smoothed by coconut milk is a joy. Serve it with aromatic Lemon Basmati Rice, flavored with cumin, black mustard seeds, and ginger.

GOAN VINDALOO FISH CURRY
WITH LEMON BASMATI RICE

SERVES 4

2 tablespoons distilled white vinegar

2 teaspoons salt

1 pound white, firm-fleshed fish, such as kingfish or cod, cut into 2-inch pieces

3 tablespoons ghee or vegetable oil

2 teaspoons ground cumin

2 teaspoons ground coriander

2 teaspoons turmeric

1 teaspoon whole black mustard seeds

1 tablespoon peeled, minced fresh ginger

1 tablespoon minced garlic

2 small Thai red chiles, minced

1 medium onion, chopped

3/4 teaspoon cayenne

8 fresh curry leaves, or 2 tablespoons freshly squeezed lime juice

1 cup canned, unsweetened coconut milk

1 small tomato, chopped

2 tablespoons grated unsweetened coconut (optional)

1/4 cup chopped cilantro

Lemon Basmati Rice (recipe follows)

1. In a medium bowl, combine the vinegar and salt. Add the fish and turn to coat. Cover and let marinate at room temperature for 10 minutes.

2. In a large skillet, heat the ghee or oil over medium-high heat and add the cumin, coriander, turmeric, and mustard seeds. Cook for just about 20 seconds, stirring so that the oil evenly coats the spices. Add the ginger, garlic, chiles, onion, cayenne, and curry leaves or lime juice. Cook until the onions are translucent, about 3 minutes.

3. Remove fish from the marinade, letting the excess drip off, and transfer to the skillet along with the spices. Gently stir until the fish is coated on all sides. Add the coconut milk, 1/2 cup water, tomato, and grated coconut, if using. Gently stir; cover. Cook over medium heat until the fish is opaque and firm, about 5 minutes. Season with salt to taste. Transfer the fish to a heated serving platter and sprinkle with chopped cilantro. Serve with Lemon Basmati Rice.

Variation: You can substitute 1 pound of boneless, skinless chicken breast for the fish, but increase the cooking time from 5 minutes to 8 to 10 minutes.

LEMON BASMATI RICE

SERVES 6

4 tablespoons vegetable oil or ghee
1 cup basmati rice
1 teaspoon whole cumin seeds
1/2 teaspoon whole black mustard seeds
1/2 teaspoon ground ginger
1 teaspoon ground turmeric
3 to 4 curry leaves, julienned, or 1 tablespoon lime zest
1 tablespoon freshly squeezed lemon juice
1/2 teaspoon salt

1. In a large saucepan bring 5 cups of water to a boil with 2 tablespoons of oil or ghee. Add rice to boiling water and cook until tender, about 8 minutes. Drain thoroughly, rinse with hot water and set aside.

2. Heat remaining oil or ghee in a large frying pan. Add the cumin and mustard seeds. When the seeds begin to pop, add the ginger, turmeric, and curry leaves or lime zest. Cook for 1 minute, stirring frequently. Add the cooked rice, then the lemon juice, and stir well. Season to taste with salt and transfer to a bowl. Let cool completely before serving.

Sacred candles on the boat on the Ganga river in Varanasi, India

❝ I went to Kashmir for one thing: saffron. The saffron of Kashmir is the finest in the world, with long threads and a dark red color. It is very potent, and very little of it is exported. This is the ultimate dessert for Kashmiris who want to cool off in the summer months, especially after the many spicy meals like the ones I had in the region that were laden with hot Kashmiri chiles. It is cool, soothing, and redolent of magical saffron. ❞

KASHMIRI APRICOT AND SAFFRON PUDDING

SERVES 4

1/4 cup slivered or sliced almonds
1/2 cup vermicelli or angel hair pasta broken into 1/2-inch pieces
2 cups whole milk
A pinch of saffron threads
1/4 cup dried apricots, finely diced
1/2 cup canned, sweetened condensed milk

1. Heat a large skillet over high heat. Add the almonds and toss frequently until toasted and golden brown, about 2 to 3 minutes. Transfer the nuts to a bowl and set aside. Add vermicelli and toss frequently until golden brown, about 2 to 3 minutes. Transfer to a separate bowl and set aside.

2. Reduce heat to medium, add the milk and saffron, and bring to a slow boil. Stir in the apricots and toasted vermicelli; reduce heat and simmer until the mixture begins to thicken, about 8 to 10 minutes, stirring frequently.

3. Add the condensed milk and stir to combine. Continue to simmer until the mixture is quite thick, about 5 minutes more, stirring occasionally. Remove pudding from the heat. Serve immediately or refrigerate until chilled. Garnish with toasted almonds just before serving.

Note: If you prefer a thinner pudding, use 1/4 cup more milk.

THAILAND

I traveled to Thailand for two things: the first was to satisfy my obsessive and insatiable appetite for exotic fruits by losing myself in its lush plantations; the second was to meet and stay with the Hill tribes in the north, who have managed to preserve their traditional way of life. • My survival in Thailand's villages and cities relied almost completely on street food, glorious street food, everything from sticky rice stuffed in fresh green bamboo to skewers of just about anything that once walked or crawled the earth. Street food is a way of life in this country and no matter what your status, it is savored by all, including members of the royal family, who venture out from behind the palace walls. • Thailand has four distinct regions, each quite unique. The north, which is known as the Golden Triangle, is a fertile valley and is home to several tribes of Hill people. The northeast is a vast plateau that yields both corn and cattle. Central Thailand is where its soul lies—its rice fields—as well as my personal Shangri-La of exotic fruits. To the south is the tourist capital, with its palm-fringed coast, white sand beaches, and clear waters. • To get to the essence of today's Thai kitchen, consider its culinary influences. In the 1st century AD, the "Tai" people migrated from the mountainous region of southwest China to Northern Thailand. With them came the

NIRMALA'S GUIDE TO
THE FLAVORS OF THAILAND

Fresh kaffir lime leaves, lemongrass, cilantro, basil (particularly the variety known as Thai basil), ginger, and chiles are essential elements of Thai cooking. Other commonly used ingredients include galangal root (a relative of ginger), ground peanuts, tamarind juice, coriander, fresh lime juice, and coconut milk. Fish sauce, oyster sauce, and shrimp paste are mainstays of savory sauces, and Thai food often uses fiery red curry paste to boost the heat of a dish. Almost every Thai table offers *Nam Prik,* a popular condiment made with fresh chiles, fish sauce, lime juice, shrimp paste, garlic, and a touch of sugar.

Burmese Mons and the Cambodian Khmers. At the beginning of the Christian era, traders from India began to settle in the southern peninsula, bringing with them not only Buddhism, but also a wealth of culinary and cultural influences. For centuries, the Mons and Khmers ruled until the mid-12th century when the first Thai kingdom emerged. It was called The Kingdom of Sukhothai, Sanskrit for "Dawn of Happiness." From the 17th century onward, the Thais traded with the Portuguese, the Dutch, the French, and the Japanese, all of whom had a hand in shaping what is now Thai cuisine. Portuguese missionaries who had acquired a taste for chiles while serving in South America introduced this spicy new ingredient, now a mainstay of Thai cooking. • Today, Thai cuisine remains uniquely identifiable. Incorporating the five taste sensations into each dish: sweet, sour, bitter, salty, and spicy, this cuisine is enjoyed by all with an adventurous palate.

MENU THAILAND

TRANG LEMONGRASS ICED TEA

SERVES 4

6 stalks lemongrass
2 tablespoons honey or sugar
2 cups ice cubes
Mint sprigs for garnish

1. Trim off the root end of the lemongrass and discard. Cut lemongrass (including green parts) into 1-inch pieces.

2. In a medium saucepan, combine 4 cups water and the chopped lemongrass. Bring the water to a boil and simmer for 5 minutes. Remove from heat and stir in honey until it dissolves. Cover and let cool to room temperature.

3. Pour the tea through a sieve and discard lemongrass. Fill 4 tall glasses with ice, pour the tea into glasses, garnish with sprigs of mint, and serve.

❝ Every year, Trang, the beautiful beach city in southern Thailand, holds a vegetarian festival. I had heard much about the festival, and especially about its fabulous street fare. So at 6:00 one morning, I started out on a six-hour bus trip from Phuket—during which I received several marriage proposals— and arrived at Trang. Unlike many of Thailand's more tourist-oriented destinations, this was a pretty and tranquil town, even with a festival in progress. When I got to the festival itself, I was immediately immersed in a sea of brilliant orange robes— Buddhist monks were everywhere, and their processions were a grand sight as they passed by dozens of mini food stalls selling all sorts of savory morsels. From one of these, I bought a tall glass containing a light green beverage loaded with ice. I took a sip—it was lemongrass tea! What a surprise it was to enjoy it as a brisk, refreshing drink: all my life in Guyana, we made lemongrass tea for its Ayurvedic, medicinal value, curing headaches, reducing fevers, and aiding digestion. I was wondering why it never occurred to us to put ice in our lemongrass tea, when I remembered that in Guyana, we didn't have electricity! It's equally delicious warm or cold. ❞

SPICY ALMONDS WITH COCONUT AND HONEY

> These cayenne-spiced, honey-sweetened nuts are sold throughout Thailand by street vendors, usually in a plastic bag or in a little cone made from newspaper. Thais mostly use lotus nuts, but my recipe uses almonds, which are just as delicious and more readily available. You can also use peanuts or cashews for this snack. "

SPICY ALMONDS WITH COCONUT AND HONEY

SERVES 4

1 cup unsweetened shredded coconut
1 + 1/2 tablespoons peanut oil
3 tablespoons honey
1 teaspoon cayenne
2 cups unsalted blanched almonds
Sea salt

1. Heat a large skillet over high heat. Add the coconut and toast, tossing occasionally, until it turns an even, light brown, being careful not to let it burn, about 2 minutes. Immediately transfer to a bowl and set aside.

2. Reduce heat to medium and add the oil. Stir in the honey and cayenne. When the oil and honey are combined, add the almonds and stir until they are evenly coated. Add the toasted coconut and gently stir until the nuts are evenly coated with coconut. Season with sea salt to taste. Immediately transfer nuts to a large nonstick baking sheet and spread them out to cool. Transfer to a bowl and serve.

I spent days with the people of northern Thailand, flying kites right in the middle of opium poppy fields with the local children, searching the misty forest for rare orchids and eating *larb* for days on end. Larb, despite its unappealing name, is quite delicious. It's made with lime juice, fish sauce, water buffalo meat, pounded rice, and fresh herbs topped with hot chiles. But after a week I was a bit tired of it, and longed for another local culinary find. It didn't take me too long. The next morning, I negotiated with a tribesman for a trip on the Mekong River into Laos. Ju, another tribesman sharing our boat trip, made this soup, one of the most flavorful I have ever tasted. He prepared it with freshly caught catfish in a base of curried coconut milk and gave it a fiery burst of red curry paste. It was like basking in a ray of sunshine while the cloudy mist hovered over the river that day. I make my own version with chicken. "

JU'S CURRY NOODLE SOUP

SERVES 6 TO 8

3 cups canned, unsweetened coconut milk
3 tablespoons Thai Red Curry Paste (recipe follows)
1 tablespoon turmeric
1 pound boneless, skinless chicken breasts, cut into 1/4-inch strips
1 cup vegetable or chicken stock
3 tablespoons fish sauce (nam pla)
2 tablespoons soy sauce
1 teaspoon salt, plus more to taste
3/4 pound fresh Asian-style egg noodles
3/4 cup loosely packed Thai basil leaves
2 green onions, thinly sliced

1. In a large saucepan, bring 1/2 cup of the coconut milk to a boil over medium-high heat. Add the Thai Red Curry Paste and turmeric; stir to combine. Cook until the mixture starts to thicken, stirring frequently, about 3 minutes.

2. Add the chicken strips, and turn to coat them well. Add the remaining coconut milk, stock, fish sauce, and soy sauce. Bring to a boil and reduce heat to a steady simmer. Cook until the chicken is cooked through, stirring occasionally, about 8 minutes. Season with salt to taste.

3. Bring a large pot of water to a boil. Add 1 teaspoon salt and the egg noodles to water, stirring occasionally. Cook noodles until al dente. Drain and divide evenly among four warm soup bowls. Ladle the hot soup over the noodles, garnish with fresh Thai basil and green onions, and serve immediately.

THAI RED CURRY PASTE

MAKES ABOUT 3/4 CUP

3 tablespoons thinly sliced lemongrass (bulb only, tough outer casing removed)
6 garlic cloves, coarsely chopped
4 small shallots, coarsely chopped
2 teaspoons ground cumin
2 teaspoons curry powder
4 kaffir lime leaves, julienned or 1 tablespoon lemon zest
2-inch piece of peeled, fresh ginger, thinly sliced
6 to 8 red Thai chiles, seeded and chopped
2 tablespoons chopped cilantro

1. In a food processor or blender, combine all ingredients and process to a thick paste. If the mixture is too thick to blend easily, add a few drops of cold water.

Made Ahead Tip: This paste can be made in advance and stored in an airtight container. It can be refrigerated for up to 2 weeks.

CURRY NOODLE SOUP

Thailand's floating markets are made up of an intricate network of canals that irrigate the local farms. They also sustain a unique, waterborne way of life for the Thai people. Around Bangkok, there are three floating markets, and wanting to witness the traditional Thai lifestyle, I headed for the Bang Khu Wiang Floating Market at the break of dawn one day. There I found *sampans*—wooden boats—laden with fresh flowers, fruit, vegetables, and household items, all creating a colorful, bustling scene. I asked my young sampan driver, one of the many Thai women wearing conical bamboo hats who paddled the boats, to venture down the canal into the villages. I wanted to see the local farming communities there. During our brief but exhilarating ride down the canal, we were waived over by a sampan hawker selling all sorts of delicacies. I bought coconut water and this fragrant bowl of rice salad made with fresh Thai herbs. If you have leftover rice, here is a perfect way to use it.

FLOATING MARKET BASIL RICE SALAD

SERVES 4 TO 6

2 tablespoons freshly squeezed lime juice
2 tablespoons honey
1/4 cup extra virgin olive oil
1 small red Thai chile, very finely sliced
1 tablespoon chopped cilantro leaves
1 fresh kaffir lime leaf, julienned, or 1 teaspoon lime zest
2 cups cooked white rice
1 medium crisp red apple, cored and diced
1 avocado, peeled, pitted, and diced
1 small cucumber, diced
Sea salt
Handful of Thai basil leaves, torn if large

1. In a medium bowl, whisk together the lime juice, honey, and olive oil. Add the chile, cilantro, and lime leaf; toss to combine. Add cooked rice, apple, avocado, and cucumber and gently toss. Season with salt to taste. Divide the salad among four salad bowls and garnish with fresh Thai basil.

Variations: Italian basil can be substituted for Thai basil in this salad. You can also use cooked Soba noodles or Thai purple rice in place of white rice.

Bang Khu Wiang floating market, Bangkok.

“If you drive about three hours south of Bangkok, you'll come to the quaint fishing village of Hua-Hin. In the evenings, this sleepy town comes alive, buzzing with dozens of food vendors hawking just about every kind of fish in the ocean, and zealously patronized by the local residents. The sights and scents of these evenings inspired me to create this one-dish meal, like the ones served right from the pan by food stall vendors. The many ingredients cook up quickly; just be sure you have the freshest of everything possible.”

THAI-STYLE SEAFOOD PAELLA

SERVES 4

6 medium scallops (about 6 ounces), membranes trimmed
Sea salt and freshly ground pepper
5 + 1/2 to 6 cups low-sodium fish or vegetable stock
3 stalks lemongrass, bottom halves only, cut into 2-inch pieces and lightly pounded with the side of a knife
1/4 cup plus 1 tablespoon extra virgin olive oil
4 medium shallots, finely chopped
3 garlic cloves, minced
3 small Thai chiles, seeded and minced
5 fresh kaffir lime leaves, julienned
1/4 cup loosely packed Thai basil leaves, julienned, plus more for garnish
2-inch piece peeled, grated fresh ginger
2 + 1/2 tablespoons tomato paste
1 + 1/2 cups paella rice
4 lobster tails, (about 4 ounces each) split
6 littleneck clams, scrubbed
6 small mussels, debearded and scrubbed
1/2 cup Chinese long beans cut into 1/2-inch pieces
Lime wedges for serving

1. Rinse and pat the scallops dry. Season with salt and pepper and refrigerate until ready to use. In a medium saucepan, bring the broth to a boil over high heat and add the lemongrass. Reduce heat and simmer until ready to use.

2. Coat the bottom of a medium paella pan, or large, deep skillet (about 14 inches in diameter) with about 1 tablespoon of the oil, and heat over medium-high heat. Add scallops and cook until they just begin to brown and feel slightly firm to the touch, about 1 to 1 + 1/2 minutes per side. Transfer to a plate and set aside.

3. Reduce heat to medium and add 1/4 cup of the oil. Add the shallots, garlic, and chiles and cook until the shallots become translucent, stirring frequently, about 5 minutes. Add the lime leaves, basil, ginger, and tomato paste and cook for 5 minutes more, stirring frequently. Season with a large pinch of salt and pepper.

4. Add the rice and cook, stirring, until the rice becomes translucent and just begins to brown, about 10 minutes. Slowly ladle in the simmering broth (being careful not to add the lemongrass) and bring to a boil, then reduce heat and keep mixture at a steady simmer. Cook for 20 minutes, gently shaking the pan occasionally so that the rice is evenly distributed.

5. Push the lobster tails, clams, and mussels into the rice so that they are almost covered, then cover the pan with foil. Cook for 8 minutes more, until the rice is done and the lobster is cooked through. Test a spoonful of rice just below the top layer; it should be al dente or slightly firm to the bite. If the rice is not done but all the liquid has been absorbed, add a little more hot stock or water and cook for a few minutes more. Arrange the reserved scallops and long beans over the rice, replace the foil cover and increase heat to high. Cook for 2 minutes, rotating the pan occasionally. Garnish the paella with Thai basil leaves and lime wedges. Serve hot.

The hotel attendant who cleaned my room in Bangkok told me I had to visit Chantaburi. When I asked her why, she sat me down and regaled me with descriptions of exotic fruits, especially jackfruits, which happened to be in season. I had wanted to make one more trip before leaving Thailand, so early the next morning I hopped on the first bus and headed southeast toward the Cambodian border, traveling for four hours chasing what had always been among my childhood favorites—jackfruit. Jackfruit is the largest fruit in the world that grows on trees; inside, there are large, edible bulbs of yellow, banana-flavored flesh.

Although it looks like a durian, its flavor and texture are very different. When ripe, the jackfruit is very fragrant, and once opened the flesh has the aroma of fresh pineapple and banana.

While fresh jackfruit is difficult to find here, the canned version is available for making my own jackfruit creation—this brandy-laced, bracing sorbet.

JACKFRUIT SORBET

SERVES 4

2/3 cup sugar
2 cans (20 ounces each) jackfruit, drained and coarsely chopped
1 tablespoon freshly squeezed lime juice
3 tablespoons Madeira or brandy
Slivers of lime rind for garnish

1. In a small saucepan, combine the sugar and 2/3 cup water. Bring to a boil over medium heat, stirring frequently until the sugar has completely dissolved and liquid begins to thicken slightly, about 5 minutes. Remove from heat and let cool.

2. Place the jackfruit, lime juice, and 1/3 cup water in a food processor and process until mixture is pureed and smooth. Transfer the mixture to a large bowl, add the sugar syrup and Madeira; stir until well combined.

3. Pour the mixture into an ice cream maker, and freeze according to manufacturer's instructions. If you do not have an ice cream maker, pour the mixture into an airtight container and freeze until set, about 2 + 1/2 to 3 hours. Remove frozen mixture from the container and cut into 3-inch pieces; place in a food processor and process until smooth. Return to airtight container and freeze again. Repeat the freezing, chopping, and blending process 2 to 3 more times until the sorbet reaches a smooth consistency. To serve, spoon the sorbet into dessert glasses and garnish with lime rind.

Make Ahead Tip: The sorbet can be made a week ahead and kept frozen in an airtight plastic container.

VIETNAM

Vietnam is a country of rivers, and much of daily life takes place on them. The Red River in the north and the Mekong River in the south run through this long, narrow country and are its main arteries, giving life and balance to the hundreds of smaller rivers that have fostered a plethora of fishing villages, vegetable farms, and rice paddies. At the moment, I am snacking on *sup ga*—lotus nuts—as we putter along the Perfume River of Hué. The river lives up to its name, serene and fragrant with flowers, but just around the bend, Dinh, my speedboat driver and I, meet up with the familiar sight of rush hour, Vietnamese-style: here the river teems with local activities—housewives washing dishes and preparing food, children bathing, and sampans selling everything from exotic produce and animals to the all-too familiar Coca-Cola. In the midst of all the frenetic activity, Dinh points to the riverbank, drawing my attention to a bare-chested farmer carrying a bamboo pole across his shoulders; a rice basket balanced on either side. Dinh says that *this* is the real Vietnam. It is a land of contrasts, and its food eloquently says so. • Before the Vietnam War, this quiet, exquisite country was barely known to the West. Now it is a top

THE FLAVORS OF VIETNAM

Rice and noodles, of which there are many varieties, are a must, as is the elemental fermented fish sauce (nuoc mam), which is used to season just about every Vietnamese dish. Rice paper wrappers, coconut milk, ginger, coriander, lemongrass, tamarind, green onions, garlic, mint, chiles, cilantro, peanuts, and rice wine vinegar are also staples, as are hot chile pastes and soy sauce. Sugar and sweetened condensed milk also help play major roles in creating the contrasts Vietnamese food is known for. Above all, the fish, vegetables, and other produce used so prodigiously in Vietnamese cuisine must be the freshest possible.

tourist destination. This graceful curve of a country on the South China Sea is bordered by China to the north and Cambodia to the south. It has absorbed the influences of both of these cultures and their foods, and since both China and France have exercised colonial rule here, it's no wonder that the cuisine is delightfully varied. Vietnam incorporated tofu, ginger, and soy sauce from China; from France came butter, coffee, and baguettes. Even as influences from all over made inroads, they were adapted and interpreted in a unique Vietnamese way (one sip of delectable Vietnamese coffee is a perfect example of how a non-native food can be reinterpreted to perfection). Vietnamese cuisine is always accompanied by rice or rice noodles, and a myriad of sauces, subtle spices, fruits, raw vegetables, and fresh herbs, creating an enlightened and aromatic meal.

MENU **VIETNAM**

APERITIF
- AVOCADO SMOOTHIE

APPETIZER
- CLASSIC VIETNAMESE SPRING ROLLS

SOUP
- MR. CHU'S PHO (BEEF SOUP)

SALAD
- AUNT TU'S CRAB SALAD WITH GREEN PAPAYA

ENTREE
- ROAST BEEF BAGUETTE WITH SPICY PEANUT SAUCE

DESSERT
- VIETNAMESE COFFEE GRANITA

AVOCADO SMOOTHIE

SERVES 2

1 cup ripe avocado pulp (from about 2 medium avocados)
2 cups ice cubes
1 thin slice peeled, fresh ginger or 1 teaspoon candied ginger, chopped
1/4 cup canned sweetened condensed milk
1 tablespoon sugar

1. In a blender, combine the avocado pulp, ice cubes, ginger, condensed milk, and sugar; process until smooth. Pour into 2 tall glasses and serve immediately.

❝ One morning during my stay in Ho Chi Minh City I found myself lying in my hotel bed nursing a swollen, throbbing forearm. Days earlier, when my weakness for exotic fruits had led me to a crop of water apples ripe for picking, my arm was the victim of several bees whose venomous stings left it pulsating with pain. I needed to detoxify and rid my system of the venom. Hopping onto a *xyclo,* or rickshaw, I ventured into the Ben Thanh—an area filled with food stalls. I was looking for something pure, like fruit juice. I had sampled all kinds of exotic fresh-squeezed juices like dragon fruit, jujube, and water apple, but I had never tried an avocado smoothie—a favorite among locals, especially at breakfast. After battling a sea of vendors touting their drinks, I came upon a gracious woman whose little son sat quietly next to her, enjoying a fresh mango. This is her recipe for the traditional, nutritious morning pick-me-up, with its burst of candied ginger and touch of sweetness from condensed milk. Within days, my bee stings vanished. This delicious smoothie can be made with ripe bananas if you prefer—it's just as delicious and delivers a potassium boost as well. ❞

Probably no other dish boasts the exuberance and freshness of Vietnamese cuisine than its famous spring rolls. The different textures, colors, and vivid herb flavors of these rolls make them irresistible—I stuffed myself with them in every home I visited. The rice paper skins are easy to work with: just be sure to keep the prepared rolls covered with damp towels to prevent them from drying out. As you make the rolls, keep them flat on a plate—don't stack them. Don't forget to dip these delicious appetizers into a bit of Spicy Peanut Sauce for an extra flavor punch.

CLASSIC VIETNAMESE SPRING ROLLS WITH SPICY PEANUT SAUCE

MAKES 20 SPRING ROLLS

2 ounces rice vermicelli, soaked in hot water for 15 minutes or until soft
1/2 cup (4 ounces) bean sprouts
1 medium carrot, shredded
1/2 large cucumber, julienned
1 cup loosely packed fresh herbs (a combination of Vietnamese mint, Thai basil, mint, and cilantro leaves)
Small bunch of fresh chives, cut into 2-inch pieces
1 cup loosely packed shredded crisp lettuce, such as romaine
Twenty (6-inch round) rice paper spring roll skins
Spicy Peanut Sauce (recipe follows)

1. Drain vermicelli and place in a large bowl. Add the bean sprouts, carrot, cucumber, herbs, chives, and lettuce. Gently toss so that all ingredients are well combined; set aside.

2. To soften the spring roll skins, pour a few inches of tepid water into a wide bowl. Gently lower one spring roll skin into the water for about 20 to 30 seconds, or until it is soft and pliable. Allow excess water to drip off. Transfer skin to a flat work surface.

3. Working with one spring roll wrapper at a time, place a scant 1/4 cup of the filling on the bottom half of the wrapper. Fold the bottom half of the wrapper over the filling with one hand while pushing the filling down with the other. Fold the sides inward, then continue to roll the wrapper forward. Transfer the roll to a platter and cover with a damp paper towel. Repeat with remaining spring rolls.

4. When all of the rolls have been made refrigerate until ready to serve. Serve with Spicy Peanut Sauce.

SPICY PEANUT SAUCE

MAKES ABOUT 1 CUP

1 tablespoon vegetable oil
1 teaspoon minced garlic
1/2 cup ground unsalted peanuts or creamy peanut butter
2 teaspoons red pepper flakes
2 tablespoons tamarind pulp or juice
1 tablespoon plus 1 teaspoon sugar
1/2 cup canned unsweetened coconut milk
1 teaspoon salt
1 tablespoon freshly squeezed lime juice

1. Heat oil in a medium skillet over medium-high heat. Add the garlic and sauté until soft, stirring frequently, about 1 minute. Do not allow garlic to burn. Add the remaining ingredients, stir and bring to a boil. Remove from heat and set aside to cool.

Make Ahead Tip: This sauce can be stored in an airtight container and kept refrigerated for up to 1 week.

A bat-wing junk sails through HaLong bay, Vietnam

MR. CHU'S PHO (BEEF SOUP)

Pronounced 'fuh' in Vietnam, this soup is a delicacy enjoyed at the abundant pho shops throughout the country as well as at home. Pho is a satiating meal in itself, rich with noodles, bean sprouts, and beef, fragrant with lemongrass and mint, and packing a hint of heat from Thai chile. The cooking process is extremely time-consuming, and surprisingly, most pho cooks are men. But I wanted to learn how to make this classic soup, so I headed for Cholon, the Chinese Quarter of Ho Chi Minh City, to meet Mr. Chu. I had been told that Mr. Chu was the best butcher—and also a great cook—living in the quarter. Each week, he butchers a cow and sells the meat to local residents. But the bones he saves for himself, for they are the key to making the ultra-rich stock that is the essence of this savory soup. Traditionally, the stock simmers for hours and hours, but thanks to the top-quality beef stock that is available in supermarkets today, you can enjoy this classic dish in half the time. Serve pho with a fresh squeeze of lime and eat it while it is piping hot.

MR. CHU'S PHO (BEEF SOUP)

SERVES 4

2 stalks lemongrass
8 cups low-sodium beef stock
1 small Thai or Serrano chile, sliced into very thin disks
4 tablespoons fish sauce (nam pla), plus more to taste
Sea salt
4 ounces rice vermicelli noodles, soaked in hot water for 10 minutes
8 ounces beef sirloin, sliced and pounded paper-thin
1 cup shredded crisp lettuce, such as romaine
About 1/2 cup fresh cilantro or Vietnamese Mint leaves, coarsely chopped
1/4 cup bean sprouts (2 ounces)
1 lime, cut into 4 wedges

1. Prepare the lemongrass by cutting off the green upper portion (about 3 to 4 inches from the base) using only the whitish bulb. Remove the tough outer layers that encase the bulb. Using a meat mallet or other heavy object, smash the lemongrass.

2. In a large pot, combine the beef stock, chile, fish sauce, and lemongrass; bring to a boil over medium-high heat and cook for 5 minutes.

3. Using tongs, remove the lemongrass and discard. Adjust the seasoning with salt and fish sauce to taste. Drain the soaked rice noodles.

4. Divide the noodles evenly among 4 deep bowls. Divide beef slices among the bowls, laying them over the noodles. Ladle the hot stock into each of the bowls, covering the beef slices. Top each serving with 1/4 of the lettuce, cilantro or mint, and bean sprouts. Serve with a lime wedge.

Kitchen Tip: A kitchen mallet or meat pounder is a useful kitchen tool: use it to pound and tenderize meat, evening the thickness so that the meat cooks evenly. You can also use a mallet to form chicken, turkey, veal, or pork cutlets. If you do not have a mallet, you can use a rolling pin or the bottom of a cast iron pan. Do not use a heavy bottle.

"I've had this dish in Indonesia, Laos, and Cambodia as well as in Vietnam. It's usually made with the same ingredients wherever it's prepared, but this version is from Aunt Tu, the aunt of my sampan driver who took me deep into the Perfume River, through monsoon-like rain and flooded riverbanks, to meet her. Aunt Tu's village was barely visible—just a few dilapidated shacks on stilts topped with palm-thatched roofs. A few papaya and palm trees managed to stand up in the gray water, and a few pigs, chickens, and oxen stood under the stilts. Yet a vibrant vegetable patch radiated with fresh green long beans, red chiles, and herbs. Dinh, my sampan driver, and I entered one of the houses on stilts and were immediately welcomed by Aunt Tu, several other women, and six beautiful children who, seeing me soaked and shriveled as a prune, wiped me down with old T-shirts. Aunt Tu was just thirty-six years old, but she looked almost fifty. As with many farming village women, her husband would head off to the big cities to find work for several months, leaving her and the children to work the fields. That rainy night, surrounded by the village women and by the light of a flickering oil lamp, we enjoyed this wonderful crabmeat salad with shredded fresh green papaya, crunchy peanuts, and hot chile. Aunt Tu's version has a very penetrating lime marinade which I've duplicated in this recipe. When we finished our feast, the children danced and sang as loud as they could to compete with the roar of the rain on the roof. It was a mirror of my own childhood, when my three brothers and I competed with the equatorial rains of the Amazon."

AUNT TU'S CRAB SALAD WITH GREEN PAPAYA

SERVES 4

2 tablespoons freshly squeezed lime juice
2 tablespoons fish sauce (nam pla)
1 tablespoon sugar
1/4 cup peanut oil
1 small red birdseye or Serrano chile, seeded and minced
4 green onions (green parts only), sliced 1/8-inch thick crosswise
1/4 cup coarsely chopped unsalted roasted peanuts
1 small green (unripe) papaya, peeled, seeded, and shredded
3 Chinese long beans cut into 1/2-inch pieces
1 small carrot, shredded
1/2 pound canned crabmeat, picked through for cartilage
Sea salt and freshly ground white pepper
1 tablespoon chopped cilantro, for garnish

1. In a large bowl, combine the lime juice, fish sauce, and sugar. Slowly whisk in the oil until mixture is completely emulsified. Stir in the chile, green onions, and peanuts.

2. Add the papaya, long beans, carrot, and crabmeat and toss well to combine. Season with salt and pepper to taste. Cover with plastic wrap and refrigerate for at least 20 minutes before serving. Garnish with chopped cilantro leaves immediately before serving.

❝ I was strolling through Hanoi's enchanting old French Quarter when I spotted a street vendor wearing a beautiful dome-shaped straw hat. She was selling stuffed baguettes—a favorite with locals who enjoy them filled with a variety of meats and dressed with different sauces. The heritage of this tempting street fare is clearly French. The vendor patted her bench, a small concrete block covered with banana leaves, suggesting that I take a seat next to her. During the entire half hour I sat there we communicated with a series of smiles and head nods as I ate my way through all of her goodies. The sauces in her sandwiches ranged from pungent fish sauces to *sot dau phong*—the sweet yet delicate Vietnamese-style peanut sauce featured in this recipe, as well as in the Spring Roll recipe on page 178. The sauce can be made ahead and refrigerated for on-the-spot sandwich making. ❞

An old woman working in water-lily fields in the countryside outside Hanoi, Vietnam

ROAST BEEF BAGUETTE
WITH SPICY PEANUT SAUCE

SERVES 4

One fresh baguette, about 16 inches long
1/2 cup Spicy Peanut Sauce (page 179)
About 8 ounces thinly sliced roast beef, or other type of sliced meat
1 large tomato, thinly sliced
1 cup loosely packed herbs such as cilantro, mint, and basil leaves, torn if large

1. Cut the baguette crosswise into four 4-inch pieces. Slice each piece lengthwise, making sure to cut only halfway through the bread. Press the sides of the bread open. Toast bread on a grill or under a broiler until it is hot and golden.

2. Spread Spicy Peanut Sauce on the both sides of the sliced area of the bread. Evenly arrange roast beef slices on the baguette, gently pushing them into the sandwich. Top with tomato and herbs. Slice baguette in half crosswise and serve.

Variation: Make this a vegetarian sandwich by omitting the beef and adding more of your favorite greens, such as shredded lettuce, carrots, bean sprouts or green onions.

VIETNAMESE COFFEE GRANITA

❝ Anyone who has experienced sweet, sensational, extra-strong Vietnamese coffee, laden not only with sugar but with sweetened condensed milk as well, becomes a lifelong addict. Often, the longing for Vietnamese coffee is overwhelming, yet it's not quite available at the corner deli. I've given this dessert-like beverage a slight twist, converting the warm elixir into a refreshing, cool granita that you can enjoy any time the longing overtakes you, particularly on a warm summer evening. It's easy to make—all you need is a little extra room in your freezer. ❞

VIETNAMESE COFFEE GRANITA

SERVES 4

1/2 cup sugar
3 cups freshly brewed espresso
About 1/2 cup canned sweetened condensed milk

1. In a large bowl, combine the sugar and hot espresso. Add additional sugar to taste, if desired. Allow coffee to cool to room temperature.

2. Pour coffee into a deep pan, cover with aluminum foil, and place in the freezer. When ice crystals begin to form (this should take about 1 hour) remove pan from freezer and stir with a fork, breaking up all the ice chunks, especially those that have formed around the edges. Return pan to freezer. Continue to stir, breaking up the ice as ice crystals continue to form (about every 30 minutes), until the mixture has an even granular texture, about 2 to 3 more hours.

3. Divide the granita among 4 large glasses. Drizzle with condensed milk and serve immediately.

Make Ahead Tip: This granita can be made at least two days ahead and stored, covered, in the freezer.

CHINA

China, the world's most populous country, is an enormous land whose regions and provinces differ in fundamental ways. China has astonishing landscapes of mountains, orchards, rice paddies, rivers and desert plains, yet you can also find yourself in the midst of some of the world's most congested cities, crammed with people, bicycles, traffic of every sort, and skylines to rival any American city. • China's culinary development was born out of years of famine and hardship. In order to survive in times of poor harvests, the Chinese ate everything edible, including things that would be unappetizing to most Americans. On the other hand, China also discovered the wonderful edible properties of such delicacies as tiger lilies, bamboo shoots, lotus roots, and tea (cha). Many westerners still consider Chinese food to be Chop Suey, fried rice, and fortune cookies, but it is so much more. And while the Chinese have contributed profoundly to the culture and the arts of the world, it is Chinese food that we relish the most. It has become the most prominent of all the Asian cuisines, and was the leader in sharing its riches with the west. • Each of China's provinces has a unique cooking style, and there is plenty of debate about how many of them exist. When I was in Xian, I met an Australian chef, Charlie, who advised dividing Chinese cooking into four major regions. Cantonese is, perhaps, the most familiar. Since the 16th

NIRMALA'S GUIDE TO
THE FLAVORS OF CHINA

Rice and noodles—whether cellophane noodles, egg noodles, buckwheat noodles, or dozens of other varieties—are essential to every Chinese table, depending on a region's cuisine. Beans, such as black beans, which are often fermented, bean curd (or tofu, which comes in many different textures), gingerroot, garlic, and green onions are versatile and common ingredients. Bok choy, Chinese cabbage, long beans, bitter melon, watercress, snow pea shoots, and water chestnuts should be on every Chinese shopping list. Add to it the essential flavor boosters: hot chile oil, sesame oil, sesame seeds, light and dark soy sauces, hoisin and oyster sauces, and vinegar. Spice shelves should have on hand Sichuan peppercorns (long banned for export, but now available in Chinese and specialty markets), five spice powder, star anise, and white pepper—all add subtle heat and warm sweet notes to meat, poultry, and fish dishes.

century, Guangzhou, the old city of Canton, had lucrative trade links with the rest of the world. Merchants who traveled the Silk Road brought ivory, porcelain, silk, and spices to the bustling ports of Guangzhou and Hong Kong. In addition to bringing their wares, they greatly influenced the local cuisine. The Cantonese cooking style is quite sophisticated, often using hints of citrus and curry. Cantonese fare does not rely on heavy sauces; instead it is prepared fresh, by way of roasting, steaming, smoking, and boiling. The light and lovely *dim sum* (little tastes) is an authentic example. Hunan cuisine comes from Eastern China and is famous for its spicy dishes and ample use of hot chiles—a characteristic it shares with Sichuan cuisine. Many Hunan dishes combine sweet and sour tastes, such as the orange chicken we enjoy here. Sichuan cooking originated in western China. Beef is more prominent there than elsewhere, and it is usually prepared by stir-frying, dusted with rice flour or water chestnut flour to create a rich gravy that gets soaked up by the accompanying rice. A well-known Sichuan dish is Kung Pao chicken. • Beijing (formerly Peking) cooking, from the north of China, is considered the "gem" of Chinese cuisine. Many of its culinary traditions originated with the emperors of China's many dynasties (who all had the best chefs, of course). Cooks in this region also incorporated influences from Mongolian and Muslim cuisine, including many lamb dishes. The harsh weather of the north and its bitter winters do not allow cultivation of

the crops common to warmer regions. Rice, for example, cannot be grown, so this area instead produces barley, wheat, and soybeans. The most famous specialty of this region is Peking Duck. • Regardless of the varied provincial cuisines, none is complete without rice or noodles, the centerpiece of every meal...including breakfast. And each morsel, down to the last grain of rice, is eaten with chopsticks, useful tools born of wisdom: Confucius taught that knives and forks resemble weapons, and so the idea of chopsticks came to be. By the way, never leave your chopsticks standing upright in a bowl of rice: it is considered to be very bad luck!

MENU CHINA

APERITIF
- GREEN TEA-LYCHEE MARTINI

APPETIZER
- SICHUAN PEPPERCORN-SESAME BEEF

SOUP
- MADAME SONG'S CRAB WONTON SOUP

SALAD
- LONG BEAN AND FORBIDDEN RICE SALAD

ENTREE
- HUNAN SPICY FISH with GINGERED BLACK BEAN SAUCE

DESSERT
- XIAN FIVE-SPICE BANANA ROLLS

> Healthful green tea and sweet lychee syrup make this a crisp, refreshing drink, but don't forget that adding vodka makes it an alcoholic beverage. It's easy to down several of these before you realize what hit you. "

GREEN TEA-LYCHEE MARTINI

SERVES 2

1 can (20 ounces) canned lychee, in syrup
3 ounces canned or bottled unsweetened green tea
3 ounces vodka
Mint sprigs for garnish

1. Drain 2 ounces of canned lychee syrup into a shaker. Reserve 6 lychees for garnish.

2. Fill shaker with ice. Pour in green tea and vodka. Shake well, then pour through a strainer into two chilled martini glasses. Garnish each glass with a few mint leaves and lychees skewered on a toothpick.

The Leshan Giant Buddha is the tallest stone Buddha statue in the world.

SICHUAN PEPPERCORN-SESAME BEEF

" I did most of my traveling throughout China by train—a great way to observe the everyday life of these hardworking people as you whoosh by, particularly in Sichuan Province, the rice capital of the country. After a 38-hour train ride and about 50 bowls of *congee,* or rice porridge, I arrived at Sichuan's capital city, Chengdu. I had come to see several things: the beautiful hibiscus flowers that adorn the city, the tea plantations, and the Leshan Giant Buddha, a renowned majestic masterpiece. I also wanted to experience the unique flavor burst of Sichuan peppercorns, another native ingredient, but one long banned from export to the United States. Now, however, it is available here at specialty markets (see Glossary). In Chengdu, markets seemed to be everywhere, especially on the sidewalks of busy streets. These teem with locals touting their products, from fruit, vegetables, and all sorts of animals to colorful plastic dishes and Honda auto parts. I had wandered aimlessly for hours, just taking in the true spirit of the people and the city, when my growling stomach got the better of me. Hypnotized by the aromas in the air, I arrived at an intersection filled with food carts. Smoke from roasting meats permeated the air, along with the aromas of warm spices, burnt Sichuan peppercorns and hints of crisp, clean ginger. At that intersection, I had this quickly cooked Sichuan Peppercorn Beef, briefly bathed in a rice wine marinade and sprinkled with sesame seeds. Try these with rice dumplings and plenty of hot green tea. "

SICHUAN PEPPERCORN-SESAME BEEF

SERVES 4

1/4 cup rice wine
1/2 teaspoon salt
1 pound sirloin beef, trimmed and cut into 1/2-inch cubes
1 tablespoon vegetable oil
2 tablespoons minced garlic
1 tablespoon finely chopped shallot
1 + 1/2 tablespoons oyster sauce
1 + 1/2 teaspoons red pepper flakes
1 tablespoon soy sauce
2 teaspoons light brown sugar
1 tablespoon sesame oil
2 teaspoons coarsely ground pepper
1 teaspoon crushed Sichuan peppercorns (see Note)
1 tablespoon toasted sesame seeds

1. In a medium bowl, combine rice wine and salt, then add beef cubes and turn to coat. Cover with plastic wrap and let marinate in the refrigerator for 20 minutes.

2. Heat a wok or a large skillet over high heat. Add the vegetable oil and heat until it smokes. Add the beef and cook until browned on all sides, about 2 to 3 minutes.

3. Reduce heat to medium-high. Add the garlic and shallot and sauté for 30 seconds. Add the oyster sauce, red pepper flakes, soy sauce, brown sugar, sesame oil, black pepper, and Sichuan peppercorns; sauté for 1 minute more. Transfer beef to a serving platter and sprinkle with toasted sesame seeds. Serve with toothpicks.

Note: To crush peppercorns, place in a self-sealing plastic bag and pound with a small, heavy saucepan, rolling pin, or mallet.

" Upon my return from the mainland, I spent two days in Macau. Chu, the owner of my hotel, said I looked tired and suggested a massage from Madame Song, adding that Madame also made the best wonton soup. (Finally, a dish I was familiar with!) Madame Song was elegant and petite, and wore a fresh cymbidium orchid tucked behind her right ear. She invited me into her home, where the aroma of fresh green onions simmering in chicken stock was all-pervasive. We passed several small rooms perfumed by sandalwood incense. Then we entered her kitchen, where a young couple sat giggling and gazing into each other's eyes. On the stove, a large stockpot was bubbling with broth, and the countertop was heaped with freshly prepared crab-stuffed wontons, ready to be plunked into the soup. Right then I wanted to eat—the massage could wait. But Madame Song insisted that the massage come first and escorted me and Joy, my masseuse, into a dimly lit room where I undressed and lay down on the massage table, which, to me, felt more like a soft bed. I closed my eyes, trying to block out the faint but familiar moans echoing around me, thinking back to all the massages I'd had in my travels. Suddenly, I sat bolt upright—I realized that I was in a brothel! Madame Song and Joy assured me that they give only massages, and since I was too hungry and tired to leave, I lay down again. Joy did indeed give me a decent massage, attacking all the knots I had acquired during my long train ride. Afterward, I sleepily dressed and made my way to the kitchen. Madame Song greeted me and led me to her jasmine- and orchid-laden patio where, moments later, Joy brought me a warm bowl of crab wonton soup with fresh bright green watercress and plump chicken feet. With the first mouthful I was in heaven, which was the same moment Madame Song confessed the truth. Yes, I was, indeed, in a brothel! This is Madame's family recipe, which she happily shared with me. I've omitted the chicken feet, but the barbecued pork adds meatiness. Whether you have your massage before or after—or not at all, this soup will warm your body and soul. "

MADAME SONG'S CRAB WONTON SOUP

SERVES 4

Wontons

1/2 pound fresh crabmeat, picked through for cartilage
1 teaspoon peeled, grated fresh ginger
2 tablespoons finely chopped fresh chives
1 tablespoon finely chopped parsley
1 tablespoon light soy sauce
1/8 teaspoon freshly ground white pepper
About 40 wonton wrappers

Soup

1 tablespoon vegetable oil
1 tablespoon minced garlic
5 cups low-sodium chicken stock
2 tablespoons light soy sauce
2 tablespoon rice wine vinegar
1 tablespoon sesame oil
1/2 cup boneless Chinese barbecued pork, cut into thin strips (about 8 ounces)
1/2 cup canned sliced water chestnuts, drained
1 cup loosely packed baby spinach leaves
Green onions thinly sliced on the diagonal for garnish

1. Make the wontons: Place crabmeat in cheesecloth and squeeze to release as much liquid as possible. Combine the crabmeat, ginger, chives, parsley, soy sauce, and white pepper in a medium bowl and toss well to thoroughly combine ingredients.

2. Working one at a time, place about 1/2 teaspoon of the filling in the center of each wonton wrapper. Moisten the sides of the wrapper with water and then fold in half diagonally to form a triangle, squeezing out any air from the center. Press the wonton firmly all around to seal it. Moisten the bottom corners with water and fold in so that they overlap one another. Pinch tightly to seal. Transfer wontons to a plate and keep covered with a damp cloth as you make the remaining wontons.

3. Make the soup: In a large pot, heat the oil over medium heat and sauté the garlic until soft, stirring frequently, about 2 minutes. Add the chicken stock, soy sauce, vinegar, sesame oil, and barbecued pork and simmer for about 8 minutes. Add prepared wontons and water chestnuts; cook for 5 minutes more.

4. Remove soup from heat and add the spinach leaves. Divide soup among 4 warmed bowls and garnish with sliced green onions.

Make Ahead Tip: You can make the dumplings ahead of time and freeze them in an airtight container. When you need them for the soup, simply defrost them. You can also steam or fry the dumplings and enjoy them on their own. Personally, I like to steam them and drizzle them with truffle oil before serving. You can buy the barbecued pork at any Chinese restaurant.

Try to visit your area's Chinatown or speciality food market to buy bundles of firm, Chinese long beans for this salad, an elegant, fragrant garlic- and ginger-laced side dish for an Asian meal. If you cannot, substitute regular green beans, trimmed, and cook until just done. Forbidden Rice is tiny and black, and was, at one time, forbidden to all except the exalted members of the Chinese imperial court. Luckily, now everyone is royal enough to savor it. 99

LONG BEAN AND FORBIDDEN RICE SALAD

SERVES 4

1 cup cooked "Forbidden" rice (Chinese Black rice), cooled
1 tablespoon sesame oil
1 tablespoon vegetable oil
2 tablespoons minced garlic
1 small shallot, finely chopped
1 pound Chinese long beans or string beans, ends trimmed, cut into 2-inch pieces
2 tablespoons peeled, grated fresh ginger
1 small Thai chile, seeded and finely chopped
3 tablespoons hoisin sauce
2 tablespoons light soy sauce
Sea salt and freshly ground pepper

1. In a medium bowl toss the cooked rice with the sesame oil. Cover and set aside.

2. In a wok or a large skillet, heat the vegetable oil until it smokes. Add the garlic and shallot and cook for 30 seconds, stirring frequently. Add the beans, ginger, and chile and stir so that the ginger is evenly distributed. Cover and cook for 2 minutes, or until the beans are barely tender.

3. Add the hoisin sauce and soy sauce to the wok and stir to combine. Sauté for 1 minute. Transfer beans to a large serving bowl and let cool slightly. Toss the beans with the rice and season to taste with salt and pepper. This makes a wonderful side dish.

Workers carrying bricks to repair an old temple.

HUNAN SPICY FISH
with GINGERED BLACK BEAN SAUCE

SERVES 4

1/4 cup cornstarch

4 sea bass or other firm-fleshed white fish fillets, about 6 to 8 ounces each

Sea salt and freshly ground pepper

1/4 cup vegetable oil

2 garlic cloves, minced

1 tablespoon finely chopped shallot

1/4 cup canned black beans, drained and coarsely mashed

2 tablespoons peeled, grated fresh ginger

2 Thai chiles, seeded and finely chopped

1/4 cup sesame oil

1/4 cup rice wine vinegar

1/4 cup light soy sauce

1. In a measuring cup, combine the cornstarch and 1/3 cup cold water, mix well and set aside. Rinse the fish and pat dry; season with salt and pepper. Heat a large skillet over high heat. Add the oil and heat until smoking. Coat the fish with the cornstarch mixture and immediately transfer to pan. Do not coat the fish ahead of time or the cornstarch coating will become gummy.

2. Sauté fish until golden brown, about 4 to 5 minutes, then turn. Sauté until golden and firm, about 3 to 5 minutes, depending on the thickness of the fish. Transfer to a plate and cover with aluminum foil to keep warm. Leave the cooking oil in the pan.

3. Make the sauce in the same pan: Reduce heat to medium-high and add the garlic and shallot to the oil. Sauté for 15 seconds stirring constantly. Increase heat to high and add the beans, ginger, chiles, sesame oil, vinegar, and soy sauce. Stir to combine; sauté 2 minutes more. Season to taste with salt and pepper. Place fish on a serving platter and spoon the sauce over the fish. Serve with fluffy steamed rice and steamed vegetables such as bok choy or snow peas.

Variation: The fish can be pan-seared without the cornstarch coating.

“ Meat is a luxury in China, so fish dishes abound there. But the fish must be absolutely fresh—caught, cleaned, and cooked right on the boats as fishermen catch them. The Hunan province boasts many lakes yielding freshwater fish. While this dish is usually prepared with whole fish, using fillets eliminates the bones, so it's easier to eat. No matter where I ate fish in China, it never tasted "fishy," so be sure to ask your fishmonger what came in fresh that morning. Like many recipes that showcase fresh ingredients, this entrée is easy to make yet full of flavor. ”

XIAN FIVE-SPICE BANANA ROLLS

Outside my hotel in Xian, the streets were lined with food vendors. At one stall I found these fantastic dessert rolls. Ever since I figured out the recipe, I've been making them for my six-year-old nephew, Shane, who loves them. It's a wonderful way to use up extra egg-roll wrappers and overripe bananas. Sprinkled with confectioners sugar and black sesame seeds, they are more than just a pretty picture—each mouthful gives you something sweet, something smooth, and something crunchy. The candied ginger is an extra bright surprise when you bite into one of these. "

XIAN FIVE-SPICE BANANA ROLLS

MAKES 12 ROLLS

2 large ripe bananas, peeled
1 teaspoon five spice powder
2 tablespoons finely diced candied ginger
1 tablespoon confectioners sugar, plus more for garnish
12 (6-inch square) spring roll wrappers
Vegetable oil, for frying
Black sesame seeds for garnish, optional

1. In a small bowl, mash the bananas and add the five spice powder, ginger, and confectioners sugar; mix well.

2. Working one at a time, place a spring roll wrapper on a flat surface with one of the edges pointing toward you (as you look down the wrapper should be a diamond shape). Place about 1 tablespoon of the banana mixture just above the bottom point of the wrapper. Moisten the top and sides of the wrapper with water. Fold the bottom corner up and over the filling, then fold both sides in toward center. Roll the egg roll up (away from you), towards the top corner. Transfer to a plate and continue to prepare the remaining banana rolls.

3. Slowly heat enough vegetable oil for deep-frying (about 3 inches) in a medium frying pan over medium heat until a deep-fry thermometer reads 365°. Fry the Banana Rolls in small batches, 2 or 3 at a time, until golden, about 2 minutes, gently turning with tongs once or twice so they brown evenly. Remove rolls and transfer them to a plate lined with paper towels. Pile on a platter, pyramid-style, dust with confectioners sugar, and sprinkle with black sesame seeds, if desired.

Variation: You may use toasted sesame seeds instead of black sesame seeds.

TIBET

When I was four years old, my grandfather began to tell me stories about a mystical, magical land a continent away from our home in Guyana. He told me it was a land "on the roof of the world"—a beautiful place called "Shangri-la," a true utopia. He said that Hindu gods dwelled there, on Mount Kailash. Of course, what he was describing was Tibet. Since its invasion by China in 1950, it has been an official part of the People's Republic of China. • When I grew up and my interest about new and exciting cuisines took shape, I wanted to learn more about the foods of this exotic place. My quest began in Kathmandu, the capital of Nepal. On my first day there, I asked a local shopkeeper for a map of Tibet. Instead, he gave me a map of China and pointed a friendly finger toward a nearby chai stand. There, the *chai-walla,* or tea server, brought me a warm, aromatic cup of milky chai overflowing with white froth, looking like the most luscious cappuccino. He secured his spectacles in order to get a better look at me, and what his eyes said was that this was no place for a woman. I opened my map and traced my finger along the Friendship Highway, from Kathmandu to Tibet's capital, Lhasa. I knew I had to see it. I scanned the chai stand for someone who looked as if he'd make a good driver for two weeks. Soon I had spotted Kesh, and what he didn't

THE FLAVORS OF TIBET

Simple yet versatile, basic ingredients in Tibetan kitchens are barley, wheat, bean curd, ginger, shallots, and garlic. Frequently used spices include turmeric, cumin, Sichuan peppercorns, star anise, and white pepper. These add light spiciness to foods, but are never overpowering. Yak butter, yak milk, and yak meat are, of course, essential to the Tibetan diet, sustaining the population in the harsh climate. Vegetables such as cabbage, carrots, and beans are often lightly sautéed to make simple, delicious meals.

understand in English he picked up very quickly in U.S. dollars. I hired him on the spot. • Little did I know that for two solid weeks, most of my travels would be about checkpoints and the stamping of permits. I fruitlessly offered a few bribes to serious-looking Chinese officials, each of whom wanted to know why a single woman was traveling alone. There was very little in the way of diplomacy. At one of these checkpoints, I mistakenly said that I was headed for Tibet in search of authentic Tibetan food. The mere mention of Tibet, as I discovered, is taboo, and so we were delayed for hours. In the end, it took my warm Patagonia jacket and four packs of Kesh's cigarettes to get us through. • For the next few days as we traveled the Friendship Highway, I saw Shangri-la just as my grandfather had described it to me: there were magnificent waterfalls, lush green mountains, and valleys blanketed with wildflowers and thousands of butterflies. Even the more arid, desolate landscapes gave way to streams and rivers flowing with clear, ice-cold water from the glaciers high above. Finally, after crossing the Great Plains, we approached Lhasa, where Tibetan nomads graze their yaks. Imagine a cross between a water buffalo and a Pekingese dog, and you have a yak. They are very friendly, but distinctly aromatic. But sadly, in Lhasa itself I am no longer in Shangri-la: instead, it is clogged with Chinese noodle shops and Sichuan-style cuisine. I was looking for real Tibetan food—simple,

basic fare that is subtly spiced. For Tibetans, food is about survival and nourishment—everything they eat must maintain their bodies in some of the most brutal weather on earth. Finally, in search of true Tibetan cuisine, I found myself in homes where Tibetans still cherish their culture and traditions—most often in rural parts of the country or in monasteries. Try your hand at making some of these recipes. They are quite easy to prepare and will give you a sense of the authentic flavors and textures of Tibetan cuisine. From his far away exile in India, the Dalai Lama would surely approve.

MENU **TIBET**

APERITIF
• TIBETAN BUTTER TEA (PO CHA)

APPETIZER
• MAYA'S TIBETAN MOMOS (STEAMED DUMPLINGS)

SOUP
• TIBETAN CHEESE SOUP

SALAD
• TOFU SALAD

ENTRÉE
• JASMINE'S BEEF STEW with KOPAN MASALA

DESSERT
• SPICED CARROT PUDDING (BARFI)

TIBETAN BUTTER TEA
(PO CHA)

The traditional key ingredient in this classic Tibetan beverage is yak milk, but because we don't see too many yak in our neck of the woods, I've used half and half instead. It's just as well: yak milk is an acquired taste for the timid palate—it is thick and tastes like warm salted yogurt. This Po Cha recipe is from Maya, a friend of a woman I met at the Bakhor market in Lhasa. It's a family recipe that originated in the Tibetan region of Pemagul, where it is made with blocks of black tea and then fused with cream, butter, and sensuous spices such as star anise. I use sugar in my version, but traditionally it is unsweetened. This drink is very soothing.

SERVES 2

2 tea bags (black tea)
1 whole star anise
1/4 teaspoon salt
2 tablespoons butter
1/2 cup half and half
Sugar

1. In a medium saucepan, combine 2 + 1/4 cups water, tea bags, and star anise; bring to a boil over medium heat. Add the salt, butter, and half and half; boil for 5 minutes more. Remove saucepan from heat, strain the tea, and sweeten to taste with sugar.

EVERYDAY
WORLD CUISINE

MAYA'S TIBETAN MOMOS
(STEAMED DUMPLINGS)

MAKES APPROXIMATELY 40 DUMPLINGS

2 tablespoons ghee or extra virgin olive oil
1 medium onion, grated
3 garlic cloves, minced
1 tablespoon peeled, grated fresh ginger
2 teaspoons ground turmeric
2 teaspoons ground cumin
1 teaspoon crushed Sichuan peppercorns or 1/2 teaspoon ground cayenne
2 tablespoons soy sauce
1 pound (about 7 cups) shredded green cabbage
1/4 cup firmly packed chopped cilantro
Approximately 40 wonton wrappers
Nonstick vegetable spray

1. In a large saucepan heat ghee or oil over medium heat. Add the onion, garlic, and ginger; sauté until soft, about 5 minutes. Add the turmeric, cumin, peppercorns, and soy sauce; continue to cook for 2 minutes more, stirring occasionally.

2. Add the shredded cabbage to the saucepan and cook, turning occasionally, until soft, about 10 minutes. Remove from heat and add the cilantro, toss to combine, and allow to rest until cool, about 20 minutes.

3. To make the wontons, place a wonton wrapper on a work surface and lightly brush with water. Keep stack of wonton wrappers covered with a damp cloth. Place about 1 teaspoon of the filling in the center of each wonton. Moisten the sides of the wrapper with water and then fold in half diagonally to form a triangle, squeezing out any air from the center. Press the wonton firmly all around to seal it. Moisten the corners with water and fold in so that they overlap each other. Transfer wontons to a baking sheet and cover with a damp cloth. Repeat until all of the filling has been used.

4. Fill a saucepan large enough to hold a steamer insert with 1/2 inch of water. Bring to a steady simmer over medium heat. Generously spray the surface of the steamer insert with nonstick vegetable spray. Place as many dumplings as will fit into the steamer in a single layer without touching each other. Cover and steam over medium heat for 10 to 12 minutes. Remove dumplings as they are done and keep warm. Repeat with remaining dumplings. Serve with chili sauce.

MAYA'S TIBETAN MOMOS

Kesh, my driver, and I are about to go our separate ways, but before saying our farewells we decide to stroll the back alleyways of Lhasa. I wanted to get a glimpse of something uniquely Tibetan, and fortunately, Kesh knew some of the merchants. One of them offered us *cholos*, a soup made of yak milk, yak cheese, and ginger, topped with Sichuan peppercorns. Because blue cheese is similar in flavor to yak cheese, it makes a perfect stand-in. Flavorful and satisfying, with hearty potatoes and hints of spice, this is truly an unusual, authentic Tibetan dish.

TIBETAN CHEESE SOUP

SERVES 4

2 tablespoons extra virgin olive oil
1 medium onion, chopped
1 tablespoon minced garlic
1 teaspoon peeled, minced fresh ginger
1 small red or green chile such as jalapeño or Thai, seeded and finely chopped
1 teaspoon curry powder
1 medium russet potato, peeled and cubed
2 tablespoons crumbled blue cheese
4 + 1/2 cups low-sodium vegetable stock
3/4 teaspoon ground white pepper
Chopped chives and croutons for garnish

1. In a medium saucepan, heat the oil over medium heat and sauté the onion, garlic, ginger, and chile until soft, about 8 minutes, stirring occasionally.

2. Reduce heat to low, add the curry powder, and cook for 1 minute. Add the potato and cheese; stir until cheese is melted.

3. Add the vegetable stock, increase heat to medium and bring to a steady simmer. Cook until the soup thickens slightly, about 20 minutes, then stir in the pepper. Divide soup evenly among 4 warmed bowls. Garnish each serving with chives and croutons, and serve immediately.

❝ I've never been a big fan of tofu, but this salad, which I had at a hotel in Lhasa, was an exception. Light and easy to make, it packs plenty of flavor and has a hint of honey for sweetness. The tofu absorbs the complex flavor mix as it briefly marinates in the dressing. ❞

TOFU SALAD

SERVES 2

1/4 cup extra virgin olive oil
1/4 cup rice wine vinegar
1 tablespoon honey
1 tablespoon soy sauce
1 tablespoon sesame oil
1 tablespoon peeled, minced fresh ginger
Pinch of salt
1 package (14 ounces) firm tofu, cut into 3/4-inch cubes
4 ounces mixed salad greens
1 small carrot, shredded
1 small cucumber, shredded

1. In a large bowl, whisk together the olive oil, vinegar, honey, soy sauce, sesame oil, ginger, and a pinch of salt. Add the tofu and toss well to coat. Cover with plastic wrap and marinate in the refrigerator for 15 minutes.

2. In a large serving bowl, toss the salad greens, carrot, and cucumber. Place the tofu and desired amount of the marinade on top of the salad and serve immediately.

Tibetan sutras.

213

> At the Bakhor market in Lhasa I found Jasmine, a street food vendor touting her yak butter. She invited me to sit down and share her lunch—it is moments like this during my travels that are the most fortuitous and memorable. Today, Jasmine's lunch is Shamday with Kopan Masala, a Tibetan stew made with yak meat and potatoes.
>
> At this point in my trip, I craved the taste of spices, and this rustic dish amply fulfilled my wish. The yak meat had cooked for hours and was falling apart like the most savory short ribs. In this version, flank steak does very well. The aromatic *kopan masala* is both a marinade and the sauce in which the meat cooks. It has hints of cinnamon, cloves, chile, cumin, turmeric, and coriander—a captivating mix that particularly enhances this stick-to-your-ribs meal. It is typical of Tibetan food to keep a light hand when using hot spices. "

JASMINE'S BEEF STEW
WITH KOPAN MASALA

SERVES 4 TO 6

Marinade
1 cup plain yogurt
1 tablespoon smoked paprika
1 teaspoon curry powder
2 teaspoons garam masala
1 tablespoon soy sauce
2 teaspoons ground ginger

Steak
3 pounds flank steak, cut into 3/4-inch cubes
2 tablespoons ghee or extra virgin olive oil
1 large onion, finely chopped
1 tablespoon minced garlic
2 cinnamon sticks, each about 2 inches long
3 bay leaves
2 small tomatoes, peeled, seeded, and diced
Sea salt

1. In a large bowl, combine the yogurt, paprika, curry powder, garam masala, soy sauce, and ginger; stir to combine. Add the beef and turn to coat. Cover the bowl with plastic wrap and marinate in the refrigerator for several hours or overnight.

2. Heat a Dutch oven over medium-high heat. Add the ghee or oil and sauté the onion and garlic until translucent, stirring frequently, about 5 minutes. Add the cinnamon sticks and bay leaves. Continue to cook until the onions brown, about 5 minutes more.

3. Add the beef, all of the marinade, and the tomatoes. Cook over high heat until the juices from the meat are released and the mixture begins to boil. Reduce heat to medium and simmer, uncovered, for 20 minutes. Reduce heat to a slow simmer, cover, and continue to cook for 40 minutes more. Remove cinnamon sticks and bay leaves; season with salt to taste. Serve with white rice or warm pita bread.

TIBET

❝ If you've never considered carrots for dessert, now is your chance to truly appreciate their sweet, hidden talent. This is a warm, spicy pudding-like dessert that I've also found at street markets in Nepal, India, and Pakistan, where it is made with coconuts. Don't be fooled: this is a decadent dessert, so much so that it's the Tibetan ruse for getting children to eat their vegetables. ❞

SPICED CARROT PUDDING
(BARFI)

SERVES 8

2 cups (about 4 medium) grated carrots
2 cups half and half
8 tablespoons (1 stick) butter, melted
1 cup loosely packed brown sugar
1 teaspoon ground cardamom
1/2 teaspoon ground nutmeg
1/2 teaspoon ground cloves
1/2 teaspoon ground cinnamon
1 cup currants or dark raisins
About 1 cup slivered almonds, toasted

1. In a medium saucepan, combine the carrots and half and half and bring to a simmer over low heat. Cook until the carrots are very tender, about 30 minutes. Add the butter, brown sugar, cardamom, nutmeg, cloves, cinnamon, and currants; stir to combine. Continue to cook over low heat, stirring constantly, until the mixture is quite thick, about 20 minutes.

2. Remove saucepan from heat and allow to cool slightly. Divide mixture evenly among 8 small bowls. Garnish each serving with toasted almonds and serve immediately.

Variation: If you don't like nuts or are allergic to them, you can garnish this with a drizzle of sweetened condensed milk instead.

Having fun with Tibetan children in Lhasa.

JAPAN

I am an avid tea drinker. So when I was in Japan, I took one of its famous bullet trains from Tokyo and headed to the fields of Shizuoka, where the pristine green valleys and vast farmlands make you feel healthy by just looking at them. While I was there I had the opportunity to see firsthand the tedious task of making matcha green tea. Matcha is a high-grade powdered green tea used in formal tea ceremonies in Japan. The veins are removed from the tea leaves to ensure that there are no fibers, then ground into a fine powder. The taste of matcha (try my ice cream recipe, page 229) is a perfect introduction to the sophisticated yet simple flavors of Japan. • Japan, the land of the rising sun, is simply enchanted. It is home to tranquil, misty forests and serene temples, yet the nightlife of its cities comes alive with excitement, teeming with people and neon-streaked streets. • The four main islands that make up Japan are a haven for food perfectionists. Fastidiously prepared bento boxes are a good example; I wish my own lunch box could look more like them! Its fertile fields produce the country's prime source of sustenance, rice (which is also transformed into sake, Japan's preferred beverage). Seafood is pristine and fresh, and surrounded by the sea, Japan avails itself of exotic sea-dwelling

NIRMALA'S GUIDE TO
THE FLAVORS
OF JAPAN

Miso, used for making soups and flavoring dishes, and nori, or seaweed, are mainstays of Japan's kitchens, as is the most important food of all: rice. Dried bonito (a kind of fish) is usually flaked and used as a flavoring for soups and sauces. More familiar ingredients include tofu (soy bean curd), rice wine vinegar, sake, soy sauce (of which there are many grades), and fresh ginger and green onions. Condiments include sinus-clearing wasabi, sesame paste (frequently used as a dipping sauce), and the spice mixture *shichimi togarashi* (seven spice seasoning), made primarily with ground red pepper, sesame seeds, nori flakes, bits of mandarin orange peel, black hemp seeds, white poppy seeds, and sansho (Sichuan peppercorn). Panko, breadcrumbs that are grated into shards rather than ground, lend fried foods an especially crunchy coating. Japan is a tea-drinking country, famed for their elaborate tea ceremony. There are dozens of varieties of tea, ranging from green tea to white tea, whole leaf to ground leaf. The Japanese are also fond of mayonnaise, thicker and richer than the American variety. Kewpie is a popular brand, sold in cute plastic squeeze bottles.

delicacies often not seen anywhere else. • The roots of Japanese cuisine date to the Heian period (794 - 1285 AD) at which time food preparation was an art, meticulously made and exquisitely presented. Back then, two main meals a day with several snacks in between were the norm. In the late 1100s, a simpler, more Zen-like cuisine evolved, featuring small portions of vegetables that were coordinated by color (yellow, white, black, green, and red), taste (salty, bitter, sweet, sour, and *umami*), and season. During the 14th through 16th centuries, Japan began open trade with the outside world, which brought new culinary influences. The Chinese contributed tea, soy sauce, bean curd, and chopsticks as eating utensils. The Portuguese introduced tempura batter for coating and deep-frying foods, as well as a popular sponge cake called *castella.* The Dutch brought potatoes, sugar, and corn. • During the Edo period (1603 – 1857) Japan, fearing attack, retreated into itself, undergoing centuries of self-imposed seclusion from the rest of the world. But by the Meiji period (1868 – 1912), Japan had once again opened and renewed trade with the west. Since then, regardless of its outside influences, true Japanese cuisine lives by just one simple rule: the simplicity and freshness of seasonal bounty, presented and savored in as natural a state as possible.

MENU JAPAN

APERITIF
- POMEGRANATE SAKE COSMO

APPETIZER
- COCONUT TEMPURA OYSTERS with WASABI MAYONNAISE

SOUP
- DAIKON-MISO SOUP

SALAD
- CRAB AND GINGER SOBA NOODLE SALAD

ENTREE
- PORK CUTLET with GINGERED SNOW PEAS

DESSERT
- MATCHA ICE CREAM

> " I adore sake, so whenever I make Cosmopolitans for my friends, I always infuse the mix with some sort of exotic fruit and use sake instead of vodka. It's a surprising twist on the ever-popular cocktail. "

POMEGRANATE SAKE COSMO

SERVES 2

2 ounces sake
1/2 ounce Triple Sec
1 ounce sweetened pomegranate juice
1/2 ounce freshly squeezed lime juice
Lime peel and pickled ginger for garnish

1. Fill a shaker with ice cubes. Pour the sake, Triple Sec, pomegranate juice, and lime juice over the ice. Shake well and strain into chilled martini glasses. Garnish with a twist of lime peel and pickled ginger.

COCONUT TEMPURA OYSTERS

> To me, there is nothing more exhilarating than being at a fish market at 5 AM. I had always been thrilled by New York's Fulton Fish Market (now relocated to the Bronx) and London's Billingsgate...but when I visited the Tsukiji Fish Market in Tokyo, I was truly in awe. It is the largest wholesale fish market in Asia, a massive shed housing thousands of just-caught fish. Fishmongers bargain with both the local residents and chefs for enormous tuna, squid, oysters, and finfish of all colors, shapes, and sizes. The excitement and cacophony of shouting, chopping, and knife-sharpening conspired to whet my appetite for fresh fish. After I'd had my fill of the market, I headed for one of the wonderful food stalls in Tsukiji for some breakfast. I had fresh oysters drizzled with a thin wasabi sauce, which inspired this idea—I've coated the oysters in a unique coconut batter which fries up golden and crunchy, while the tender oyster within retains its briny flavor. "

COCONUT TEMPURA OYSTERS
WITH WASABI MAYONNAISE

MAKES 24 OYSTERS

24 shucked oysters
Vegetable oil for deep-frying
1/2 cup all-purpose flour
1/2 teaspoon salt
1/2 cup ice water
2 large egg yolks, lightly beaten
1/4 cup unsweetened shredded coconut
Wasabi Mayonnaise (recipe follows)

1. Pat the oysters dry and set aside. Slowly heat enough vegetable oil for deep-frying (about 3 inches) in a medium frying pan over medium-high heat until a deep-fry thermometer reads 365°.

2. Combine the flour, salt, 1/2 cup ice water, and egg yolks; stir to combine. Fold in the coconut. Dip the oysters in coconut batter a few at a time and deep-fry until golden brown, about 2 to 3 minutes. Drain on paper towels. Serve with Wasabi Mayonnaise.

WASABI MAYONNAISE

MAKES ABOUT 1/2 CUP

1/3 cup mayonnaise
2 teaspoons wasabi paste or powder
2 tablespoons honey

1. Combine all of the ingredients in a small bowl and whisk well to combine. Cover and chill until ready to serve.

> People often ask me to show them how to make miso soup. I think they have the mistaken notion that Japanese food is difficult to prepare, but it just isn't so. If there is an Asian market near you, you can make this very simple, healthful version of miso soup, which is immensely flavorful and very high in protein. I have omitted tofu, which is a traditional ingredient in miso soup, replacing it with daikon radish, which gives this soup a crisp, refreshing taste. "

DAIKON-MISO SOUP

SERVES 4

5 cups low-sodium vegetable stock
1/2 cup peeled, diced daikon radish
1/4 cup white or yellow miso paste
1/2 cup loosely packed, julienned nori (Japanese dried seaweed)
2 green onions, thinly sliced, for garnish

1. In a medium saucepan, combine the stock and radish; bring to a boil, then reduce heat to a simmer. Add the miso paste and whisk to dissolve, being careful not to let the mixture boil. Remove soup from heat, stirring in the nori and divide among 4 warm soup bowls. Sprinkle with green onions and serve hot.

Cooking Tip: To julienne the seaweed, use kitchen shears.

These lucky rakes, purchased during the Day of the Rooster, bring wealth for the coming year.

CRAB AND GINGER SOBA NOODLE SALAD

SERVES 4

1/2 pound Jumbo lump crabmeat, picked through for cartilage
1 teaspoon black sesame seeds
2 tablespoons chopped cilantro
1 tablespoon chopped parsley
1 tablespoon freshly squeezed lime juice
1/2 pound soba noodles
2 tablespoons sesame oil
1 tablespoon peeled, grated fresh ginger
2 tablespoons light soy sauce
Sea salt
Chives for garnish

1. In a medium bowl, combine the crabmeat, sesame seeds, cilantro, parsley, and lime juice. Toss to combine; cover with plastic wrap and refrigerate until ready to use.

2. In a large saucepan, bring water to a boil over high heat. Add the noodles and cook for about 3 minutes or until al dente, or just firm to the bite. Drain and immediately rinse with cold water. Transfer noodles to a large bowl and toss with sesame oil, ginger, and soy sauce.

3. When ready to serve, coil a nest of sesame noodles at the center of each of 4 plates. Divide crabmeat mixture equally among each serving, placing it in the center of the noodles. Sprinkle with sea salt and garnish with chives. Serve at room temperature.

" For my train ride from Tokyo to Nara, I bought a small salad to have for lunch. It didn't have the extravagance of crabmeat as this recipe does, but it was a wonderful gingery noodle dish with various pickled vegetables, a very traditional food in Japan. On the way, I stopped at Shizuoka, a serene city with lush tea plantations and a spectacular view of Mount Fuji. What a perfect place to enjoy both the view and my lunch! Alas, I had forgotten to bring chopsticks, but the village girl in me came through as I began to eat with my fingers. I quickly learned from the disapproving stares of the local residents that this is simply not proper dining etiquette in their country. "

EVERYDAY
WORLD CUISINE

" When you're tired of the same old breaded pork chops for dinner, try these thin cutlets, dressed up Japanese-style with sweet teriyaki sauce—not from a bottle, but homemade in a flash and flavored with ginger, orange juice, and rice wine vinegar. You can even make this dish with thin cuts of chicken or beef. The panko breadcrumbs, which resemble tiny shards of bread instead of the usual ground breadcrumbs we're used to, make the chops extra-crispy. When you serve them with fresh snow peas that have been gently gingered and a bowl of steamed rice, you have a perfectly balanced, delicious family meal. "

PORK CUTLET
WITH GINGERED SNOW PEAS

SERVES 4

Vegetable oil for deep-frying
4 boneless pork cutlets, about 4 ounces each
Sea salt and freshly ground pepper
About 1/4 cup all-purpose flour
2 eggs, lightly beaten
1 + 1/2 cups panko breadcrumbs
2 cups hot cooked white rice
Teriyaki Sauce (recipe follows)
Gingered Snow Peas (recipe follows)

1. Preheat a wide, deep skillet over medium-high heat. Slowly heat enough vegetable oil for deep-frying (about 3 inches) until a deep-fry thermometer reads 365°.

2. Trim any excess fat from the pork to ensure that the meat does not curl when fried. Pound the pork with a kitchen mallet to 1/4-inch thick. Season cutlets with salt and pepper, then dust lightly with flour. Dip the cutlets into the eggs and then coat with the panko breadcrumbs. Firmly press the breadcrumbs onto the cutlets with your fingers.

3. Deep-fry the cutlets, two at a time, turning once, until golden brown on both sides, about 5 minutes total. Drain on paper towels. Repeat with remaining cutlets.

4. To serve, cut the pork into 1-inch strips and spoon a little of the Teriyaki Sauce over them. Serve the remaining sauce on the side. Serve the pork with white rice and Gingered Snow Peas.

226
IN NIRMALA'S
KITCHEN

TERIYAKI SAUCE

MAKES ABOUT 1 CUP

1/4 cup sake or dry white wine
2 tablespoons sugar
1/4 cup soy sauce
2 tablespoons rice wine vinegar
1/2 teaspoon ground ginger
2 tablespoons freshly squeezed orange juice

1. Combine all ingredients in a small saucepan. Cook over medium heat, stirring frequently, until the sugar has dissolved, about 2 to 3 minutes.

Make Ahead Tip: Teriyaki sauce can be made up to two days ahead and refrigerated in an airtight plastic container.

GINGERED SNOW PEAS

SERVES 4

1 pound fresh snow peas, or frozen snow peas, thawed
1 tablespoon extra virgin olive oil
1 garlic clove, crushed
1 tablespoon peeled, grated fresh ginger
3 tablespoons sake or dry white wine

1. Trim the ends of the snow peas. In a medium skillet heat oil over medium heat, add the garlic, ginger, snow peas, and sake or white wine, and sauté for 2 to 3 minutes, or until peas are tender.

A tray of typical Japanese appetizers.

MATCHA ICE CREAM

I have always been an avid tea drinker with a perpetual romance with tea houses and tea plantations around the world. Matcha is a particular kind of high-grade green tea that is used in Japan's formal ritual tea ceremony. First, the veins are removed from the tea leaves to ensure that no fibers are present, then the leaves are ground into a very fine powder. It can be added to a variety of sweet and savory dishes, but it is nicest to experience the purity of matcha's flavor by savoring it on its own. You can also use it to make this truly refreshing summer dessert—serve this ice cream with fresh berries if you like. Matcha tastes like nothing else you've ever eaten, so expect your palate to thank you with requests for more.

MATCHA ICE CREAM

SERVES 4

1 + 1/2 cups whole milk
1 + 1/2 cups heavy cream
5 large egg yolks
1/2 cup sugar
1/8 teaspoon salt
1 tablespoon matcha (green tea powder)

1. In a medium saucepan, heat the milk and cream over medium heat until small bubbles appear. Immediately remove from heat and set aside. Do not allow mixture to boil.

2. In a medium bowl, beat the egg yolks and gradually whisk in the sugar and salt. Continue whisking for 3 minutes. Temper the eggs to prevent scalding them by slowly whisking in a few tablespoons of the warm milk and cream mixture. Continue to pour in the remaining milk and cream mixture while continuously whisking, making sure that no lumps form.

3. Return mixture to saucepan and cook over low heat, stirring frequently. As soon as the mixture thickens (it should coat the back of a spoon), about 10 minutes, remove from heat and set aside.

4. In a small bowl, whisk the matcha with 1/4 cup hot water until dissolved, then pour it into the custard, whisking to combine. Pour the mixture through a sieve into a large bowl. Cover with a clean kitchen towel and allow to cool to room temperature.

5. Pour the custard mixture into an ice-cream maker, and freeze according to manufacturer's instructions. If you do not have an ice cream maker, pour the mixture into an airtight container and freeze until set, about 2 + 1/2 to 3 hours. Remove from the container and cut into 3-inch pieces. Place in a food processor and process until smooth. Return to airtight container and freeze again. Repeat the freezing and chopping process 2 to 3 times until a smooth consistency is reached.

Make Ahead Tip: The ice cream can be made up to a week ahead, and frozen in an airtight container.

AUSTRALIA

As a child, I was mesmerized by the food and culture of native peoples, perhaps because at an early age I spent my summers with the Arawak Indians of my country, Guyana. As I grew, so did my interest in other indigenous groups, including the Maori of New Zealand, and the aborigines of Australia. • Australian aborigines were early hunter-gatherers, and they have thrived for more than 40,000 years in their vast savannahs, coastal plains, and red deserts. "Bush Food," or aboriginal cuisine, has long been a varied fare. Their foods came from the wild—almost half from plants—and much of it eaten raw. They feasted on a variety of fruits, nuts, and seeds, as well as roots and tubers. Figs, macadamia nuts, green plums, bush tomatoes, and seeds of native plants such as wattleseed (which, when roasted and ground, has a coffee-like flavor) are among the better-known foods from these sources. They also had available an abundance of seafood (cockles were a favorite), wild game, and enormous emu eggs. Even kangaroo meat helped to provide the much-needed protein necessary for a balanced diet. • When European settlers arrived in the early 1800s they viewed the aborigines as primitive hunter-gatherers and dismissed their agricultural knowledge of the land. Many native foods

THE FLAVORS
OF AUSTRALIA

With the influx of immigrants to Australia, the continent's pantry has been revolutionized. Popular ingredients include lemongrass, chiles, lemon myrtle, sake, basil, bush tomatoes, bunya nuts, and spices from all over the world. Polenta, couscous, and short-grain rice for risotto are also staples. Fresh shellfish (yabby, a freshwater, lobster-like crustacean is abundant) and finfish of all kinds swim the surrounding ocean. In Australia's sub-tropical territories, you'll find fresh fruits and vegetables, including Asian varieties such as jackfruit, long beans, papaya, and bok choy. Native spices such as bush tomato and wattleseed are being put to more and more creative new uses.

and techniques took a back seat to "more civilized" European fare and customs. Fortunately, thanks to post-World War II immigration from Southeast Asia and the Middle East, Australia now boasts a contemporary, multicultural cuisine renowned throughout the world. This massive continent has introduced some of the world's most talented chefs, and local artisans meticulously cultivate fresh produce. Australia's vineyards yield superb wines, as America has recently discovered, and its dairy farms create some of the best cheeses in the world.

MENU AUSTRALIA

APERITIF
• AUSSIE MINT SMOOTHIE

APPETIZER
• BUSH TOMATO AND ASPARAGUS FRITTATA

SOUP
• CHARLIE'S OXTAIL SOUP

SALAD
• AUSSIE SHRIMP-ON-THE-BARBIE SALAD

ENTREE
• GRILLED OSTRICH FILETS with PRESERVED LEMON POLENTA CAKES

DESSERT
• WATTLESEED ICE CREAM

AUSSIE MINT SMOOTHIE

SERVES 4

2 cups diced honeydew melon, plus 4 slices for garnish

1 cup plain yogurt or lemon yogurt

2 cups seedless green grapes, frozen, plus more for garnish

1 teaspoon dried Australian mint or 1/4 cup loosely packed fresh mint leaves, plus more for garnish

2 teaspoons freshly squeezed lime juice

1 tablespoon sugar

1. In a blender, combine the honeydew, yogurt, frozen grapes, mint, lime juice, and sugar; process until smooth. Add additional lime juice if desired, and sugar to taste. Evenly divide smoothie among 4 tall glasses and garnish with slices of honeydew, grapes, and mint. Serve immediately.

❝ Aside from great scuba diving and an exhilerating nightlife, Cairns possesses a hidden secret: a tropical rainforest covered with lush greenery, abundant vegetation, and dense sugarcane fields. I had come to Cairnes for its famous native Australian mint, which I had long known to be unique but had yet to taste for myself. In my quest, I arrived at one of the small Aborigine communities surrounding the rainforest, and that afternoon the village leader and I sat under a giant eucalyptus tree sipping mint tea sweetened with sugar cane juice. We talked for hours about unique Aborigine seeds, nuts, and fruits. Then off we went through fields of towering sugarcane, making our way to a vast, green pasture. There we gathered the highly unusual native Australian mint. It is unlike any other variety of mint I have ever tasted—delicate in flavor, but with an underlying peppery bite that is both aromatic and palate-pleasing. Of course, this refreshing summer smoothie can be made using regular fresh mint—either way it makes a perfect after-dinner drink, one that I often serve guests after a particularly spicy dinner. ❞

BUSH TOMATO AND ASPARAGUS FRITTATA

I'm not big on breakfast (sorry, mom), but after a 10-hour drive dodging kangaroos, two of which cracked our windshield and nearly hoofed me in the face, I was ready to eat just about anything. The night drive had taken me and Charlie, my driver, from Adelaide on the southern coast of Australia to the tiny town of Parachilna. I had wanted a taste of life on the prairie, but when we reached our shabby hotel we were dismayed to discover that it did not have a kitchen. We were greeted by a curly-locked Aborigine, and before I could even ask for a room, he whipped out two emu eggs, asking if I wanted to buy them as souvenirs. Each egg was the size of a small cantaloupe. I smelled them and shook them, and when I asked if he had a frying pan his eyes widened in horror. Charlie and I smiled at each other and got to work gathering firewood and fishing the cigarette lighter from the car. Soon we had a small fire going outside the hotel, and I produced my supply of the Aboriginal spice called *akudjura,* or bush tomato. That's how we created our breakfast of emu eggs (each is the equivalent of 10 chicken eggs) with ground bush tomato, which was decidedly delicious. At home, I decided to add crisp asparagus, as it marries beautifully with the fruity, yet slightly tangy flavor of bush tomato. This is a delightful way to get kids, including my ten-year-old niece, Nadiya, to eat eggs, especially when you use different cookie cutters to cut the frittata into fun shapes.

BUSH TOMATO AND ASPARAGUS FRITTATA

SERVES 4

6 large eggs
1/2 teaspoon salt
1/4 teaspoon freshly ground pepper
2 tablespoons unsalted butter
1 tablespoon olive oil
1 pound asparagus trimmed and cut into 1/4-inch pieces
2 tablespoons ground, dried bush tomato or 1/4 cup finely diced sundried tomato
1/2 cup grated Parmesan cheese
1 tablespoon chopped chives

1. Preheat the broiler. Whisk the eggs with salt and pepper until fluffy and set aside.

2. In a 10-inch ovenproof nonstick skillet, heat butter and oil over medium-high heat. Add the asparagus and sauté for 2 minutes. Add the bush tomato; sauté 3 minutes more.

3. Pour the eggs over the bush tomato-asparagus mixture. Using a spatula, pull the eggs toward the middle of the pan until they begin to set. Reduce heat to medium-low and cook until the frittata is almost set but top is still uncooked, about 2 minutes.

4. Evenly sprinkle Parmesan cheese over the top of the frittata and transfer skillet to broiler. Broil until the top is golden brown, about 5 minutes. Let the frittata cool to room temperature. Sprinkle with chives, cut into large wedges, and serve.

Charlie, my driver in Australia, is Aborigine and we spent a great deal of time together during my journey there. Charlie is multi-talented: he's an accomplished player of Australia's native instrument, the didgeridoo, he paints, and he is also an excellent cook. His clan is in the northern territory, near famous Ayers Rock, and that is where he took me to meet his Aussie friends and made us this wonderful soup, which he prepared using kangaroo tail. I don't know of any kangaroo tails available in the U.S., so I make this luscious soup with oxtails, which are plentiful. The beauty of this soup is that it is cooked to the point at which the meat falls away from the bones, and the consistency of the meat is gelatinous so that it simply melts on your tongue like warm butter. The flavor is deep and rich—and out of this world. Try this soup with a piping hot crusty baguette.

CHARLIE'S OXTAIL SOUP

SERVES 8

2 tablespoons extra virgin olive oil
3 pounds oxtail, cut into pieces
1 large onion, chopped
2 garlic cloves, crushed
1 tablespoon peeled, minced fresh ginger
1 cup dry red wine
2 large carrots cut into 1/2-inch pieces
2 stalks celery, chopped
1 large potato, peeled and cut into 1/2-inch pieces
2 bay leaves
About 5 cups low-sodium beef stock
Sea salt and freshly ground pepper

1. Heat oil in a large saucepan over high heat. Add the oxtail pieces and arrange in a single layer, pressing them firmly down so they make good contact with the bottom of the pan. Brown well on all sides. Using tongs, transfer meat to a platter; set aside.

2. Pour excess fat from the pot leaving about 2 tablespoons; reduce heat to medium-high. Sauté the onion, garlic, and ginger until soft, about 5 minutes.

3. Add the wine and stir well with a wooden spoon to loosen all the brown bits from the pan. Continue to cook until the wine is reduced by half. Return meat to the pan and add the carrots, celery, potato, and bay leaves. Pour in 5 cups beef stock, or enough to cover the oxtail pieces completely. Adjust seasoning with salt and pepper. Bring to a boil, then reduce heat and simmer, covered, until meat can be easily pulled off the bones, about 3 hours. Skim off excess fat; remove and discard bay leaves. Serve hot.

AUSSIE SHRIMP-ON-THE-BARBIE SALAD

With such a rich coastline, it's no surprise that seafood is a major part of Australian cuisine. In Cairns, I had the good fortune to befriend Aaron, who was born in Jamaica but lives in Cairns where he runs a food shack next door to the Holiday Inn. Aaron and his boat, Shirley, will take you scuba-diving for next to nothing, but I'd rather enjoy his food—including his terrific jerk chicken. This is Aaron's recipe for sublime grilled jumbo shrimp. He makes them to top off a fresh, simply dressed green salad.

AUSSIE SHRIMP-ON-THE-BARBIE SALAD

SERVES 4

1/2 cup extra virgin olive oil, plus more for dressing salad
1/3 cup freshly squeezed lemon juice
2 tablespoons minced garlic
2 tablespoons minced shallot
1 tablespoon chopped fresh thyme leaves
1 tablespoon chopped flat-leaf parsley
1 tablespoon chopped cilantro
1/4 teaspoon kosher salt
12 jumbo shrimp (about 1 + 1/2 pounds), peeled and deveined
4 cups mixed salad greens, washed and dried
Balsamic vinegar
Sea salt and freshly ground pepper

1. Soak four 8- or 10-inch bamboo or wood skewers in water for several hours or overnight.

2. In a large bowl, whisk together the oil, lemon juice, garlic, shallot, thyme, parsley, cilantro, and salt. Add the shrimp and toss to coat. Cover bowl with plastic wrap, transfer to refrigerator and marinate for 1 hour.

3. Heat a charcoal or gas grill until very hot and brush the grill with oil. Remove shrimp from the marinade, letting excess drip off. Thread 3 shrimp onto each of 4 skewers.

4. Place shrimp on grill and cook for about 4 minutes on each side, or until seared and cooked through. Arrange salad greens on a large serving platter and drizzle with oil and vinegar. Place skewers on the bed of lettuce and sprinkle with sea salt and freshly ground pepper. Serve immediately.

GRILLED OSTRICH FILETS
WITH PRESERVED LEMON POLENTA CAKES

SERVES 4

4 ostrich filets, about 4 ounces each
Sea salt and freshly ground pepper
Preserved Lemon Polenta Cakes (recipe follows)

1. Heat a gas or charcoal grill until very hot. Season filets with salt and pepper and grill 3 minutes on each side.

PRESERVED LEMON POLENTA CAKES

3 tablespoons unsalted butter
2 tablespoons minced shallot
1 tablespoon peeled, minced fresh ginger
1 small red Serrano or other small red chile, finely minced
2 cups low-sodium chicken stock
3/4 cup polenta (do not use prepared polenta)
1/4 cup finely chopped preserved lemons
1 cup grated zucchini
Sea salt
About 3 tablespoons olive oil

1. Preheat oven to 300°. Heat butter in a large saucepan and sauté the shallot, ginger, and chile until soft, about 2 minutes. Add the stock and gently bring to a simmer. Slowly sprinkle the polenta into the boiling stock while continuously whisking, making sure that no lumps form. Once all the polenta has been incorporated, reduce heat to low and continue to stir frequently with a wooden spoon until it begins to thicken, about 10 minutes.

2. Stir in the preserved lemon and zucchini; season to taste with salt. Remove polenta from heat and allow to cool. Divide the mixture into four portions and carefully shape each portion into individual cakes about 3-inches in diameter.

3. Heat oil in a large skillet over high heat. Cook the polenta cakes until golden brown, about 5 minutes on each side. Drain on paper towels and keep warm in oven until ready to serve. Serve with Grilled Ostrich Filets.

It's difficult to describe the flavor of wattleseed, which I discovered in Australia's northern territory, but I haven't stopped experimenting with them since the day I found them. The taste is mocha-like (although the seeds are caffeine-free), with touches of hazelnut and chocolate. In my excitement to develop new recipes using these magical seeds, I created my own special wattleseed ice cream. Here, the seeds are first steeped to flavor the custard base, then are mixed back in for crunch. 99

WATTLESEED ICE CREAM

SERVES 4 TO 6

4 cups heavy cream
2 tablespoons Wattleseed (Nirmala's Kitchen brand) or ground coffee
6 large egg yolks
1/2 cup sugar

1. In a medium saucepan, combine the cream and wattleseed and cook over medium heat just until small bubbles begin to appear around the edges. Remove from heat and let mixture steep for 30 minutes. Strain mixture through a fine sieve into a bowl. Transfer the wattleseed left behind in the sieve to a separate small bowl and set aside.

2. In a medium bowl, whisk together the egg yolks and sugar until well combined. Whisk the cream mixture into the egg mixture, then transfer to a medium saucepan and cook over low heat, stirring constantly, until the custard is thick enough to coat the back of a wooden spoon, about 5 minutes. Remove from heat and add 1 tablespoon of the reserved wattleseed.

3. Pour the custard into an ice cream maker, and freeze according to manufacturer's instructions. If you do not have an ice cream maker, pour the mixture into an airtight container and freeze until set, about 2 + 1/2 to 3 hours. Remove the frozen custard from the container and cut into 3-inch pieces. Place in a food processor and process until smooth. Return to airtight container and freeze again. Repeat the freezing and chopping process 2 to 3 times until a desired consistency is reached.

Scuba diving around the Great Barrier Reef.

NEW ZEALAND

My destiny with New Zealand actually began in an airport in Papua New Guinea. It was there that I met Albert, a bronzed, handsome Maori native whose face was tattooed with traditional symbols. We sat next to each other in our waiting room seats, separated only by a large palm branch broom that he carried. We began a slow conversation that soon morphed into a four-hour tête-à-tête as we waited for our now-grounded flight to be rescheduled. With nowhere to go, Albert and I tried to get some sleep on the betel nut-stained concrete floor. That night, Albert intoxicated my senses with stories of New Zealand's Maori culture and its culinary treasures, one of which he happened to have a jar of on hand: delicious golden honey from the South Island. I knew I had smelled something sweet. • The next morning, my eyes opened to Albert's beautifully etched face, inches from mine. I knew I had to take a detour. Instead of the Solomon Islands, I flew to New Zealand. • As Albert tells it, his Maori people came from a legendary homeland called *Hawaiki*. Some have speculated that this mythical place did in fact exist, somewhere in Polynesia, and that it was quite exquisite. The Maori were master navigators, using stars, cloud patterns, the direction of sea birds in flight, and the color of the sea as guides throughout the Pacific Ocean. The great navigator Kupe is said to have discovered New Zealand, which

THE FLAVORS OF NEW ZEALAND

The Maori don't traditionally use spices, but New Zealand's settlers have influenced its kitchens with the many flavors of the Pacific Rim. Honey, cheese, cilantro, chiles, and some spices like cumin and curry powder are essentials. Meats include lamb and venison. Fresh seafood, such as oysters, clams, and mussels is abundant and plays a major part in Kiwi cuisine. The traditional *kumara* (a kind of sweet potato) continues to be a major ingredient, as is taro. And of course, fresh fruits, especially passion fruit and the familiar kiwi (also known as Chinese gooseberries) are always close at hand.

he called *Aotearoa,* or Land of the Long White Cloud, in about 800 AD, whereupon he returned to his homeland and left directions for getting there. Centuries later, around 1350 AD, a great migration took place from Hawaiki to Aotearoa. They came in seven great waka canoes, built to withstand the roiling seas. On board were hordes of people and their possessions, including foods such as taro and *kumara,* the Maori version of sweet potatoes. • The Maori prospered in their new home, and *kai* (food) was sacred to them. Originally, the Maori refrained from using seasonings but with time, their palates began to crave new flavors. They added dried shellfish to their dishes, and for sweetness, the juice of berries and flax bulbs. To heighten the flavor of wild game, the meat was wrapped in taro leaves before steaming it in a *hangi,* or earthen oven. Today, these native foods are all but lost. Only if you're lucky enough to be a guest in a Maori home, will you get to experience these traditional flavors and methods. • Today, the food of New Zealand is known as Kiwi cuisine (the kiwi, a flightless bird, has become New Zealand's national symbol). The flavors vary, with a fusion of European, Asian, and Polynesian influences. Also reflected in the cuisine are a few Maori influences, including the use of *pikopiko* (fern tips) and *kawakawa*, a kind of seasoning. This melding of traditional flavors with newer ones is what makes Kiwi cooking such an exceptional cuisine, one I would never have experienced if not for Albert who, like the great Kupe, pointed me in the right direction.

MENU NEW ZEALAND

KIWITINI

APPETIZER
• PEAR AND SMOKED BRIE MELTS

SOUP
• PETER'S COCONUT-CURRY CLAM CHOWDER with RUTABAGA

SALAD
• ROCHELLE'S GINGER-HONEYED VEGETABLE SALAD

ENTREE
• AUNT CAMILLE'S SPICE-CRUSTED RACK OF LAMB with MASHED GINGER-LIME
SWEET POTATOES

DESSERT
• PASSION FRUIT AND RIESLING DELIGHT

" Visit any salad bar in America today and you'll find fruit salads chock full of kiwi, the pretty deep green fruit native to New Zealand, where it is known as the Chinese gooseberry. Because they've been so overexposed here, I've never been a big fan of these fuzzy-skinned oval-shaped fruits— but when I found myself at a food stall on the beach in the romantic city of Russell, New Zealand's first capital, I enthusiastically enjoyed a non-alcoholic version of this kiwi-based refresher. At home, I added a touch of sweetness with honey, an orangey aura of Triple-Sec, and a tangy twist of lime, ending up with this tasty new cocktail. "

KIWITINI

SERVES 2

1 small ripe kiwi, peeled and sliced
1 teaspoon honey
2 + 1/2 ounces vodka
2 + 1/2 ounces Triple Sec
1 + 1/2 ounces white grape juice
2 teaspoons freshly squeezed lime juice

1. Set 2 slices of kiwi aside for garnish. In a small bowl, mash the remaining kiwi with a fork, then combine with honey in a shaker and shake well. Fill shaker with ice. Add vodka, Triple Sec, grape juice, and lime juice; shake well. Strain into chilled martini glasses and garnish each with a slice of kiwi.

PEAR AND SMOKED BRIE MELTS

" One of the most enjoyable experiences I had in New Zealand was winery hopping—New Zealand's wines are world-renowned and wine making is a hugely successful industry. But before I sip, I must eat, so when these dainty little morsels were served at a vineyard in Mooreland, on the South Island, I ate more than my fair share. The host kept giving me strange looks for devouring all of her delicious hors d'oeuvres, so naturally, I ended up buying four bottles of her superb Riesling. Nowadays, I serve these melting morsels at my own wine parties. They're also the perfect size and shape for children to enjoy… minus the Riesling. You can easily make substitutions with equally delicious results—try apples instead of pears, or fontina, mozzarella, or any soft Mexican cheese in place of brie. "

PEAR AND SMOKED BRIE MELTS

MAKES 9 APPETIZERS

6 slices white or rye bread, crusts removed, trimmed to form uniform squares
4 tablespoons unsalted butter, softened
1 tablespoon mayonnaise
1 tablespoon grainy mustard
1 teaspoon honey
1 medium ripe but firm pear, peeled, cored, and thinly sliced
About 4 ounces smoked brie, thinly sliced
1 tablespoon extra virgin olive oil

1. Butter each slice of bread on one side and set aside.

2. In a small bowl, combine the mayonnaise, mustard, and honey; mix well. Spread the mayonnaise mixture on the unbuttered side of 3 pieces of the bread. Place the pear slices and then the cheese slices evenly over the mayonnaise mixture. Cover the open-face slices with the remaining slices to bread, buttered side facing up.

3. In a large skillet, heat oil over medium heat until hot but not smoking. Add the sandwiches and fry until golden brown, about 2 minutes. Carefully turn and fry on the other side until golden brown and cheese is bubbly. Remove sandwiches to a cutting board and carefully cut each into thirds. Serve immediately.

I made new friends in New Zealand—a native Maori woman named Janice and her husband Peter, a Kiwi, or Caucasian New Zealander. One cool morning, Janice and Peter took me on a digging expedition for the island's famed green-lipped clams, essential to making this fabulous Pan-Asian-style chowder. Armed with just hand shovels and buckets, we started digging at 7 AM. To passers-by, we must have looked like we were digging for Atlantis. We dug for three hours, ending up with two bucketsful of clams—it was quite an adventure. The flavor of these green-lipped shellfish (New Zealand also boasts delicious green-lipped mussels) is out of this world. Green-lipped clams are often called New Zealand clams here in the U.S. If you can't find them, by all means use the littleneck clams available at any fish market. My contribution was to intensify the flavor by using curry powder and rutabagas instead of potatoes.

PETER'S COCONUT-CURRY CLAM CHOWDER WITH RUTABAGA

SERVES 4

2 tablespoons unsalted butter
1 large onion, grated
1 teaspoon minced garlic
Pinch of salt
2 teaspoons curry powder
1 + 1/2 cups chopped celery (about 3 stalks)
2 tablespoons all-purpose flour
2 cups peeled and diced rutabaga or russet potatoes (about 1 large rutabaga or 2 potatoes)
1 + 1/2 cups canned unsweetened coconut milk
1 cup whole milk
1 pound shucked green-lipped or littleneck clams
Sea salt and freshly ground pepper
1/4 cup chopped parsley for garnish
Oyster crackers

1. Heat the butter in a large saucepan over medium-high heat. Add onion, garlic, and a pinch of salt; sauté until soft, stirring frequently, about 5 minutes. Add the curry powder and celery and cook for 3 minutes more, stirring frequently.

2. Add the flour, and stir continuously for 2 minutes. Add the rutabaga, coconut milk and milk; bring to a boil. Reduce heat to low and cover. Simmer chowder until the rutabaga is fork tender, about 10 minutes. Add the clams and cook for 2 minutes more. If necessary, add more milk to reach desired consistency and season to taste with salt and pepper. Garnish with parsley and serve with oyster crackers.

252

IN NIRMALA'S KITCHEN

On the advice of a friend, I ventured down to beehive country beneath the snow-capped mountains of South Island. I yearned for the decadent taste of fresh, raw honey oozing between my fingers and coating my cheeks, just like Winnie-the-Pooh. Rochelle, a local organic honey farmer, invited me to help harvest some of her honeycombs. Looking like Martians dressed in our protective white suits, we headed for the hives. The buzzing was positively orchestral—but I didn't mind because I knew I was protected by my bee suit. I wish I had had one when I was young, climbing our bee-laden fruit trees in Guyana. Rochelle's delicious honey crop inspired this salad of pretty colors and contrasting flavors. "

ROCHELLE'S GINGER-HONEYED VEGETABLE SALAD

SERVES 4 TO 6

6 medium carrots, peeled and cut into 1 + 1/2-inch rounds
1 pound asparagus, trimmed and cut into 2-inch pieces
3 tablespoons honey
3 tablespoons balsamic vinegar
1-inch piece of peeled fresh ginger, finely chopped
1 tablespoon toasted sesame seeds
Sea salt and freshly ground pepper
1/4 cup extra virgin olive oil
1 pint red or yellow cherry tomatoes

1. Have a bowl of ice water ready. Bring a small pot of water to a boil over medium-high heat. Blanch the carrots for 2 minutes then add the asparagus, and blanch for 2 minutes more. Drain and immediately plunge the vegetables into ice water to stop the cooking.

2. In a small bowl, whisk together the honey, vinegar, ginger, and sesame seeds for the dressing. Add salt and pepper to taste. Slowly drizzle in the oil and whisk continuously until the dressing is emulsified. Toss blanched vegetables and tomatoes with dressing in a large bowl and serve.

Early dawn on the Cook Islands.

New Zealand's lamb is the best in the world, and this dish—a fresh, delicate rack of lamb with a spiced crumb crust—was prepared especially for me. My new-found friends, Janice and Peter, brought me to visit their Aunt Camille who lives about forty miles from Auckland where she owns an enormous, lush organic sheep farm. Aunt Camille is a gracious woman whose laughter is contagious—she lives by herself but hires two strapping young men from the nearby village to help with chores. Mainly, she rears her flock to sell to a local processing facility so that we lamb-lovers in the rest of the world can feast on the delicacy. On this day, the minute we entered her home the aroma emanating from her kitchen seduced my senses. The savory herbs blended harmoniously with the distinctive lamb flavor, and as a partner, *kumara*, the Maori version of sweet potatoes, were sweetened with honey and spiced up with ginger, chile, and lime. This is a sublime choice for a dinner party entrée. "

AUNT CAMILLE'S SPICE-CRUSTED RACK OF LAMB
WITH MASHED GINGER-LIME SWEET POTATOES

SERVES 4

1 rack of lamb, about 1 + 1/2 pounds, Frenched (see Note)
1/2 teaspoon salt
1 teaspoon freshly ground pepper
About 1/4 cup extra virgin olive oil
2 garlic cloves, minced
1 teaspoon ground ginger
1 tablespoon chopped fresh rosemary
1 teaspoon ground cumin
1 teaspoon ground turmeric
1 teaspoon ground coriander
1/2 cup panko breadcrumbs
1 + 1/2 tablespoons Dijon mustard
Mashed Ginger-Lime Sweet Potatoes (recipe follows)

1. Preheat oven to 425°. Season the lamb with salt and pepper. In a large pan set over high heat, sear the lamb on all sides so that a golden brown crust forms. Transfer lamb to a large plate and cover with aluminum foil.

2. In a large bowl, combine the olive oil, garlic, ginger, rosemary, cumin, turmeric, coriander, and breadcrumbs; mix well (the mixture should hold together). Add additional oil if necessary.

3. Lightly coat the lamb with a thin, even layer of mustard, then coat with the spiced breadcrumb mixture on all sides, pressing firmly. Transfer lamb to a large roasting pan. Cover the bones with strips of aluminum foil to prevent them from burning. Roast until the lamb is medium rare, about 20 minutes (the internal temperate should read 125° on an instant-read thermometer). Remove lamb from oven, and let rest for 5 minutes. Slice the rack between the bones to form individual chops and serve with Mashed Ginger-Lime Sweet Potatoes.

Note: Frenching is the cutting away of the fat and meat at the ends of the bones on rib chops, crown roasts, and rib roasts. This process is primarily used for its attractive presentation. My butcher Sal from Queens does a superb job. You can ask your butcher to do it for you, or you can do it yourself: Using a sharp knife, pare and strip away about 1 to 2 inches of the meat and fat below the tips of the bones.

AUNT CAMILLE'S SPICE-CRUSTED RACK OF LAMB

MASHED GINGER-LIME SWEET POTATOES

SERVES 4

2 pounds sweet potatoes, peeled and cut into 1-inch cubes
2 teaspoons kosher salt
1 garlic clove, peeled
1 tablespoon extra virgin olive oil
1 tablespoon peeled, grated fresh ginger
1 tablespoon minced shallot
1 small Thai or jalapeño chile, seeded and minced
3 tablespoons unsalted butter, cut into pieces
2 teaspoons honey
1 tablespoon finely chopped cilantro
1 tablespoon freshly squeezed lime juice
Sea salt and freshly ground pepper

1. Place potatoes in a large saucepan and fill with enough cold water to cover by 1 inch. Add salt and the garlic; bring water to a boil. Reduce heat and simmer until tender (potatoes should be easily pierced with a paring knife) about 6 to 8 minutes.

2. Meanwhile, in a small skillet, heat the oil, then add the ginger, shallot, and chile. Sauté until soft and fragrant, stirring frequently, about 2 minutes. Remove from heat and set aside.

3. When the potatoes are done, drain them and return to them to pot along with the garlic. Add the cooked ginger mixture, butter, honey, cilantro, and lime juice; mash to desired consistency. Season with sea salt and pepper to taste and serve immediately.

> New Zealand produces excellent Riesling, a wine with a slightly flinty, intensely fruity yet acidic flavor. It's the perfect choice for these individual, refreshing desserts—they'll perk up your palate after just about any meal. Prepare the mixture and then pour it into martini glasses to chill. The supermarket brand gelatin-in-a-box never tasted like this! ''

PASSION FRUIT AND RIESLING DELIGHT

MAKES 4 WINE GLASS DESSERTS

2 tablespoons unflavored gelatin (from about 3 packages)
2 cups canned or bottled passion fruit juice
1 cup sugar
1 tablespoon freshly squeezed lemon juice
3/4 cup Riesling
Fresh mint leaves for garnish

1. In a large bowl, soften the gelatin in 1/4 cup hot water. In a medium saucepan, combine passion fruit juice and sugar and slowly bring to a boil over medium-low heat until the sugar is dissolved, stirring frequently.

2. Pour the passion fruit mixture into the gelatin mixture. Add the lemon juice and Riesling. Let cool slightly, then stir and pour into 4 stemmed wine glasses; refrigerate for 8 hours or overnight. Garnish with a sprig of mint to serve.

Entrance to the Waitomo caves.

257

NIRMALA'S GUIDE TO
EXOTIC
INGREDIENTS

This glossary reflects my life-long passion for ethnic and exotic ingredients. I became familiar with many of these as a child when my family and I cultivated them on our farm and cooked with them at home in Guyana; others I discovered later in life while on my extensive travels around the world. It is my philosophy that we should always be aware of what we eat because each food we consume plays a critical role in the way our bodies develop and thrive, or sicken and weaken. • Become familiar with the ingredients you use: know where they come from, feel them, taste them, smell them, experiment with them. Discover their flavor possibilities and their nutritive values. This glossary is a quick resource for learning more about them, and where they may be purchased. I have included all of the special ingredients called for in my recipes, but have also added many other interesting foods from around the world. You won't find any formal Latin or botanical names listed here; merely easily recognizable points of reference that will lead you to a better knowledge of what you eat.

MY FAVORITE TOOLS: MASALA BRICK AND MACHETE

Ackee Ackee has been the national fruit of Jamaica since it was introduced to the West Indies via West Africa in the 18th century. Consuming this fruit in its unripe state can be fatal. This pear-shaped fruit is harvested when the pinkish skin bursts open, revealing three black seeds. The safest way to enjoy ackee is to buy it in cans, which are available at Caribbean specialty food stores. The texture of ackee is a bit like scrambled eggs—its taste is a little bland, but when combined with salt cod, green onions, and Scotch bonnet peppers, it's simply divine. Ackee can also be served with salted pork and bacon.

Agar-Agar This double-named substance is a vegetable gelatin made from several types of seaweed that are processed by boiling and then drying. The finished product is either a refined white powder, or transparent, crinkly, long strands. Agar-agar is widely used in Asian desserts because in the absence of refrigeration, the gelatinous substance can be stored safely. It is also a perfect vegetarian or halal ingredient as it does not contain any animal by-products the way other gelatins do. In Japan, agar-agar is called *kanten*. It can usually be found in Asian markets in clear plastic bags.

Aji (see Chiles)

Allspice Allspice berries are round and dark brown. They are native to Jamaica, Central America, and Morocco. The fruit of a tropical evergreen tree, every part of it is fragrant, but the berries in particular have a warm aroma and taste like a fusion of nutmeg, cinnamon, and cloves (hence the name allspice). It is an essential ingredient in Caribbean Jerk blends, and lends delicious flavor to breads, cakes, and pies. I like to use a few allspice berries in marinades because they nicely balance the other elements. Whole and ground allspice berries can be found in jars in the spice section of most supermarkets.

Amchur or Amchoor Unripe mangoes that have been sun-dried and then ground to a powder produce amchur. Light brown in color, it is used in Indian cooking and is an essential ingredient for making Chaat Masala, a citrus-y and spicy blend often used to top off savory lentil dishes. Amchur gives food a tangy, sour flavor, making it a good substitute for lemon, tamarind, or lime juice in recipes. You can find amchur in Indian markets and at some specialty food stores.

Ancho Chile (see Chiles)

Aniseed Aniseed, also called anis or anise, is native to the Middle East and today is also widely cultivated throughout Europe and Central America. It has a sweet, warm, licorice-like flavor that is delicious in breads and  biscuits. It also complements seafood and pasta sauces. Anise is the predominant flavor in Ouzo, the well-known Greek liqueur. If necessary, fennel seeds can be substituted for aniseed in recipes. It is available in jars in the spice section of most supermarkets, and at specialty food stores.

Annatto or Achiote These dark reddish-brown seeds commonly used for coloring are native to tropical South America. Annatto seeds are either fried in oil or soaked in water to extract a bright yellowish-orange color. The seeds are then discarded and the remaining oil or water is used to cook food, giving it a bright hue similar to that of saffron. The seeds have a faint, flowery scent and a slightly peppery taste. Annatto is an essential ingredient in Latin American and Mexican cuisines, and is also used in the Philippines to make pipian, a pork and chicken dish. In Jamaican dishes annatto gives ackee and codfish a gorgeous pink color, and in Venezuela it is used to make a spice blend called *aji criollo*, which includes garlic, red chiles, and other spices. Annatto seeds can be found at Latin American specialty food stores and at some online sources.

Argan Oil The Argan tree is native only to Morocco where Berber women have used the oil pressed from its fruit in cooking for centuries. It has also been used as a medicinal aid because of its high vitamin E content. The fruit is green and resembles olives, but is a bit larger and rounder. Harvesting the fruit is a tedious task. Inside each fruit is a kernel which, when stone-pressed, releases a reddish-colored oil. It lends a rich, smoky, nutty flavor to foods and is often used for drizzling over pasta and salads. It is also used in the preparation of amlou, a Moroccan condiment made with ground almonds and honey, which is valued for its aphrodisiac qualities. I like it as a delicious spread on toast or pita bread. Argan oil can be found at gourmet stores and online.

Asafoetida or Hing Powder Asafoetida is a gum-like resin that is extracted from a species of giant fennel plant. It is native to Iran and is also harvested in Kashmir. It is extensively used in Indian cooking (it's an essential ingredient in Chaat Masala, a citrus-y and spicy blend often used to top off savory lentil dishes). The gum is dried and ground, then wheat flour is added to form a free-flowing light brown powder. Asafoetida has a very strong, unpleasant odor that resembles rotten eggs. The taste is very acidic and musky when sampled on its own, but when cooked in a curry it lends a very pleasant flavor. Asafoetida can be found in the spice section at Indian and specialty food stores.

ASIAN NOODLES Dozens of different noodles take center stage in cuisines throughout the world, but the one thing they share is that they are all made from ground grains. Some are made from mung beans, some from rice, and some from buckwheat, and eggs can be added to make egg noodles. Fresh noodles lend quite a different textural experience to certain dishes, but in most cases, dried noodles are what you find in home kitchens. Here are just a few Asian varieties:

•**CELLOPHANE NOODLES** These are made from dried mung bean flour (they are sometimes called mung bean threads, glass noodles, or cellophane vermicelli) and water. They are not the same as, nor are they interchangeable with, rice vermicelli, which is made with rice flour. Cellophane noodles truly live up to their name: they are transparent when soaked and cooked. They have a slightly slippery texture and are as thin as angel-hair spaghetti. Look for them in packages at Asian specialty food stores.

•**EGG OR YELLOW NOODLES** The most popular kind of noodle in Asian dishes, egg noodles (or yellow noodles) are made with flour and eggs, and range in widths from spaghetti-thin to coarse, thick, and as wide as ribbons. They are great in soups and stir-frys and are used to make lo-mein. You can usually find them in packages next to the wonton wrappers in the refrigerated section of Asian specialty food stores.

•**RAMEN NOODLES** Real ramen noodles are basically a type of thin Chinese egg noodle, popular in Japan. The Japanese take pride in making their own fresh ramen, which they enjoy with savory broth topped with slices of pork and green scallions. Every chef or housewife in Japan has a unique recipe. It is nowhere like the plastic packaged ramen that appear in the soup aisle of our supermarkets. If you want to make your own bowl of ramen, you can use fresh egg noodles, which are sold in the refrigerated sections of Asian supermarkets.

•**RICE VERMICELLI OR RICE NOODLES** Rice vermicelli is a thin noodle made from rice flour and water. It is white and almost opaque. The best quality rice noodles come from Thailand and Vietnam, where they also come in a variety of sizes and thicknesses. The flat, fettuccine-looking rice noodles are sometimes called rice sticks. Rice noodles are used in soups, and are essential in the popular Thai dish, pad Thai, as well as in stir-frys. Look for them at Asian specialty food stores.

•**SOBA NOODLES** These hearty noodles are made from buckwheat flour and are sometimes flavored with green tea. They are usually light brown in color, and have a wonderful nutty flavor and chewy texture. Soba noodles are used in soups and stir-frys, and are staples in Japanese and Korean cuisines. They can usually be found in the pasta section of almost any supermarket.

•**SOMEN NOODLES** Somen are made from wheat flour, water, and a bit of oil. They are delicate, white, hair-thin strands. They are usually cooked and served cold with a dipping sauce and are a staple of Japanese cuisine. Somen can be found at Asian specialty food stores, some supermarkets, and at some online sources.

•**UDON NOODLES** These thick whole-wheat noodles are commonly used in both Japanese and Korean cuisine. They are available fresh in Asian markets in the refrigerated section or dried in grocery stores.

261

BITTER MELON

Australian Mint Native to its namesake, this versatile variety of mint is used in desserts and as a seasoning in butter sauces, breads, and salad dressings. It is also excellent with seafood, chicken, and pork. Australian mint is dark green in color, has an exquisite aroma and flavor reminiscent of peppermint with a hint of sweet berries. You can find it at specialty food stores.

Avocados The avocado is a green, oval-shaped fruit with leathery skin that encloses soft green pulp and a large brown seed, or pit. Sometimes called an Alligator Pear, avocados are native to the tropical Americas, and the trees on which they grow are commonly found in home gardens throughout the Caribbean and Hawaii. Some cultures consider it an aphrodisiac, but on a more practical note, its nutritive profile is very valuable: one avocado contains 17 vitamins and minerals, and has more potassium that most other fruits and vegetables. Avocados ripen only after being picked. When looking for a ripe specimen, lightly press the skin. If the fruit yields to pressure and feels semi-soft, it is perfect. Avocados are available at almost any supermarket.

Balachan or Trassi Balachan is a very pungent paste made from tiny fermented shrimp. Almost all southeast Asian kitchens have some sort of smooth dried shrimp paste on hand. The most common shrimp pastes found are in jars or cans from which the paste can be easily scooped; others come in solid block form that must be sliced or cubed. Solid shrimp paste must always be cooked before eating. The best way to do this without having your home end up smelling like a fish market is to slice off a piece of the paste, wrap it in foil with the edges tightly closed, and grill it on top of a stove burner for 2 to 3 minutes on each side. When you open the foil, the cooked paste should be crumbled. I recommend buying the kind that comes in jars, which can be found at Asian markets, specialty food stores, and some online sources.

Bamboo Shoots Bamboo shoots are the whitish parts of young bamboo plants. If not properly boiled, these shoots can be toxic, so I recommend buying the canned version instead. Drain and rinse them well several times before using. Bamboo shoots complement stir-fry dishes very well—crisp and refreshing, they have a tender, asparagus-like flavor. If you want to use the fresh shoots, you can usually find them in Asian markets immersed in water, like tofu. The canned version is available at Asian markets and most supermarkets in the ethnic foods section.

Banana Blossom Unopened, this is a gorgeous, purplish-colored blossom that is eaten as a vegetable in southeast Asia. In Sri Lanka, it is called plantain flower, while in Australia it is known as banana bell. In the Philippines, it is added to kari-kari, a delicious, savory, and spicy beef stew. In Thailand, it is sliced and eaten raw with a condiment known as nam prik. The banana blossom is an acquired taste: it is bland, with the texture of an artichoke heart. This is a seasonal item that can be found fresh at Indian and some Asian markets in the fruit section during the summer months. Canned banana blossoms are also available at Philippine, Thai, and other specialty food stores. The canned version works best in spicy stews or curry-based meals. Their beautiful shape also makes them wonderful for serving salads.

Banana Leaves Banana leaves make ideal food wrappers because they preserve moisture and impart a light fragrance to food, whether steamed or grilled. In southern India and in the Caribbean, banana leaves, which are very large and long, are used as plates and serving ware. In Guyana, my mother used them as serving trays, placing fruits and sweets as offerings to her numerous Hindu Gods. In almost every Asian country, the leaves are shaped into quaint cups, cones, or square packets to enclose a variety of fillings. Unfortunately, these beautiful leaves are nearly impossible to find fresh unless you live in the tropics. Sometimes, though, you can spot them in the freezer section of southeast Asian and Latin American specialty food stores.

Barberry Barberries are ripe, dried berries from a species of the Berberis tree. The tree grows in certain regions of Europe and Africa. The berries are red in color and resemble small dried cranberries—in fact, when I climbed Mount Kilimanjaro they were my trail mix. Their flavor and aroma are somewhat fruity and pleasantly acidic. Barberries are primarily used in Iranian and Asian cuisines for their sour flavor; in India they are used for making desserts. You can find the berries at Middle Eastern specialty stores and some online sources.

Basil There are numerous varieties of basil including lime, holy, licorice, Thai, cinnamon, clove, camphor, lettuce leaf, and purple. The leaves are usually chopped or julienned and added at the end of cooking to release the oils that contain their sweet floral fragrances and flavors. Another familiar variety is sweet, or European, basil, and it is indispensable in Italian cooking. Mostly available fresh in the summer months, it marries well with salads, pasta, and savory tomato sauces. You can briefly keep basil fresh in the refrigerator with the stems set in a container of water, or you can preserve them in oil or vinegar. I like to preserve them by pureeing the leaves with a little water, then freezing the paste in ice cube trays. European basil can be found at most supermarkets and produce stands.

Basmati Rice (see Rice)

Bay Leaf Also known as bay laurel, this herb is widely cultivated in its native eastern Mediterranean region. Yet bay laurel trees also grow wild along the northern California coast, deliciously perfuming the air for motorists along the way. The leaves are indispensable in dozens of European soups, stews, and casseroles. Fresh bay leaves have a sharp, bitter edge while the dried version has a more distinct aroma and is less bitter. If you have leftover fresh bay leaves, you can lay them on a flat surface, such as a baking sheet, and store them in a dark, well-ventilated place until they become brittle, then seal them in an airtight container. Dried bay leaves should always be sage green in color, never brown or yellowish. They can keep for up to a year. Dry bay leaves can be found in jars in the spice section of most supermarkets. Look for fresh bay leaves at specialty food stores.

Bean Curd or Tofu Introduced by the Chinese, bean curd is made from soybeans and is a rich source of protein. It's an ideal food for vegetarians because its texture makes it a good substitute for meat, and it is easy to digest. There are several varieties of bean curd, even

some that are flavored, but the most popular ones are soft, firm, and extra-firm. In the fresh produce section of Asian specialty stores, you'll find fresh tofu immersed in tubs of water, but all varieties are also available packaged in plastic in most supermarkets. The natural flavor of tofu is nearly tasteless until it is combined with other ingredients. Deep-fried tofu, which looks like thick slices of banana bread, can be found at Chinatowns across the country; it has to be rinsed in very hot water before cooking to remove the excess oil.

Besan Flour Sometimes called channa powder, chickpea flour, or gram flour, this pale yellow flour is made from ground chickpeas. Besan flour is used to make batters for meats, fish, and vegetables, and it can also be used as a thickener. Besan flour is available at Indian specialty stores.

Betel Leaf The betel leaf is a thick, smooth, heart-shaped, dark green leaf that is broad at one end and pointed at the other. In India, it is called *paan*. Usually sold in bunches, betel leaves taste similar to mustard greens, but with a warm, pleasing undertone. Hindus use it for religious purposes, and when filled with fragrant herbs and spices it is chewed after meals to refresh the palate. Look for betel leaves at Indian specialty stores.

Bilimbi Bilimbi is native to Indonesia, though today it is widely cultivated in home gardens throughout South and Central America and all of southeast Asia. This

smaller cousin of the star fruit grows on the bark of the tropical bilimbi tree. It is used to make chutney and is a souring agent in curry dishes. You can find it in the frozen section of many Indian supermarkets.

Birdseye Chile (see Chiles)

Bitter Melon Also known as bitter gourd or kerela, bitter melon is a staple vegetable in Asian cuisines. The oblong, dark green melon has short, tooth-like spines and comes in a variety of sizes ranging from 2 inches to a foot long. As its name indicates, bitter melon is an acquired taste, and the seeds and inner membrane must be removed before cooking. In India, bitter melon is stuffed with vegetables and spices, then deep-fried. In

China, it is often stir-fried with beef and black bean sauce, which nicely offsets its bitter flavor. It is used in many other Chinese dishes as well. Bitter melon is available at Indian specialty stores and at Chinese markets. If there is a Chinatown near you, an open stall or shop will be sure to have it.

Black Limes, Dried Limes, or Oman Limes

These are whole, sun-dried limes used in Middle Eastern cooking. They start out as small fresh limes that are then boiled in salt and placed under sunny skies to dry. The resulting crisp, hard skins are pierced with a fork and the limes are added whole to stews and to fish, lamb, and rice dishes, to which they lend a sweet, warm, lemony taste. The darker the lime, the more pungent the flavor. These versatile fruits are available at Middle-Eastern specialty stores.

Black Rice or Forbidden Rice (see Rice)

Blood Oranges

Sweet-tart in taste and bright red inside, blood oranges are delicious in salads, along with slightly bitter greens like arugula or watercress. Some varieties are more acidic; their juice is used in sauces. Today they are cultivated in the Mediterranean and part of California. Blood oranges are usually available at most supermarkets in late spring.

Breadfruit

This fruit (which tastes nothing like bread) is native to the Pacific Islands and southeast Asia. Each fruit is about the size of a cantaloupe, but the skin is very tough and knobby-looking. It ranges in weight from one to eight pounds and grows on trees that can reach 50 feet high. Breadfruit must be peeled in the same way a pineapple is in order to reveal the thick white flesh inside which can then be boiled, baked, steamed, or fried. The texture of breadfruit is similar to mashed potatoes, for which it is often a substitute, but with a slightly sweeter

flavor. Thinly sliced, breadfruit makes terrific fried chips. In the Tahitian islands, it is fermented into a potent drink called *mei*. Here, breadfruit is usually available in cans, but some West Indian and Latin American specialty food stores may have fresh fruits immersed in tubs of water.

Brie

Perhaps the most famous of all the French cheeses and a world favorite, brie is a soft cow's milk cheese. It is slightly pale and off-white in color and is quite savory. It has a buttery consistency and taste, and today's varieties of Brie include the popular plain, smoked (the cheese is smoked over hardwood chips), and various herbed options. Brie is available at most supermarkets and at cheese shops.

Bush Tomatoes or Akudjura

For thousands of years, the aboriginal people in the Northern Territory of Australia have handpicked bush tomatoes, which are actually berries. Also known as akudjura, these cranberry-shaped fruits are dark brown and have a fruity, caramel-like flavor with a slight tang. When they are picked, they're sun-dried and then coarsely ground. They are used to flavor casseroles, beef stews, and wild game. Ground bush tomatoes are also sprinkled over antipasti or used as an ingredient in chutney. It works well as a coating for grilled fish, particularly salmon and tuna. Bush tomatoes can be found at online sources and at specialty food stores, but you can substitute fresh tomatillo (see Tomatillo)— a tangy, tomato like vegetable native to Mexico.

Candlenut or Kemiri

Candlenuts are native to Indonesia's Maluku (formerly the Moluccas) Islands, Australia, and Southeast Asia. They look like macadamia nuts and are oil-rich, making them a good thickening agent. Many Malaysian, Indonesian, and South Pacific dishes include candlenuts. Macadamia nuts or almonds can be substituted in recipes, but they will taste a bit sweeter than candlenuts, which have a hint of bitterness. These nuts are not to be eaten raw, as they can be toxic. They are used solely for cooking. You can find candlenuts at Indonesian and Thai specialty stores, or at online sources.

Capers Capers are among the culinary delights of the Mediterranean, where they grow wild or are farmed. The unopened green flower buds of this shrub are the size of champagne grapes and are never eaten raw—they are either pickled in vinegar or packed dry in salt, which must be soaked and rinsed off before use. The taste of pickled capers is somewhat lemony, with a piquant, fresh, salty taste. They complement tapenades, fish, and chicken very well, and add a nice sensation to salad dressings. Capers can be found in jars at almost any supermarket.

Carambola (see Star Fruit)

Caraway Seeds Caraway is indigenous to North Africa, the Middle East, and the Mediterranean. Without it there would be no rye bread for corned beef, but it has many other uses as well. It is the dominant flavor in Kümmel, a strong liqueur, and it is also used to flavor cakes, sausages, and Indian and Tunisian spice blends. Caraway has a distinctive taste that is slightly earthy with a hint of aniseed. It is often mistaken for cumin, but if you take a close look at both of them, the shapes of the seeds are different. When you buy caraway seeds, they should be brown and have a slight curve. They're available in jars in the spice section of almost any supermarket.

Cardamom Cardamom is one of the most ancient of spices. It originated in the tropical forests of Sri Lanka, and is grown in tiny green pods on grass-like plants with long slender stalks. Today it is an essential ingredient in Middle Eastern, Indian, and African cuisines. There are three kinds of cardamom: green, white, and black. Green is the variety that is used most— the pods are about the size of black eye peas and have a distinctive lemony, flowery aroma and a warm, bittersweet, fruity flavor. The white variety is essentially green cardamom that has been bleached. Black cardamom pods are twice the size of the green ones—they resemble dried prunes and have an earthy aroma with hints of pine and mint. For maximum flavor when cooking with cardamom, lightly bruise the pods so that they slightly open. The pods contain about a dozen or more tiny, intensely aromatic seeds in which cardamom's true flavor is contained. Green and white cardamom are used as a base for desserts, beverages, and rice pilafs, while the black variety is used in savory dishes. Cardamom can usually be found in jars in the spice section of almost any supermarket.

Cashews (see Cashew Apple)

Cashew Apple Native to northeastern Brazil, the cashew apple is a fruit about the size of a small pear. This  tall tree bears fruit with reddish skin and a dark brown cashew-shaped pod at the bottom. The cashew apple is actually harvested for its nuts, but the apple itself is also used to make Feni, a distilled liquor from Goa in India. The apple is the only part that can be eaten raw—the nuts present a problem during harvesting, as the their protective pods are surrounded by toxic oil. The cost of processing cashew nuts makes them pricier than most other nuts. Cashew apples can be found in my backyard in Guyana, but cashews are available in any supermarket.

Cassava Also known as manioc, yucca, or gari, cassavas are the potatoes of Latin America, Africa, and the Caribbean. Native to South America, this long, slender tuber has a brown skin and starchy white flesh that tastes a bit like sweet potatoes. Plain boiled cassava can replace potatoes in any meal. You can also cut cassava into lengthwise slices and deep fry them. When dried and ground, the result is cassava flour, or *gari*, as it is called in Africa. I like to use the flour to make crêpes. In the Pacific Islands, cassava is called *pia*, and in South America it's known as manioc root, or yucca. Cassava can be found in both fresh and powdered form at Latin American specialty food stores.

Cassia Cassia, sometimes confused with cinnamon, is actually related to a species of the laurel tree native to China. The trees, which have a thick, tough-looking bark are now cultivated in Vietnam and other Southeast Asian countries. The advantage cassia has over cinnamon is that its aroma and flavor are much more intense, the result of a higher content of volatile oils. Cassia, which is darker in color than cinnamon, is widely used in Chinese cooking to flavor meat dishes, and it is an essential spice in five spice powder, a Chinese seasoning. It is usually found in powdered form and is sometimes sold as cinnamon in supermarkets, but you can find the real thing at Chinese specialty stores or at some online sources.

Cellophane Noodles (see Asian Noodles)

Chayote Chayote is a light green, oval-shaped fruit native to the Americas. This fruit loves sunshine and its vines are seen in home gardens throughout Mexico and Central America. When small, the fruit is about the size of a lemon and you can eat it skin and all. When chayote grows larger it is used for cooking, though it must be peeled and the single inner seed removed. Chayote can be used in salads in place of cucumber, or can be stuffed and baked like zucchini or eggplant. In fact its flavor is light and crisply zucchini-like. It is sometimes called chayote squash and can be found in most supermarkets.

Cherimoya Native to South America, this green, bumpy-skinned fruit is often seen in specialty food stores or in Latin American markets, but it is also widely grown in New Zealand and California. It is a cousin to the soursop fruit, which is also known as guanabana. Commonly referred to as simply moya, the fruit has a thick, soft, but inedible skin; inside are shiny black seeds. The pulp is milky white and has a captivating taste that blends the flavors of banana, pineapple, papaya, and mango, among others. It has a creamy texture, and is ripe for eating when it slightly yields to pressure, similar to an avocado. Cherimoya juice or Soursop juice is available in both canned and frozen pulp forms in Latin American grocery stores. The label will say Soursop or Guanabana. It makes a fabulous shake.

Ciku (see Sapodilla)

Chipotle Peppers (see Chiles, Jalapeño)

CHILES To me, no exotic cuisine is quite complete without the addition of fresh or dried chile peppers, of which there are dozens that vary in shape, size, color, and level of heat. Chiles are native to Mexico and the tropical Americas, but have migrated to all parts of the world.

Spanish and Portuguese explorers brought these fascinating fruits to Europe and Asia, and Christopher Columbus brought several varieties back to Spain from his voyage to the New World where they evolved to become pimentos. Today, hundreds of chiles are grown around the world, each region boasting its own unique variety. Once harvested, chiles can not only be used fresh, but can be dried, powdered, shredded, crushed, pickled, and made into chile oils, sauces, and numerous other condiments. Some chiles are devilishly hot, while others are more gentle. The heat level of each variety is indexed according to "Scoville" units, which range in levels from zero up to 350,000 units! Named for William L. Scoville who developed it in 1912, the Scoville Organoleptic Test determines the potency of different chile peppers, measured in multiples of 100 units. Removing the seeds from chile peppers can reduce the intensity of their heat. The oils in some peppers can be quite potent, so many people opt to wear plastic or rubber gloves when handling them. The heat levels of the chiles listed here are rated on a scale of 1 to 10, with 1 being the mildest and 10 for extremely hot.

•**AJI AMARILLO 7/10** These famous chiles are common in Peru where they're also called *cosqueno*. They have a light fruity aroma, but with a kick; they are shaped like jalapeños but are wrinkly. Aji is used in making wonderful potato dishes, as well as with seafood and wild game. I like to use them when I make ceviche (page 53). You can find these chiles in the freezer section of most Latin American stores. They are also available in canned and powdered forms.

•**ANCHO CHILE** (see Poblano Chile)

•**BIRDSEYE CHILE 8-9/10** Also called bird pepper, these fiery, tiny, slender peppers are used both fresh and dried. The name derives from the shape of the beak of the bird that feasts on them; their color is either green or red. These are also sometimes called Thai chiles, and are used in preparing many Thai dishes. Whenever you enjoy spicy Indian or Asian food, it is likely that the spiciness is from these chiles rather than the other spices in the dish. The smaller the chile, the hotter it is, so I recommend using medium-sized ones that are not as overpowering. These chiles can be found at South Asian specialty stores.

•**CAYENNE CHILE 7-8/10** Cayenne chiles are either green or red, quite slender, and very hot. They hit about 150,000 units on the Scoville scale.

Widely used in Indian and Cajun cooking, these have not only a good kick, but wonderful flavors as well. Cayenne chiles can be found at specialty food markets.

•**CHIPOTLE CHILE** (see Chiles, Jalapeño)

•**HABANERO CHILE 10/10** Also called Scotch bonnet, Red Savina, or Congo peppers, these are the hottest of chiles. They are native to the tropical Americas and the West Indies. Habaneros are called Scotch Bonnets in Jamaica, Congo pepper in parts of Africa, and in Guyana we call them "Boiler fire," but whatever you call them, they rack up a whopping 300,000 units on the Scoville scale. They are small, round, and almost block-like in shape with deep lobes, and come in several festive colors: bright to deep orange, red, and purple. Habaneros are used in sauces, soups, stews, and chutneys, and are the essential ingredients in Caribbean Jerk blends. They can be found in either fresh, canned, or powdered forms at specialty food stores and are always at my table as a condiment.

JALAPEÑO CHILE 5-6/10 A staple in Mexican cooking, jalapeños are small, oblong, dark green or red. Once they're dried and smoked, they are called chipotle peppers. In chipotle form, they are small and light brown, relatively mild, and are commonly used in beef and chicken stews. They can be found either canned or fresh in most supermarkets.

•**KASHMIR CHILE 7/10** In India this chile is called lal mirch and is widely grown in the northern region of Kashmir. It is slender and dark red in color, with a distinctive sweet flavor and just a mild bite. Mostly, it is used for giving Kashmiri specialties a glowing red color without imparting too much heat. Kashmir chiles can be found at Indian markets in either whole or powdered form.

•**PASILLA CHILE 6/10** These chiles are native to Oaxaca, Mexico. When they are roasted, their color deepens to almost blood-red. Pasillas, which are also known as *chile negro,* have a smoky taste with hints of licorice and are used in sauces and vegetable dishes. In their fresh state, they are called chilaca chiles. They are available at Latin American specialty stores.

•**PIMENT D'ESPELETTE 6/10** I happened to discover this unique long red pepper while I was in the Basque region of France where a pepper festival is held in late October. During the festival, the facades of many homes are decorated with strings of dried espelette, harvested during the early months of spring. Piment d'Espelette is grown in just about a dozen villages in this region and are protected with the AOC (Appellation d'Origine Contrôlée) seal to ensure that their flavor remains pure. Originally, these peppers were native to Mexico and came to France by way of Christopher Columbus. They have an almost fruity taste and aroma with a refreshing bite. In the U.S., Piment d'Espelette can be found ground or in paste form at specialty food stores and at some online sources.

•**POBLANO CHILE 3-4/10** These mild, heart-shaped peppers are large and have thick "walls" that make them perfect for stuffing. Usually, you see them as chiles rellenos on Mexican menus. When poblanos are dried, they are called ancho chiles. As anchos, they are a deep brown color and are used for making sauces, including the famous Mexican moles. Poblanos can be found fresh at Latin American or Mexican specialty stores, or as ancho chiles in canned or powdered forms. Ancho chile powder can be found at some online sources.

•**ROCOTO CHILE 8/10** Native to Peru and other parts of the Andes, these round, plump, orangey-yellow to red peppers are used fresh in condiments or cooked in stews. In the U.S., look for whole, frozen rocotos at Latin American specialty food stores. I like to use them in my ceviche, which always brings back fond memories of Peru.

•**SCOTCH BONNET CHILE** (see Habanero Chile)

•**SERRANO CHILE 7/10** These peppers are essential to Mexican cooking. They are slender and green or greenish-yellow, about one to two inches long and have pronounced heat with a fresh chile taste. Serrano peppers can be found at most supermarkets.

•**THAI RED CHILE** (see Birdseye Chile)

•**WIRI-WIRI OR HUNGARIAN CHERRY PEPPER 6-7/10** I grew up eating this pepper in Guyana. It is great for pickling and for making hot sauce—it is quite hot with a refreshing citrus-y bite. Grown in the West Indies, South America, Africa, and parts of Europe, these round cherry-looking chiles can be either red or green, and may be found fresh at West Indian specialty stores.

YOUNG COCONUT

Chinese Barbecued Pork Slow-roasted Chinese pork is usually found in Chinese restaurants, hanging in the window. If you've visited any of the many Chinatowns throughout the country, you've probably seen the reddish-colored meat hanging from wire racks next to glistening mahogany-colored roasted ducks and chickens. Chinese pork is hard to find unless you live near a Chinese community where it is sold by the pound. There are no substitutes for it unless you make it at home yourself which is a tedious task.

Chinese Cabbage Chinese cabbage is broad and

oblong in shape, with closely packed pale green leaves and wide white stems, and has a very delicate mustard-like flavor. It is often used in soups, stir-frys, dumpling fillings, and is the main ingredient in the famously spicy-hot Korean condiment, kim chi. Chinese cabbage, usually labeled as Napa cabbage in the U.S., is available at most supermarkets.

Chinese Chives These long, flat-bladed chives have a light onion-garlic taste that is much stronger than that of the chives usually available in U.S. markets. They are also sometimes called garlic chives. They are solid dark green in color and about 6- to 12-inches long. When purchasing them, choose bunches that show no wilted or bruised blades. They're great for sprinkling over salads, soups, and baked potatoes—and add special panache to omelettes or scrambled eggs.

Chinese Long Beans (see Long Beans)

Chinese Sausage or Lop-chong These sausages resemble chorizo sausage in color but breakfast

sausage in size. They're dark red with bits of visible fat. Their flavor is a bit tangy because they're made with pork and paprika. Then they are cured and air-dried, intensifying the flavors. You can usually see Chinese sausages hanging in Chinatown shop windows throughout the U.S. They make a great substitute for chorizo, and add wonderful flavor and texture to stir-frys and fried rice.

Chorizo Abundantly used in Mexican and Latin American cuisines, chorizo is made up of coarsely ground pork flavored with paprika, garlic, and other spices. Slice them and add them to soups, stews, and casseroles. Or just slice them and fry the slices in fruity olive oil to make a delicious tapas dish. Chorizos are now available at most supermarkets and specialty food stores.

Cilantro This ancient herb is indigenous to southern Europe and is sometimes called Chinese parsley or coriander. It looks a lot like parsley, with which it shouldn't be confused because its flavor is very different. Some people say cilantro is an acquired taste. It has a pungent aroma which some people might not like. All parts of the cilantro plant are used in Asian and Indian cooking. The seeds of the herb are called coriander, which is the base of most curry blends and spice rubs. Always chop cilantro leaves just before using to preserve their oils and flavor, and add them toward the end of cooking, as the flavor dissipates if heated for too long. Because of its strong flavor, use cilantro sparingly.

Cinnamon This spice comes from the bark of an evergreen tree from the laurel family—it is ancient, and native to Sri Lanka, although it is now also cultivated in Saigon. Fine cinnamon is collected from the narrow roots of the bark, then rolled by hand and placed in the sun to dry. When dried, they form beautiful auburn-colored rolled quills. Cinnamon is what you love in your latte, with its warm, sweet scent. It is used in many desserts and beverages.

Cloves I've been chewing cloves as a breath sweetener for as long as I can remember. Native to the Maluku (formerly the Moluccas) Islands of Indonesia, cloves are the unopened flower buds of a tree from the myrtle family that can grow up to 15 feet tall. The flowers grow in clusters; the buds are greenish-pink and become redder as they mature. The buds are harvested and sun-dried for 4 to 5 days, by which time they have turned the brown color we're familiar with. Cloves have an intense flavor that can actually leave a tingling sensation in your mouth, and an equally intense aroma that can perfume your entire home. Clove oil is prized for its medicinal value as well: the next time you have a toothache, ask your pharmacist for a bottle of clove oil and dab some on to dull the pain. Whole and ground cloves can be found in jars in the spice section of almost any supermarket.

Coconut There is barely a part of the coconut tree that I haven't used in some way. More than just a source of food and drink in tropical parts of the world, it's also

very useful in satisfying a variety of household and cooking needs. As a child I used the coconuts' fern-like branches to make brooms; the husks are used for washing dishes and for making mats. The wood is used to build huts, and the shells are polished and fashioned into cooking utensils in addition to various ornamental and other objects. The fruit of the coconut palm, the coconut itself, is indispensable in many of the world's cuisines. From young, or green, coconuts (these are also sometimes a deep yellow color) comes the clear liquid called coconut water that is used in cocktails (page 20) and refreshing beverages. When the coconut matures, it turns gray or dark brown, and by removing the outer thick, dry, fibrous husk, the hard round coconut fruit is revealed. A good-size coconut is about the size of a grapefruit. Contrary to what most people believe, coconut milk does not come from inside the coconut. To make it, the shell of the coconut must be cracked with a hammer (or in my kitchen, a machete). The water is discarded, then the white flesh is dug out, then cut into small pieces and put in a food processor or blender with some warm water so that the blades won't jam. A little more water is added, the mixture is removed from the blender, and then rubbed together with the fingertips for a couple of minutes. The resulting mushy substance is strained through cheesecloth or a fine sieve, and the result is coconut milk. Any coconut milk you don't use in recipes can be stored in ice cube trays in the freezer. Of course, it's much less labor-intensive to buy coconut milk in cans or in powdered form, both of which are available at many supermarkets and specialty food stores. Unless you are

making a dessert that uses coconut, never substitute coconut cream for coconut milk—this is a thick, sweetened liquid that is mostly used for making desserts and sweet drinks, as is the shredded coconut you see in bags in the baking section of your supermarket. Coconuts are available at supermarkets and at Asian and Latin American specialty food stores.

Coconut Oil Made from the white flesh of the coconut, coconut oil is extensively consumed in Southeast Asia because it is less expensive than other oils. This is a heavily saturated oil that turns white when stored at cool temperatures, and clear light brown when stored at warmer temperatures. As a little girl I made it from scratch and sold it to villagers to be used as a hair conditioner and body cream.

Coconut Water, Clear (see Coconut)

Coriander Seeds Coriander seeds are essential to many spice blends used all around the world. Native to Asia and parts of the Mediterranean, these round brown seeds have a spicy, floral fragrance and a sweet, almost citrus-like flavor. To enhance the flavor of coriander seeds in almost any dish, lightly toast them in a pan on top of the stove, then crush or grind them before using. Coriander seeds as well as ground coriander are available in jars in the spice section of your supermarket, or at specialty food stores.

Corn Husks Corn husks cover and protect ears of corn. These are removed from the corn and dried, after which they resemble flat, papery, pale yellow sheets. They're used for wrapping tamales and other foods, retaining the moisture of the fillings during cooking. The dry husks must first be soaked in water for about an hour before using. They are available at most Latin American specialty food stores and at some online sources.

Cornstarch The starchy substance derived from corn, cornstarch is used as a thickening agent. It is a fine white powder that usually comes in boxes. To avoid lumps in the gravy or sauce of a dish, a tablespoon or two of cornstarch should be mixed with a little cold water. Stir constantly, and within minutes the sauce will thicken. Cornstarch can be purchased at any supermarket.

Couscous Couscous is a very starchy staple food native to North African countries such as Tunisia and Morocco. It is actually semolina that has been coarsely ground, moistened, and rolled with flour. Today there are  many varieties and sizes of couscous, including flavored versions and the large pearl-shaped Israeli couscous, which is wonderful in soups. Couscous is available in boxes or in bags at almost any supermarket.

Culantro This intense version of cilantro with a bitter note grows wild in the West Indies and Southeast Asia. Usually sold in bunches or in bags, its deep green leaves are slender and have serrated edges. Its aroma and taste are quite pungent and sharp, so it should be used sparingly. In Trinidad, where it's called *shado beni*, it is extensively used in cooking and is the key ingredient in fish and meat marinades. In Puerto Rico, it's called *recao*, which is used for making the delicious marinade, sofrito. If a recipe calls for culantro, regular cilantro is an adequate substitute. Culantro can be found in Latin American and West Indian specialty food stores in the fresh herb section.

Cumin Cumin is native to Egypt's Nile Valley, but today it's widely cultivated in Africa, India, the Middle East, and the Americas. This ancient spice was used for medicinal purposes in ancient Egypt. Cumin is commonly used in Indian cooking—pale brown, it looks similar to caraway seeds, but it is not curved, and tastes completely different. Cumin is used in just about every spice blend. As with coriander, to maximize the aroma and flavor of cumin, first lightly toast the seeds in a pan on the stove, then coarsely crush them. You can sprinkle them over many foods, giving them a warm, earthy, slightly bitter flavor. Black cumin, or kala jeera, is smaller and darker in color, and has a sweeter smell and more mellow flavor. It is commonly used in Kashmiri and Iranian cooking.

Curry Most people aren't aware that curry is not, in itself, a separate spice. Curry simply means "sauce." Saying you don't like curry is just like saying you don't like sauce. The typical curries most of us are familiar with are the yellow Indian curry dishes. It is turmeric that gives them their yellow color, and chiles that give them heat, not spices. The word curry derives from *kari*, the Tamil word for sauce, which was adapted and reinterpreted by the British during the Raj, when they occupied India. Curry is actually a mix of many ingredients, and every Asian country has its own version of it. Today, it is usually categorized as mild, hot, very hot, yellow, green, or red. The standard ingredients for curry powder include turmeric (for color), coriander, cumin, fennel seeds, fenugreek seeds, and red cayenne chiles. Curry powders are available at almost any supermarket and at Indian and Asian specialty food stores.

Curry Leaves Curry leaves are cultivated in India, Thailand, and now in Australia. What bay leaves are to American cooking, *khadi*, as curry leaves are known in India, are integral to its cuisine. These fresh, small, shiny dark green leaves emit a tantalizing citrus aroma when cooked, but sadly, this sensation is missing in the dried version. Chennai (formerly known as Madras) is the only region of India that includes curry leaves in their curry powder blend; elsewhere, the leaves are added at the end of a curry dish. The leaves partner well with fish curries, and other seafood and rice dishes. Fresh curry leaves can be found in plastic bags in the fruit section of Indian specialty food stores. Unused leaves can be frozen.

Daikon Radish There are several kinds and shapes of Asian radishes: there are round ones, long, tapered ones, and short, stubby ones. Colors can range from pure white or rose pink to dark red or green. The daikon's taste and texture are similar to the radishes we're used to here. Daikon suits salads and soups well. They're also delicious on their own, cut into paper-thin slices. You can find them at most Asian specialty food stores.

Dashi Dashi is Japanese fish stock that is made with dried bonito (flaked tuna) and dried kelp, a kind of seaweed. It gives a flavor boost to fish dishes and soups, the way a mild fish stock would. Dashi is available in concentrated form at Asian specialty food stores. It must be diluted in water before using.

Dates Native to the Middle East, dates are truly ancient, biblical fruits. They grow on date palm trees, and many different countries now cultivate a variety of them. Both Middle Eastern countries and California yield fruits of different textures, colors, shapes, and degrees of sweetness. Unripe dates can be cherry red or golden yellow, but dried dates, the ones we see in our supermarkets, are usually dark to golden brown in color. Dates are naturally sweet, and so offer limitless possibilities for flavoring sweet and savory dishes alike. Try stuffing dried, pitted dates with a little mascarpone or cream cheese as a deliciously simple hors d'oeuvre or healthy snack. Fresh Barhi dates, which are becoming available here, are large round globes that grow on branches. When fully ripe, they are bursting with sugar, and eating them is just like eating candy. Dried dates, either pitted or unpitted, are more commonly available at almost any supermarket. They freeze well and, in fact, when frozen they are easier to chop for recipes that call for chopped dates.

Dende or Palm Oil This bright orange oil is very popular in South America and Central America. It is made from the kernels of a palm tree native to Africa, but is now also widely cultivated in Brazil. Because corn oil and olive oil are luxuries in some South American countries, dende oil is used there for cooking instead. It also gives food a distinctive color and is often used in preparing seafood with coconut milk. Its one drawback is that the oil is high in saturated fat (though not animal fat). Dende oil can be found at South American specialty food stores.

Dhal In the West we call them split peas or lentils, but in India, dhal actually refers to a vast variety of pulses. The one we're most familiar with in Indian restaurants here is channa dhal, which is either yellow or green, and the peas can be whole or split. Usually, these peas are cooked, pureed, and served as an accompanying side dish to the main meal. Dhal flour, which is used for making batters for fritters is generally ground yellow split peas. A variety of other dhal peas can be found at West Indian, Middle Eastern, and Indian specialty food stores.

Dibbis Dibbis is date syrup: ripe dates are boiled down to a pulp and then strained. In Iraq, it is used as a sweetener. Dibbis makes a wonderful substitute for honey or maple syrup—I like to use it on pancakes and waffles. It can be found in jars at Middle Eastern specialty food stores.

Dill Dill is native to the Mediterranean and is a well-loved herb around the world. Grown for its feathery leaves, dill is used in hundreds of ways in dips, salads, marinades, sauces, garnishes, and much more. Dill seeds are used in many Indian spice blends. Both the fresh leaves and seeds have the warm, refreshing flavor of anise. Fresh dill can be found in the produce section of almost any supermarket, as can the dried version, which is usually in jars in the spice section.

Dragon Fruit This exotic-looking cactus fruit originated in Central America but is now cultivated in Florida and California. In Asia, it is called *pitaya*. It has a striking fuchsia skin with slightly protruding "scales" (hence its name); inside, the flesh can be either white, pink, or magenta, with many tiny, edible seeds. Dragon fruit has a delicately sweet but mildly acidic flavor that resembles a fusion of pears and kiwi, and its fragrance is reminiscent of jasmine and orange blossoms. The flowers and leaves are also edible when cooked. These fruits make wonderful salads, drinks, and sorbets, and even a great snack when eaten out of hand. Best of all, they are high in vitamin C. Dragon fruit is seasonal and can be found at specialty food stores between August and November. If there is a Chinatown near you, it is often sold from outdoor carts or at markets.

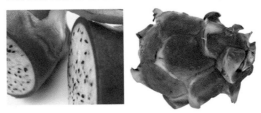

CINNAMON

Dried Salt Cod or Baccalá This form of dried, salted codfish is a staple in Latin American, Caribbean, Italian, and Portuguese kitchens. It must be soaked several times in warm water to remove the salty taste and soften the flesh. It can be pureed with other ingredients and served with polenta as a main course, or in casseroles. It can also be pureed with other ingredients, formed into balls and deep-fried. Dried salt cod, which is also called baccalá, or bacalau, can be found either in plastic bags, wooden boxes, or as whole dried fish in most seafood stores and some specialty food stores.

Drumstick or Shijan Tree The fruit of the Shijan tree is often referred to as a vegetable called a drumstick. It is also referred to as the horseradish tree but is not at all related to the familiar American condiment. Native to India, the tree has drooping branches that range from 9- to 15-inches long, with fern-like leaves. The leaves are oval and less than an inch wide. All parts of the tree are edible—flowers, shoots, and pods; the long, round, pointy pods are called drumsticks and are cut up and boiled like beans. Their flavor is mild and sweet. You can usually find them in cans at Indian specialty food stores. The leaves of the drumsticks are used in curries to lend them a tangy flavor. Fresh drumsticks can be found at most Indian grocery stores. The seeds of the drumstick tree yield ben oil, which is used for oiling machinery and watches, and as an ingredient in the manufacture of soaps, cosmetics, and perfumes.

Durian Durian is a large, round or oblong fruit that is completely covered with strong, sharp thorns. When ripe, the inside of the durian splits into five capsule-like parts, each of which contains brown seeds that are covered with a thick, firm, creamy-yellow pulp. It has a distinctly powerful, unpleasant aroma, so

much so that it is suggested that it be cut outdoors. When cooked, however, its sulfuric odor disappears and it becomes a prized ingredient in Asian cuisine. The durian is native to Malaysia where it grows on trees in the rain forest or jungle to heights as tall as 40 feet. Durian is a seasonal fruit available in the summer and fall, and can be found at Asian specialty food stores.

Edamame One of my favorite things on a Japanese menu, these verdant green beans in fuzzy pods are not to be missed. I like to boil them for 2 to 3 minutes, drain, drizzle with sesame seed oil, and sprinkle with sea salt. Cook with them the same way you would with fava beans.

I usually get them fresh in the summer and fall months; look for firm pods. You can also find them in the frozen section of Asian supermarkets.

Edible Flowers Several flowers that we think of as purely ornamental actually make delicious ingredients in salads, beverages and, of course, are beautiful garnishes. The most commonly used edible varieties are nasturtiums, which have a peppery quality, and pansies, which have a pear-like flavor. Other flowers include jasmine blossoms, hibiscus, chamomile, lavender, and squash blossoms (squash blossoms are often stuffed with a variety of fillings and either fried or sautéed). It is important to note that these flowers are not the ones you buy at your local garden center or florist. They usually come in clear plastic containers and are labeled as edible. You can find them at most specialty food stores.

Egg Noodles (see Asian Noodles)

Fennel Fennel is native to the Mediterranean. The plant is completely edible—the stems, leaves, and bulbs are used to flavor salads, sauces, and fish dishes. Fresh fennel has the scent and flavor of anise with hints of licorice; when sliced raw, it is a great addition to orange salad. Sliced and sautéed, baked, or braised, the bulbs make wonderful side dishes. Fennel seeds are considered a spice. They resemble cumin seeds but are larger and lighter in color, and have a strong flavor with a bittersweet aftertaste. Fennel seed is an essential ingredient in Malaysian and Thai curry blends, and in India, they are included in the after-meals betel leaf "chew," or are roasted and eaten as a breath freshener.

Fenugreek Seeds These tiny hard seeds are brownish-yellow in color and are native to Asia and southern Europe. When you smell curry powder, fenugreek is the dominant spice that leaves a lingering fragrance. The seeds have a bitter taste and are among the most potent of Indian spices. They're an essential ingredient not only in curry powder but also in many Middle Eastern and African spice blends. Fenugreek is available at specialty food stores and at some online sources.

Feta Cheese This Greek cheese can be made from either cows', goats', or sheeps' milk. It is thick and firm but easily crumbled, making it wonderful sprinkled on salads or atop a baked dish or casserole. Depending on which kind of milk it's made from, feta cheese offers different degrees of tanginess, although it is never overpowering. It is essential in the classic Greek salad. You can find feta cheese at almost any supermarket, specialty food store, or cheese shop.

Fiddlehead Ferns Usually called simply fiddleheads, these young ferns have been a foodstuff of New Zealand's native Maori people for centuries. They call the ferns *pikopiko*, and eat them steamed with mussels, or *kuku*. There's no need to travel that far to enjoy these dainty treats, though—I've had them in Canada, Japan, Australia, and Indonesia, as well as right here in the U.S. Fiddleheads are

tightly furled fern fronds—when completely curled up, they have the shape of an overcooked shrimp. They're very pretty to look at with their fresh green color, and they have a very enjoyable, mild taste similar to asparagus. Fiddleheads usually come with a light brown, papery leaf near the center to protect the delicate fronds, so they should first be soaked to facilitate removing the papery layer. They are delicious simply steamed, and are terrific additions to stir-frys. In general, you can use them the same way you do broccoli or asparagus. Early spring is the season for fiddleheads and the season isn't very long, so enjoy them while you can. They're available at most specialty food stores and at farmers markets.

Fingered Citron or Buddha's Fingers This exotic-looking fruit is partially split into five or more finger-like segments. The fruit is seedless and has no flesh but is extremely fragrant, like a fusion of tangerines and pineapples. The rind is yellowish in color and tastes exceptional when grated and used in desserts. In Asia, Buddha's fingers are placed as offerings on temple altars.

I like to place a few of them in a large glass jar, pour vodka over them and let them rest, covered, for two weeks. The result is not just a delicious infused vodka, but a stunning feast for the eyes as well. Winter is the season for these wonderful fruits; you can find them at specialty food stores, Chinese markets, and at some online sources.

Fish Sauce Fish sauce is made from fermented fish. Some less expensive versions are made with shrimp or other tiny fish. While the aroma is quite pungent, it dissipates and evolves into a salty flavor when cooked. It heightens the flavor of hundreds of Asian dishes, and elevates the taste of ordinary vegetables and seafood. Fish sauce comes in bottles—you'll find it next to soy sauce in Asian markets, and in some supermarkets or specialty food stores. Qualities of fish sauce vary, so experiment with several brands before deciding which flavor best suits your palate.

Five Spice Powder This aromatic, flavorful spice blend is used in Chinese cuisine. Its primary use is to flavor roasted meats and casseroles. The five ingredients are ground fennel, cassia, Sichuan peppercorns, cloves, and star anise—just imagine how delicious and fragrant a combination this is. Five spice powder is sometimes available in jars in the spice section of your supermarket, but Asian and other specialty food stores are a better bet.

Galangal A cousin to the ginger family, galangal is native to Java and China. This rhizome looks similar to ginger but is paler in color and has beautiful pink shoots. Sometimes called Thai ginger, it is commonly used in Thai cooking—its flavor is citrus-like and not quite as pungent as ginger. Its aroma is piney. Galangal can be found refrigerated in Thai or Asian specialty food stores, usually next to the lime leaves and lemongrass.

Garam Masala This is a famous blend of Indian spices that adds mesmerizing fragrance to all Indian dishes. "Garam" means hot; "masala" means a mixture of spices. As in many ethnic cuisines, every family has its own prized version of masalas to enhance meat and vegetable dishes. The basic spices used in masalas abide by certain Ayurvedic practices that prescribe heating up the body, such as cumin, black peppercorns, cloves, and nutmeg. Garam masala can be found in jars or plastic bags at Indian and other specialty food stores, and at some online sources.

Gari (see Cassava)

Ghee Ghee is pure clarified butter, which is butter with all of the water and milk solids skimmed away, leaving only the clear liquid. It is made from cow milk. Because there is no milk content, ghee will not burn, so it can be heated to very high temperatures. In Middle Eastern kitchens, ghee is made with goats' or sheeps' milk and is called *semneh*, *smen*, or *sman*. It imparts a warm, sweet, nutty flavor to foods. Look for it in jars or cans at Indian or specialty food stores.

Ginep The ginep, or gineppe, is a tree fruit native to South American countries and can be found throughout the Caribbean in home gardens or on the carts of street vendors. Often, street vendors can be seen selling ginep fruit in bunches at traffic stoplights in various ethnic neighborhoods in the U.S. as well. The fruit grows in clusters on the trees' branches and resemble small limes. Their skins are smooth and thin, but leathery, and the glistening pulp inside is either salmon or yellowish in color. The pulp is translucent, gelatinous, and juicy, and clings to the teeth. When ripe, ginep is sweet, but if unripe, it's more acidic. Most of the fruits have a single large, yellow-white seed, while some have two hemispherical seeds. The edible kernel is white, crisp, starchy, and astringent. Look for ginep at Latin American and Caribbean specialty stores.

Ginger This ancient rhizome has a pungent flavor that is basic to Asian cuisines. It is similar to its cousin, galangal, but its skin is much tougher. Ginger is very versatile: it can be grated, chopped, or sliced, and the liquid can be squeezed from it to produce delicious ginger juice. Slightly peppery and with what can be a potent bite, ginger is widely cultivated throughout the world and available at almost any supermarket. To soothe an upset stomach, a sore throat, or to head off the onset of a cold, place a few slices of peeled, fresh ginger in a cup of boiling water, add a touch of honey and let steep for a couple of minutes. Two cups a day should fix things—it does for me. And who could have sushi without pickled ginger, sitting pretty in pink or yellow in your bento box.

Grains of Paradise (see Pepper)

Grape Leaves These large green leaves that grow on grapevines are used for wrapping foods. Their size is ideal for this purpose, making wonderful packets that seal in moisture and flavor (page 127). They are mostly used in Greek and Middle Eastern cuisines. Grape leaves are usually sold in jars or cans, preserved in brine. The brine

must be completely rinsed off before using the leaves to remove the saltiness. If you happen to live near a vineyard, fresh grape leaves can also be used to hold fillings and wrap foods: boil them for about 1 minute to make them soft and pliable. You can find the brined leaves at specialty food stores and at some online sources.

Greek Yogurt Greek-style yogurt is thicker and creamier than American yogurt, but it has a slightly higher fat content. It is typically used in Greek desserts—add a drizzle of honey and you have a perfect after-dinner treat. Greek yogurt is becoming increasingly available here; look for it at specialty food stores.

Green Plaintains (see Plantains)

Green Tea, Unsweetened, Canned (see Tea)

Green Tea, Powdered (see Matcha)

Guava Native to South America and the Caribbean, guavas come in many varieties. The one thing they all have in common is the center core: a large ball made up of tiny hard seeds and edible sweet pulp. The scent of ripe guavas can perfume your entire home and garden, giving off an aromatic blend of passion fruit, overripe bananas, pineapples, and limes. Some guavas can be found in Asian markets—they are dark green and oval-shaped with whitish-pink flesh, and are about the size of an apple. Other varieties may be bright yellow, pink, or deep red, and as large as cantaloupes or as tiny as globe grapes. The paste made from guavas is a very popular dessert in Latin American countries, where it is served with a variety of soft or semi-soft cheeses. Guava is also used in many desserts and beverages. You can find canned guava, guava juice, guava paste, and guava jelly at Latin American specialty food stores and at your nearest Chinatown. They will be fresh in the spring and summer months.

Habanero Peppers (see Chiles)

Harissa This remarkable Tunisian sauce is made with chiles, caraway seeds, cumin, coriander, garlic, and olive oil. You can find it in tubes or jars in a paste form, or there is a dry version which looks a rub for a steak. You can use the paste version for stews or sauces, and the dry version can be made into a wonderful dip by adding olive oil. Its fiery flavor has spread to other neighboring countries such as Morocco, Algeria, and Israel. You can find it in Middle Eastern stores, specialty food shops, and some online sources.

Hibiscus (see Edible Flowers and Sorrel)

Hoisin Sauce Made with a combination of soybean paste, garlic, vinegar, and salt, the Chinese use hoisin as a dipping sauce for spring rolls and for glazing pork and roast duck. To give my barbecue sauce an Asian flavor I add a few tablespoons of this wonderful condiment. You can find hoisin sauce in most supermarkets.

Jackfruit Jackfruit grows on a species of fast-growing evergreen tree native to India and is quite common throughout Asia and tropical regions as well. A single jackfruit can grow as long as three feet and weigh as much as 100 pounds. It is light green, then deepens to yellow-brown when ripe. It is covered with hard, knobby spines like the durian, but unlike the durian, when ripe the jackfruit yields segmented yellow flesh that has a heavenly perfume, almost like bubble gum. It can be eaten raw or used in desserts and beverages. The variety called green jackfruit is the size of a cantaloupe but its exterior is the same to a ripe jackfruit, and is used as a vegetable. Inside the green jackfruit are segments of white seeds that are encased in a stringy white tissue (see page 193). Both are used for cooking savory dishes and curries, and the edible seeds can be boiled or roasted. Both kinds of jackfruit (and their close relative, breadfruit)

can be found in cans at southeast Asian and West Indian specialty food stores, which will most likely have them fresh during the autumn months.

Jalapeño Peppers (see Chiles)

Japanese Eggplant Sometimes also called Asian eggplants, this variety is long and slender, as well as slightly smaller—about four to eight inches long. They have a purplish hue and a texture that is quite different from the "black beauty" variety we're used to. Japanese eggplant cooks much faster and has a more intense flavor, as their water content isn't as high as regular eggplants. You can sometimes find Japanese eggplants at your supermarket; if not, almost any Asian specialty food store that sells produce will have them.

Jicama Jicama (pronounced hickama) is a tuber, and it has a mild, sweet, crisp white interior, similar to a crunchy apple, but it looks like a giant white radish or a potato. The skin peels off easily, and then the jicama can be cut up and eaten raw. It is delicious julienned and used in salads, and makes a wonderfully different lunchbox or brown bag treat. Kids will enjoy them because of their sweetness and it is also a favoriate with dieters, as it low in calories and has no fat. It is also known as yam bean. Jicama is usually available at specialty food stores.

Kaffir Lime and Kaffir Lime Leaves

Native to southeast Asia, the kaffir lime tree bears bumpy, wrinkled limes that yield very little juice. It is the rinds that are grated and used in cooking. The glossy dark green leaves are indispensable in Thai cooking, and are usually used shredded or crumbled. Both the fruit and the leaves have the bursting flavor and aroma of citrus. In fact, you can substitute regular limes or lemon myrtle leaves for kaffir lime's flavor, although the result won't be exactly the same. You can usually find kaffir limes and leaves in the refrigerated section of Thai specialty food stores.

Kefalotyri Cheese

A Greek cheese, kefalotyri is made from ewe's milk, and is white or yellow-ish in color. Kefalotyri is a hard cheese with a tangy, sharp aroma, very much like Italian Romano, for which it can be a substitute; it's perfect for grating over cooked dishes. Kefalotyri can be found at most specialty food stores and cheese shops.

Kenchur

Although kenchur is a member of the galangal family, it has its own distinct, strong citrus aroma that is quite different from that of galangal or ginger. It is used in Asian cooking much the same way as galangal and ginger, and it's also added to curries and stir-frys. In Malaysia, it is called *cekur*; in Thailand, *pro hom*. Kenchur looks like a slender version of ginger and can be found in the refrigerated section of Thai specialty food stores.

Kim Chi

An authentic Korean meal is not complete without this requisite condiment, which is basically aged cabbage with a very hot kick. Considered a relish, the cabbage is fermented along with turnips, radishes, or cucumber, and sometimes even fish, as the main ingredient. There are countless varieties of kim chi, as each Korean family has their own recipe. Crushed red pepper, garlic, salt, water, chopped green onions, cucumber, ginger, apples, pears, anchovies, clams, and many other ingredients can be added to enhance its flavor. Kim chi is usually available in jars in the refrigerated section of Asian specialty food stores.

Kokam or Kokum

Kokam is a dark purple fruit that grows on evergreen trees in southern India. Once the ripe fruits are harvested, the rinds are removed and allowed to dry. The rinds are then used as a souring agent for Indian curry dishes. Kokam is also sometimes boiled in sugar syrup to make a delicious purple-colored drink that is very popular in southern India. It can be found in dried slices at the spice section of Indian specialty food stores.

Kombu (see Seaweed)

Krupuk or Shrimp Crackers

We know them as shrimp crackers—those dried, brittle pink or multi-colored "chips" that can quickly become addictive. They are made from tapioca flour, dried ground shrimp, and salt. When deep-fried, they swell up and become crisp and puffy, like fried pork rinds. These crackers are popular snacks in Asian homes, and they make a fun, colorful garnish as well. They also make great "scoops" for peanut dipping sauce (page 179). You can find krupuk in bags at many Asian and South Asian specialty foods stores.

Lablab Beans or Seem

Also known as Hyacinth Beans, Lablab beans grow on a twining vine that has vibrant, bright purple flowers and edible pods that grow from 2- to 5-inches long. Their flavor is similar to American broadbeans, and they're used to make savory Indian dishes. String beans can be substituted in a pinch. Lablab beans can be green or purple, and are seasonal. Look for them during the autumn months in Asian and Indian specialty food stores. (The seeds should not be eaten raw as they can be harsh on the digestive system and are toxic.)

Lemongrass

Lemongrass, with its strong, aromatic leaves and stems, has become widely available in the U.S. It grows in close bunches, as wild grasses do, and is native to Sri Lanka and southern India. Lemongrass is extensively used in Thai, Vietnamese, and Malaysian cuisines, to which it lends a lemony flavor without the acidity or sharpness of lemons. The entire lemongrass stalk can be boiled to make wonderful soup stocks and aromatic teas. Usually,

however, it is the whitish bulb at the bottom of the stalk that is chopped and used as an ingredient. Several layers of the stalk must first be removed before reaching the pinkish insides. If lemongrass is not available for a recipe, lime leaves or freshly squeezed lime juice can be substituted. Look for lemongrass stalks at some supermarkets, and at Asian and other specialty food stores. Unused lemongrass freezes well.

Lemon Myrtle Native to Australia, lemon myrtle has long been used by the Aborigines for medicinal purposes. This tall plant produces slender, 3- to 4-inch long leaves, which are dried and ground. I use ground lemon myrtle in fish, pasta, or vegetable dishes. Its flavor is a unique and refreshing blend of lime, lemon, and lemongrass. Ground lemon myrtle and dried lemon myrtle leaves are available at specialty stores and some online sources.

Longan The longan is often called the "little brother" of the lychee fruit. Sometimes called dragon's eye, the longan belongs to the same family as the rambutan and the lychee. The longan is round and a little larger than an olive. It has a thin, rough, caramel-colored shell that is easily peeled, starting at the stem. The pulp inside is translucent white and surrounds a large round brown pit, hence the name dragon's eye. Longan has sweeter flesh than the lychee but it's not as juicy, and there isn't as much of it due to the size of the pit. Longan is available in cans in Asian specialty food markets, but look for the fresh fruits during the summer months when they are in season.

Long Beans These beans, which can grow as long as three feet (they are also sometimes called yard beans) are from the black-eyed pea family. The beans grow in pairs and their colors can vary from jade green to light purple. They have soft, edible seeds. Long beans make a great variation on American green beans, and they can be eaten raw, blanched and tossed into a salad, or chopped and used in stir-frys or as a side dish. Long beans are crisp and refreshing, with an almost asparagus-like flavor. Look for them at Asian, West Indian, and other specialty food stores.

Lychee Fruit Lychees are from southeast China. They are sphere-shaped, pinkish-red fruits about an inch or so in diameter with thin shells similar to the longan. When the shell is peeled off, the lychee's flesh is translucent white and encloses an elongated, dark, glossy seed. As with the longan, the best way to start peeling lychees is from the stem end. When you put the entire fruit in your mouth, it tastes sweet and as juicy as a watermelon, with a slight hint of acidity. Be sure to discard the pit, or seed. Fresh lychees are a seasonal treat—they're available during the summer months at Asian and other specialty food stores or at open-air markets in local Chinatowns.

Canned lychees, which are sometimes available at supermarkets as well as Asian specialty stores, are a good substitute. Lychee juice, which is delicious in cocktails, is also available in cans.

Mahlab This is a small kernel from a variety of black cherry that is native to the Mediterranean. The kernels are tear-shaped and light brown in color, and they emit an unusual rose scent and floral flavor but leave a slightly bitter aftertaste. Mahlab is used to flavor cakes, pastries, and biscuits in Middle Eastern cuisines. While mahlab is available in powdered form, I tend not to use it because after a while it loses both flavor and aroma. Instead, I recommend buying the fresh kernels and grinding them in a spice grinder when you're ready to use them. Middle Eastern specialty food stores will have mahlab.

Mango To my mind, mangoes are the world's most popular fruit. There has barely been a country I've visited in which I haven't encountered them. There are hundreds of varieties of mangoes, each with a distinctive color, pulp, juice, shape, and size. The mango tree is deep-rooted and dome-shaped, and is believed to have originated in the Indo-Burmese region. In the Hindu religion, both the wood and the leaves of mango trees are used for religious rituals as offerings. Green mangoes, which are unripe and sour, are used for making wonderful chutneys and as an ingredient in savory curries. Ripe mangoes are used in sweet curries, beverages, and desserts. If you don't want to bother with the mess of preparing a whole mango, the juice and pulp are widely available in cans or bottles at most specialty food stores. But nothing quite beats a juicy fresh mango, and to select one, the fruit should feel heavy (a sign that there's plenty of juice inside), and its skin should slightly yield to pressure, as with an avocado. The fragrance should be floral with hints of spice; if so, the flavor will be too. Mangoes are usually available all year long at many supermarkets.

STAR FRUIT

Manioc (see Cassava)

Manouri Cheese Another of Greece's beloved cheeses, manouri can be made from either goats' or sheeps' milk. It is white, soft, and creamy, and is reminiscent of Italian ricotta cheese, but with a hint of citrus. Ricotta can substitute for it if manouri is not available. Manouri is used for making the famous Greek pastry, spanakopita, and is also considered a dessert cheese. Look for it at specialty food stores and cheese shops.

Mastic Mastic is the resinous sap that is collected from small shrub-like trees on the Greek island of Chios. The translucent droplets are referred to as "tears." Mastic is a very versatile substance: it is used for the consistency and texture it gives to ice cream and popular sweets like rice pudding and "Turkish Delight." It can also be chewed just like gum, and is even used in the manufacture of some varnishes. If you feel like experimenting with mastic, look for it at Middle Eastern and Greek specialty stores. They usually come in small plastic bags and look like small crystals.

Matcha This highly-prized powdered green tea is used in the elaborate, traditional Japanese tea ceremony. It is also a natural food color, giving soba noodles their greenish tinge, as well as an ingredient in delicately delicious green tea ice cream. It also makes a decadent latte. Matcha comes from gyokuro tea leaves that have been steamed and dried—a time-consuming process in which all of the leaves' veins are removed. The pure dried leaves, called *tencha*, are then stone-ground into a powder so fine that it has the consistency of baby powder. Matcha green tea powder tastes like fresh flowers, and can be found in fine tea shops and specialty food stores.

Matzoh, Matzah, or Matza Matzoh is the thin, brittle unleavened bread that is traditionally eaten during the Jewish Passover holiday. Its sole ingredients are flour and water, although there are egg matzohs for children and those with delicate digestions, as well as some flavored with onion. Matzoh is also ground into a medium- to fine-textured meal that is used in baking, as well as for breading foods and thickening soups and gravies. The finest textured meal is used for making cakes. It is also delicious when prepared as "Matzoh Brei"—crumble one or two matzohs into a bowl, cover with

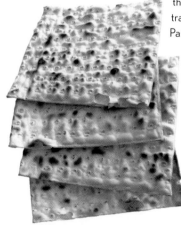

boiling water and let rest for one minute; then drain well, mix with a beaten egg, and fry in lots of butter (if cooking kosher, fry it in margarine). You can eat this plain with salt, or with a little applesauce on the side. Matzoh is available at almost any supermarket all year long, although during the Passover season, it is sold separately marked "Kosher for Passover."

Melokhia Native to Egypt but also grown in parts of India, melokhia is a tiny, flat, round green vegetable, the leaves of which are about the size of a penny. When cooked, it becomes glutinous; in fact, if you're an okra lover, you'll love melokhia just as much because the flavors are similar. It is the essential ingredient in Egyptian melokhia soup. You can find this unusual item in the freezer section of Middle Eastern specialty stores.

Mint Mint is surely one of the world's favorite flavors. From dental rinse to ice cream, it is the dominant flavor in hundreds of foods, beverages, and various food-related products. Native to Europe and the Mediterranean, there are many varieties of mint, each with a very different taste (if you've ever tried peppermint gum and spearmint gum, you can taste the difference right away). In fact, spearmint and peppermint are the most commonly used varieties. Fresh mint is bright green and very fragrant, with a sweet, sharp aroma and notes of

menthol. It can also have a fiery bite. Whether it's used in sauces or desserts, tossed into salads, or used as a beautiful garnish, mint is extremely versatile and refreshing, which is probably the reason for the pleasurable, palate-cleansing phenomenon known as after-dinner mints. Dried mint is usually used in making Middle Eastern and Mediterranean spice blends—it has a pungent aroma but lacks the sweet, vibrant taste of fresh mint. Bunches of fresh mint are usually available all year long at almost any supermarket. Even if you don't use it for cooking, place a bunch of mint in a vase of water and let the lovely aroma perfume your home.

Mirin Mirin is Japanese sweetened rice wine made from glutinous rice. It is only used for cooking, not drinking. It has a lower alcohol content than sake, and just a touch will heighten the flavors of seafood or steamed vegetables. When a recipe calls for mirin, you can substitute white wine with a pinch of sugar or use sweet sherry. Mirin is available in bottles at almost any supermarket, and at Asian specialty food stores.

Miso Miso is fermented soybean paste combined with salt. It is high in many nutrients and in protein, and low in fat. As a Japanese favorite, miso comes in different flavors, textures, and colors. The most commonly used miso is white miso, which has less salt than red miso paste. Dissolved in boiling water, miso makes a delicious and nourishing soup. While miso is available in dried form, I prefer to use the paste, which comes in plastic pouches. Once opened, though, the paste must be refrigerated. Miso and miso pastes are available at Asian and some other specialty food stores.

Mora Berries A cousin of our American blackberries, mora berries grow wild in South America. They taste very much the same as blackberries but have a hint of citrus. Blueberries or blackberries can easily stand in for mora berries, but for the real thing, look in the freezer section of Latin American specialty food stores.

Mustard Seeds These tiny seeds are about the size of caviar eggs. They're native to Europe and southeast Asia, and along with the oil extracted from them, are commonly used in Indian cooking and for pickling. They are, of course, the main ingredient in all of the various mustards we enjoy on sandwiches, hot dogs and dozens of other favorites. Mustard seeds come in white, black, or a reddish-brown color; the black seeds are larger and hotter than the other two and are a little harder to find. Mustard seeds can usually be found in jars in the spice section of most supermarkets, at specialty food stores, and at some online sources.

Nigella Seeds Small, black, and irregularly shaped, nigella seeds resemble black sesame seeds. They are often called onion seeds; in India they are known as *kalonji*. The seeds do not have a strong aroma, but once chewed they reveal a wonderful, mouth-filling flavor and a slight scent of oregano. You sometimes find nigella seeds sprinkled on top of rye bread, but usually, they are ground and used in Iranian and Indian spice blends. They're essential in preparing planch phora, an Indian spice blend made with cumin, fenugreek, mustard, nigella, and fennel seeds. Look for them at Indian specialty food stores.

Nori (see Seaweed)

Nutmeg and Mace Native to the Maluku (formerly the Moluccas) Islands of Indonesia, nutmeg is a thick, fleshy yellow fruit that is produced only by female trees. When ripe, the fruit splits open to reveal an exotic-looking lacy red membrane known as mace, which is ground and used as a separate spice. The lacy covering encases a hard brown shell, and when the shell is cracked, the nutmeg appears. Mace and nutmeg both are warm to the taste with hints of citrus and clove, and have a sweet, pine-like aroma, although mace has a slightly more delicate flavor. Nutmeg is best when purchased whole and grated into foods as needed. This can be done using a regular hand grater, or in special nutmeg mills that look like peppermills. Ground mace retains its flavor well and is usually used in making North Indian and Moroccan spice blends, including garam masala and curry powder, as well as in stuffings and sausages. It is also used as a flavoring in cakes and other desserts. Whole nutmeg, as well as ground mace, can be found in jars in the spice section of your supermarket.

Okra People either love okra or hate it. It is pod-shaped and native to Africa, although it traveled to the Americas and the Caribbean by way of African slave laborers who were brought there. The pods are emerald green and can grow anywhere from 2 to 9 inches long. Outside, the pod is slightly fuzzy; inside are many tiny white seeds surrounded by a thick, glutinous liquid. If too large, okra can be fibrous, so it's best to look for small, firm ones—about 2 to 3 inches long. The stem end is wider than the opposite end which comes to a point. Some people dislike the mucilaginous quality of the juice inside the okra pods. It is better for them to buy the larger ones, which won't have as much liquid, and deep fry them. The small ones are delicious on their own, simply steamed and served with melted butter, but okra is most famous for its use in the famous Louisiana specialty, gumbo. In

 Southeast Asian countries and in East Africa, okra is stuffed with spices and deep-fried. Spring is okra season: look for it at most supermarkets and at open-air farmers markets.

Orange Blossom Water This delightful liquid essence is an indispensable pantry item in Middle Eastern kitchens. Orange blossom water is used to flavor all sorts of desserts because its flavor and aroma truly live up to its name: it is a fusion of sweet oranges and their fragrant blossom petals. Orange blossom water is available in bottles at Middle Eastern or other specialty food stores, and is interchangeable with its sister essence, rose water.

Ostrich This enormous, flightless bird, often depicted with its head in the sand, is from Africa and parts of Southeast Asia. An ostrich can weight up to 300 pounds and grow to 6 feet tall. The U.S., Australia, New Zealand, and Africa are now home to the industry of ostrich farming, and ostrich meat is becoming readily available. Ostrich meat, which is  usually cut into medallions like filet mignon, is slightly gamier than beef, but it is very lean, which makes it low in fat and a good choice for dieters. It must be cooked very carefully though, as just one or two minutes too long on the grill will leave it inedibly dry. Look for ostrich medallions at specialty meat markets and at some online sources.

Oxtails Even though these are actually cows' tails, they are called oxtails. They are quite bony, but when cooked the meat becomes extremely flavorful. To me, one of the most delicious dishes is a slow-cooked soup or stew (page 238) with chunks of oxtail that have been braised until the meat falls off the bones. Oxtails are sold cut in rounds in the meat section of Latin American or Caribbean supermarkets, specialty food stores, and some meat markets.

Oyster Sauce Commonly used in Asian cuisines for adding to stir-frys, oyster sauce is a thick, brown sauce made with ground oysters, salt, water, cornstarch, and caramel for coloring. It is usually found right next to soy sauce and hoisin sauce at most supermarkets.

Palm Sugar This type of sugar is made from the sap of various palm trees. The sap is boiled down, then dried and shaped into solid brown cakes or cones. Its color can vary from light to dark brown. When needed, the amount of sugar is grated from the cake. Soft brown sugar, or jaggery (made from cane sugar), are good substitutes. Palm sugar is frequently used in Indian and Thai kitchens, and can be found at Indian and Thai specialty food stores.

Pandanus Leaf Pandan or pandanus leaf is a member of the screw pine family. It is a wonderfully aromatic leaf that is used to flavor desserts, rice dishes, and to wrap meats and seafood before cooking. The flavor is floral and delicate. You can look for these long green leaves in the refrigerated section of Asian specialty food stores, but if you can't locate any, bottled pandan essence is available for flavoring desserts. It comes in small green bottles.

Panko Breadcrumbs Panko are Japanese breadcrumbs that are coarser than regular breadcrumbs. There are two types of panko: tan, which is made with white bread and its crusts, or white, which is made without the crusts. Panko is not ground the way other breadcrumbs are, instead they are shredded or grated, resulting in long shards. Coating meats, fish, and vegetables with panko before deep frying or baking results in an incredibly crispy, crunchy texture. You can also try flavoring panko with different spices for extra effect. Once you use panko, you'll find it hard to go back to regular breadcrumbs. Panko is available at almost any supermarket or at Asian specialty food stores.

Papadum Also called papads, papadum are seasoned wheat and lentil flatbreads. These are thin and brittle, and they fry up quickly when cooked. Papads are usually served with savory chutneys at Indian restaurants as an appetizer. For a healthy snack, you can also bake the flatbreads in a toaster oven instead of frying them. Pre-packaged papads can be found at Indian specialty food stores.

Papaya The papaya is one of the oldest fruits, dating back to prehistoric times. There are many varieties of it, and it is widely grown in the tropics and subtropics. Some papayas are the size of a mango, but they can also grow as large as a watermelon. Green papayas are the unripe fruit, and make a delicious addition to savory curries and salads, while the sweet, ripe fruits are used to make shakes, smoothies, marmalades, and salads. Papaya contains a high amount of the enzyme papain, a natural tenderizer for meats and poultry. Papaya tastes sweet, like a blend of mango and cantaloupe.

The black seeds inside the fruit are edible but have a sharp, peppery bite. My grandfather used to grind the seeds like black pepper and serve them to me after a meal to aid in digestion or to soothe an upset stomach. Fresh papaya is available year-round but if you cannot find them, look for jarred papaya in the fresh fruit section of most supermarkets.

Paprika   The peppers from which paprika is made are commercially grown in South America, Spain, Hungary, and in the U.S. Paprika is used to season, garnish, and lend color to a variety of foods, including chiles and paellas. The pods are red and/or yellow; they are dried and then ground into a fine powder. Paprika is available in several levels of "hotness," from sweet, which has nearly no heat at all, to extra-hot. Smoked paprika, or pimentón, is achieved by smoking the peppers before drying and grinding them. Its color is very deep red. The smoky flavor of pimentón is irresistible in everything from omelets to casseroles, but it should be used sparingly. Paprika is available in the spice section of almost any supermarket; pimentón can be found at Latin American and Spanish specialty food stores as well as at some online sources.

Pasilla Peppers (see Chiles)

Passion Fruit   Passion fruit is native to the Amazon region of South America, where it is said that the Spanish missionaries, who claim to have witnessed the passion of Christ in the flowers of the plant, christened it with its current name.

There are several varieties of passion fruit: the ones we most commonly see in specialty food stores are yellow and purple in color, and are about the size and shape of an egg. They are unmistakably tropical. The passion fruit's skin is smooth and tough, but inside is a juicy, yellow-orange pulp filled with edible seeds that are about the size of grape seeds. The taste is sweet-tart. Passion fruit juice and passion fruit pulp are used to make wonderfully refreshing beverages, sorbets, and other desserts. Passion fruit and passion fruit juice can be found at specialty food stores.

Poblano Peppers (see Chiles)

PEPPER AND PEPPERCORNS   Pepper, so commonly found in shakers and mills on every countertop from restaurants to home kitchens, was once so prized that the ancient Romans used it as currency. References to pepper date back as far as the first century A.D., and during the middle ages it was a hot trade commodity, widely used for its medicinal and aromatic qualities as well as flavor. Today, we can't get enough of it, and pepper still accounts for a quarter of the world's spice trade industry. Nearly everything we eat is seasoned with salt and pepper, yet we barely stop to think about where pepper actually comes from. Pepper is a fruit native to the Malabar Coast of India where it grows on vines that climb up small trees for shade. The vines can take up to 8 years to mature, and can continue to bear fruit for 20 years. The fruit grows in small green clusters; when mature they turn a vibrant red (hence red peppercorns). The hot peppery bite you taste when you use pepper lies in its outer membrane, which contains a molecule called piperine. Today, pepper is harvested in Indonesia, Brazil, Malaysia, and Vietnam. Each region's growing conditions determine the flavor of the peppercorns, and flavors can vary quite noticeably. Of the black peppercorns, Malabar is considered to be the highest quality, while Tellicherry peppercorns are the largest. Indonesian Muntok is the best of the white peppercorns, and the Sarawak variety has a milder aroma than the Brazilian and Vietnamese fruits. A wealth of different peppercorns is available at specialty food stores and at several online sources.

•**BLACK PEPPERCORNS** Black pepper is harvested when the berries are actually green. They are placed in heaps to ferment and then spread out to dry. During the drying process, the outer layer that contains the piperine responsible for pepper's bite shrivels and turns black or dark brown.

•**CUBEB PEPPER OR JAVA PEPPER** Cubeb pepper is native to Java and is sometimes called Java pepper. Sometimes, it is also referred to as tail pepper because of the small, hair-thin

FINGERED CITRON

stem that remains attached to each dried peppercorn. This is considered to be a rare pepper—the peppercorns are slightly larger than most others and have notes of allspice and eucalyptus. When cooked, these sweet spice flavors are released. Cubeb pepper is available at specialty food stores.

•**GRAINS OF PARADISE** Grains of Paradise, also known as Melegueta or Guinea pepper, is as rare as its unusual name. It is indigenous to the coastal regions of western Africa, from Sierra Leone to Angola. The Melegueta plant, however, is not related to the vine on which the peppers grow; rather it is a member of the ginger family. The spherical seeds of Grains of Paradise look very much like cardamom seeds (cardamom is another member of the ginger family), and they have a peppery bite with hints of cardamom and camphor. They are used wherever an exotic pepper seasoning is needed, such as in the cuisines of North Africa, including Moroccan and Tunisian dishes. Look for Grains of Paradise at some specialty food stores or online sources.

•**GREEN PEPPERCORNS** These are immature pepper berries—they are harvested and sold fresh, freeze-dried, or brined in vinegar to maintain their verdant color. Green peppercorns are not as potent as black pepper, although they do have a fresh pungency and light aroma.

•**INDIAN LONG PEPPER OR JAVANESE LONG PEPPER** Known by both names, these peppercorns are native to India. They resemble tiny catkins and are harvested when green, then sun-dried after which they turn a grayish-black. After drying, they measure about 1/2-inch to 1-inch long. In North and East Africa, long pepper is used in making slow-cooked stews. Its flavor is sweet and it is quite fragrant, yet it has the taste of black pepper with a biting aftertaste. Long pepper is used in many exotic Asian dishes and clear soups. It also partners well with galangal, turmeric, and kenchur in rich, thick curries. Today it is cultivated in Indonesia and parts of Africa as well as in India. Look for Indian or Javanese long pepper at specialty food stores and at some online sources.

•**MOUNTAIN PEPPERBERRY OR DORRIGO PEPPER** These pepper berries are grown in Australia. They're known as mountain pepperberry or Dorrigo pepper and are dark blue to black in color. They have an intensely peppery bite, and are used both whole and ground. When ground, the dark purplish color bleeds through cream sauces, lending them a beautiful, unusual hue. Mountain pepperberry has an earthy undertaste that lingers, and its heat slowly builds for about three minutes after eating. It's wise to use this pepper with care: for every amount of conventional pepper you use,

about one-tenth of mountain pepperberry will be plenty.

•**PINK PEPPER OR PINK PEPPERCORNS** Pink peppercorns are not a vinous pepper, but are actually the dried berries of the Baies rose plant. This rare plant grows in the French island of Reunion and in Brazil, making it an expensive pepper. Unlike the black, green, and white peppercorns, these peppers aren't really peppercorns but are referred to as such because of their shape and size. Pink peppercorns have a brittle, papery, pink skin enclosing a hard, irregular seed. When crushed, the flavor becomes fruity and almost pine-like, with a hint of juniper berries. It works very well in fish, poultry, and seafood dishes. Look for pink pepper at specialty stores or online.

•**RED PEPPERCORNS** These gaily colored, fully ripened berries are plucked from its vine when fully red and ripe with a delicate, sweet flavor. They still pack a dose of heat, however. Red peppercorns are considered the "true" pink peppercorn and its counterpart, pink pepper, is considered to be "false" pepper. You can find dried red peppercorns whole, or in brine or vinegar to keep their outer membranes intact.

•**SICHUAN OR SZECHWAN PEPPERCORNS** Long banned from import to the U.S., these unusual-tasting peppercorns are now available here. They grow on the prickly ash tree, and when they are dried they are rust-colored and have hair-thin stems and open ends. When opened, the rough skins reveal a brittle black seed, but the true spice lies in the empty husk or skin. These are mildly peppery and earthy. Sichuan peppercorns are the main ingredient in Chinese five spice powder. There are several other species of Sichuan peppercorns that originate from Nepal, Japan, and Korea. In Japan, Sichuan peppercorns are called *sancho*; in Tibet, *emma*; in Nepal, *timur*. Look for Sichuan peppercorns at Asian and other specialty food stores and at some online sources.

•**WHITE PEPPERCORNS** When mature, these ripened red berries are harvested and then soaked in water for several days until the outer red membrane can be easily removed. The resulting grayish-colored berries are then sun-dried until they turn a grayish-white color. White pepper is not as hot as black pepper. It is commonly used in Vietnamese and Chinese dishes, and in any preparation in which the color of conventional black pepper is not desired, such as some cream soups and sauces. Muntok, a white pepper from Indonesia, is said to be the very best. White pepper is usually available in jars in the spice section of almost any supermarket.

Phyllo Dough or Filo Dough

These paper-thin sheets of dough are made with flour, salt, eggs, and water. Phyllo can be layered, shaped, or shredded and baked into deliciously crispy, savory dishes and delectable, flaky desserts such as the famous honey-drizzled baklava. If you are fortunate enough to live near a Greek market, fresh phyllo dough is a true gourmet treat. But you can also easily find phyllo (sometimes spelled filo) dough in the freezer section of most supermarkets and specialty food stores. When using the frozen version, allow it to defrost completely in its plastic covering and unroll it very carefully as it can tear in an instant. As you work with the layers one at a time, brushing each with melted butter, keep the remaining stack of phyllo sheets covered with a damp cloth. Phyllo dries out in seconds if not kept moist, and once it dries out it's unusable.

Pickled Ginger (see Ginger)

Plantains

Plantains, which look very similar to bananas, are indeed from the banana family. They are native to India but are extensively used in Latin American, African, and Caribbean cooking. Green plantains are unripe and inedible raw, but once they are cooked (they can be boiled, fried, baked, or roasted) their unique flavor is a delight. Their skins are quite tough, making them difficult to peel, and the cream-colored fruit inside is quite starchy. Ripe plantains are yellow and often have black spots, so most people confuse them with bananas. These can be eaten raw—they are sweet, with golden yellow flesh, and the skins are easily peeled away. Plantains make terrific tostones (the fruit is cut into rounds, fried in oil on one side, then slightly mashed and fried on the other side), and great chips that you can often find in bags next to the potato chips in supermarkets. Fresh plantains can be found all year long at some Latin American and other specialty foods stores, as well as in some supermarkets.

Polenta

Polenta, which is actually plain cornmeal, was once considered to be peasant food. Now it's on almost every three-star menu throughout the world in dozens of guises. In northern Italy, it is a staple in every home kitchen where it can be prepared with tomato and other sauces, cheese, meat and other toppings and fillings. If you love grits, you'll adore polenta: it is made with dried yellow or white cornmeal that has been ground to either coarse, medium, or fine grade. Polenta must be cooked for quite some time and stirred constantly to prevent sticking and burning—and once bubbling it can be quite volatile. But there are also instant and prepared versions of polenta available, cutting down on time in the kitchen as well as burn concerns. These are available in most supermarkets and at Italian and other specialty food stores.

Ponzu

Ponzu is a tart, citrus-based Japanese dipping sauce. This light-yellow condiment is commonly made wih citrus juices, vinegar, and soy sauce. You can find ponzu in glass bottles in your Asian market.

Pomegranate

This ancient fruit originated in Persia (Iran), and is now used throughout the world. It is about the size of an orange, with a bumpy, leathery red skin. Inside are membranes that contain hundreds of translucent, edible red seeds, and for this reason the pomegranate has long been a symbol of fertility. The seeds have a refreshing sweet-tart taste. This is a very versatile fruit: it can be eaten out of hand, or the seeds can be scraped out and made into jellies, or used as a tasty, colorful garnish. The juice is used in delicious alcoholic and non-alcoholic beverages. Pomegranate seeds can also be ground into a powder and used as a souring agent in Middle Eastern and Indian dishes. The powdered seeds have a tart, tangy flavor and also lend a reddish color to food. Pomegranate molasses, which is made by boiling pomegranate juice down to a concentrate, is a thick, dark syrup that's wonderful for

marinating poultry and wild game. Fresh pomegranates are seasonal, usually available between August and November, and can be found in most supermarkets and specialty food stores, as can bottled pomegranate juice. Both the seeds of the fruit and the juice are very high in vitamin C.

Preserved Lemons These wonderful, unusual condiments are must-haves in Moroccan, North African, and Mediterranean kitchens. They give food an almost sweet tang. Preserved lemons are whole, ripe lemons that are cut partway through into quarters, placed in jars, and cured in salt and/or fresh lemon juice for several weeks. Once opened, any unused preserved lemons in the jar should be refrigerated. Some cooks like to use the entire fruit in cooking, while others scrape out the flesh and use only the rind, finely chopped. Either way, the excess salt should be rinsed off. You can find ready-made preserved lemons in Middle Eastern and other specialty food stores.

Pumpkin Seeds or Pepitas Pumpkin seeds are also known as pepitas. These flat, dark green seeds are encased in a yellow-white husk. Sweet and nutty with a chewy texture, these delicious seeds are very nutritious, and can be tossed over salads or on top of soups for a delicious crunch. You can find them in Latin American grocery stores, health food stores, and most supermarkets in plastic containers or plastic bags.

Purple Corn The Incas of the Andes have long used these purple kernels. Although their flavor is bland, they are used for their fabulous color, especially in the popular Peruvian beverage, chicha morada (page 80), or purple corn drink. Whole ears of purple corn can be found at Latin American specialty food stores.

Purple Potatoes South America seems to like the color purple. Like its corn, purple potatoes, which also originated there but are now cultivated in the U.S., have a subtle, nutty flavor and, of course, a terrific color both inside and out. Baking them is a good way to maintain their intense hue. Purple potatoes are usually small and slightly dimpled, similar to red-skinned new potatoes. You can find them at specialty food stores.

Purslane While little known here, purslane is consumed throughout much of Europe and Asia. It is a summertime vegetable (actually, it is a weed), and can be eaten fresh in a salad, or cooked. Purslane has tiny, thick green leaves and stems, and has a mild aroma, but the texture is a bit crunchy and the taste is slightly citrusy. In the Mediterranean, it is commonly used as a salad ingredient; in the Middle East it is used in soups and stews because of its okra-like gelatinous quality. Purslane can be found fresh at summer farmers markets and at some specialty food stores.

Queso Blanco Queso Blanco is a mild Mexican cheese used both for cooking and snacking. I love pairing it with fresh fruits. This cheese is made fresh and unfortunately has a shelf life of about a week. The beauty of this cheese is that it will become soft and creamy when heated but will not melt, which makes it perfect for stuffing chicken, burgers, bread, or deep-frying. You can find it in the refrigerated section of Hispanic stores or at most specialty cheese shops.

Queso Chihuahua This is a Mexican, pale yellow melting cheese that is terrific in savory dishes. It can also be thickly sliced, breaded like mozzarella sticks and deep-fried. Its taste is similar to a mild cheddar or jack cheese, which make good substitutes for it, too. Most Latin American markets, some supermarkets, and cheese shops will have it.

Queso Fresco This popular Mexican cheese is usually crumbled or grated over bean dishes and salads. Just like Queso Blanco this is also a fresh cheese which when heated will not melt but become creamy and soft. You can find it in the refrigerated section of Hispanic stores or at most specialty cheese shops.

Quinoa Pronounced keen-wa, this is a delicate, nutty-flavored grain that is gaining great popularity here. Indigenous to the Andes in South America, it is either golden or red in color and is among the most ancient of grains. When cooked, each grain softens and splits open to reveal the curled-up germ inside. The germ is what gives quinoa its interesting texture and slight crunch when you eat it. Quinoa is easy to prepare, and is available in either bags or boxes at health and specialty food stores.

Red Chili Oil This is an infernally hot condiment that is actually vegetable oil infused with ripe red chiles. This oil is extensively used in Chinese cuisine and can be found in bottles at Asian and other specialty food stores.

Red Curry Paste Every southeast Asian country I have visited has their own curry paste, they come in various heat levels from sweet to deadly hot and colors abound. Curry paste is made with chiles, spices indigenous to that country, and can be made with curry leaves, kaffir lime leaves, cilantro, and lemon grass. The common ingredients for the bottled version you see at your local supermarkets or Asian grocery stores is made with chiles, vinegar, cilantro, cumin, coriander, turmeric, and citrus juice. It is mainly used in soups and savory curry dishes.

Rice Noodles (see Asian Noodles)

Rice Paper Wrappers (see Rice)

RICE Countless civilizations and cultures have thrived on rice for thousands of years. Today, it's a staple in every kitchen throughout the world. Rice as we now know it comes in two types: long grain and short-to-medium grain. The rices we use in contemporary cuisines come from all corners of the world, and each has its own distinguishing texture and flavor. Long grain rices tend to cook up light and fluffy, while the short-to-medium grains yield a stickier rice. Some short grain rices, such as the Italian Carnaroli and Arborio, carry their starches inside each grain and must be slowly coaxed out; the result is neither fluffy nor sticky but somewhere pleasantly between the two. Almost every package of rice will give you preparation directions. Follow them, and you'll have perfect rice every time (the basic proportions for making rice are one cup of rice to two cups of water, although with some kinds of rice this proportion differs). In most Asian kitchens, rice is thoroughly rinsed before cooking until the white, starchy liquid becomes clear. This is how I was taught to prepare rice. This, however, also eliminates

much of rice's nutrient value. Here is a partial list of some of the world's most well-known varieties of rice (many of which are available at supermarkets; others can be found at specialty food stores and at some online sources).

•**BAMBOO GREEN RICE** This is a short grain rice that is infused with the juice extracted from young green bamboo plants. It has a stunning color and is very aromatic with a green tea-like flavor.

•**BASMATI RICE** Any Indian rice dish is made with basmati rice. It is aged for a year or longer after harvesting. The aging process lends basmati rice a unique, nutty flavor, and it smells delightfully like popcorn while it cooks.

•**BHUTANESE RED RICE** (see Red Rice)

•**BROWN RICE** The difference between brown rice and white rice is that brown rice does not go through the milling process, which strips away the thin outer layer of bran that encloses each grain. Stripping away the bran also removes many valuable vitamins, minerals, and fiber, making brown rice a healthier alternative to the processed white version.

•**CHINA BLACK RICE OR CHINESE FORBIDDEN RICE** This is a short grain, high-gluten (a kind of protein that combines with starch) rice that makes it ideal for both sweet and savory dishes such as stuffings and desserts. The rice itself is very black, but when cooked it turns dark purple. Its high gluten content gives this rice a chewy texture. In ancient Chinese dynasties, black rice was prepared and served only to emperors and members of the royal court, hence the name "Forbidden."

•**FRENCH RED RICE** (see Red Rice)

•**GLUTINOUS RICE** Glutinous rice is a staple food in some areas of Southeast Asia, including parts of Myanmar, Laos, Thailand, and Cambodia. It is sometimes called waxy rice, sticky rice, or sweet sticky rice. This short grain rice comes in purple and white varieties and is often used in desserts. In Japan, it is called mochi rice and is used to make rice cakes. In Thailand, both the purple and white varieties are used in rice pudding made with coconut milk.

•**HIMALAYAN RED RICE** (see Red Rice)

•**JASMINE RICE** Extremely fragrant, jasmine rice is a long grain variety from Thailand. Like basmati rice, it has a distinct popcorn-like aroma during cooking, and comes out bright white. It is used in Thai and Vietnamese cuisines as well as in other South Asian countries.

•**KALIJIRA RICE OR BABY BASMATI RICE** The grains of this rice grown in Bangladesh are tiny and aromatic. It cooks very quickly and is ideal for making rice pudding.

•**MOCHI RICE** (see Glutinous Rice)

•**PAELLA RICE** This is a medium grain rice that is essential for making truly authentic Spanish paella. There are several varieties, such as Valencia or Granza, which are both highly regarded. Many people often substitute regular long grain rice when making this dish but the result is never the same. Paella is mainly about the rice used; the other ingredients are condiments.

•**PARBOILED RICE** If you haven't perfected your rice-cooking technique, parboiled rice is for you: it is a long grain rice that has already been steamed, then allowed to dry. Good results are consistent, even if you overcook it. Parboiled rice is used by many time-pressed families in the U.S. as well as in packaged foods and is available in almost any supermarket. It is even used in some Caribbean and Latin American dishes.

•**PINIPIG OR POUNDED DRIED RICE FLAKES** These unusual rice flakes are made from pounded rice and often dyed with vibrant colors. They are used in Filipino kitchens for making desserts and beverages. Vietnam also has a version of it.

•**POHA RICE** Basically, poha rice is parboiled rice that starts out as a puffy cereal-looking grain. The grains are pressed by stone rollers and then dried. It is commonly used in south Indian cooking for making both savory dishes and desserts.

•**PURPLE STICKY RICE** (see Glutinous Rice)

•**RED RICE** This chewy rice is cooked with its reddish-brown bran layer. It is aromatic and nutty, though it takes a bit longer to cook than white or brown rice. Try this rice in salads or alongside meat or fish. There are several varieties of red rice on the market today, including a French red from Camargue, American-grown Wehani rice, and Bhutanese or Himalayan red rice.

•**RICE PAPER** Rice paper is either round or triangular in shape and is sold in plastic bags or packages. The sheets are brittle, paper-thin, and are made from rice flour, water, and salt. After soaking rice papers for a minute or two, they are ready to be used for making all kinds of wraps, like the famous Vietnamese spring rolls (page 178).

•**RICE VINEGAR** This vinegar is made from fermented rice. There are three types: white, which is used in sweet and sour dishes; red, which is used in seafood preparations; and black, which is used as a condiment for dipping. Both Chinese and Japanese white rice vinegars are milder and sweeter than the distilled white vinegar found in most American supermarkets. They are used for making sushi rice. Chinese black vinegar can pack quite a powerful punch, so use it sparingly. If you can't find white rice vinegar, most recipes suggest dry sherry as a good substitute.

•**RISOTTO RICE** Rice used for making risotto can also be found labeled Piedmont rice, Arborio rice, or Carnaroli rice. These are plump, short grains that, when properly cooked, are able to absorb a great amount of liquid without becoming mushy. Semi-fino, or superfine, is the best of several grades, and Arborio is considered the best variety. Never wash risotto rice or cook over too high a heat, as this will eliminate the starch that gives risotto its creamy texture.

•**ROSE MATTA RICE** This reddish-brown parboiled rice comes from southern India where it is a staple. When cooked it is plump with a hearty, nutty flavor. Try this flavorful rice with soups, salads, or as a side dish.

•**SWEET STICKY RICE** (see Glutinous Rice)

Rosella (see Sorrel)

Rosemary Rosemary is a hardy annual herb with a strong, peppery, pine-like aroma and flavor. It is native to the Mediterranean but is also cultivated in Europe and in many American home gardens and on windowsills. Rosemary's most well-known partner is lamb—a marriage made in heaven—and chopped rosemary leaves go well with vegetables, beans, potatoes, and in breads and sauces. Whole stems are often used in stews and other slow-cooked dishes where they soften and infuse their flavor throughout the dish. Branches of rosemary are sometimes placed inside whole fish before grilling. Fresh and dried rosemary are available at most supermarkets.

Rose Water Fragrant and lovely, rosewater is made from rose petals. With its sweet, distinctively mild flavor, it is used in many Indian and Middle Eastern desserts and beverages. Rosewater candy with pistachio nuts is among India's favorite sweet treats. Rose water can be found at most specialty food stores.

Safflower Native to India, the dried edible petals of the safflower plant are used in the Philippines, where they are called casubha or kasubha, for adding color to dishes such as arroz caldo and paella. This usage is similar to that of using saffron to color the original Spanish versions of these dishes. Although safflower doesn't contribute the exquisite fragrance and flavor that saffron does, it is often substituted by less-than-reputable merchants and restaurants, much the way turmeric often is as well. Compared to the thread-like stigmas of true saffron, safflower petals are shorter, straighter, and thicker. Sometimes, safflower is referred to as bastard saffron. Safflower petals can be found at Asian specialty stores.

Saffron Saffron is the dried stigmas plucked from the centers of wild crocus, a fragile, white and mauve flower that grows in parts of Kashmir, the Middle East, and Europe. Gathering saffron is extraordinarily labor intensive, which makes it the most expensive spice in the world. Each stigma is harvested by hand and then dried. Saffron has an exquisite, delicate flavor and a golden reddish-yellow color that lends a gorgeous, glowing color to food. Saffron comes in powdered form as well. Don't be fooled by cheap saffron—the real thing always comes at a price. Many markets try to claim that turmeric and safflower are actually saffron. They're not. Look for whole saffron threads in small glass vials, and powdered saffron in individual packets, at specialty food stores, some supermarkets, and at online sources.

Sago Pearls Sago pearls are made from the starch extracted from the stems of southeast Asian sago palm trees. The starch is ground and pressed through a sieve. For export, the starch is formed into several sizes of round beads, similar to tapioca. It has a bland taste and is very glutinous, which makes it excellent in porridges, puddings, and bubble tea. Sago pearls can be found at Asian markets.

Sake Sake is fermented rice wine and is drunk extensively in Japan as an alcoholic beverage in addition to being used in cooking. Sake is either dry or sweet, like vermouth. Many people believe that drinking sake warm is the proper way to consume it, but experts say that this is only a way of masking the flavor of poor-quality sake. Sake is becoming very popular in the U.S., with tastings and lectures being frequently held in many cities. You can buy sake in almost any wine shop.

Salt Cod, Dried (see Dried Salt Cod)

Sambal Sambal is a multipurpose condiment combining several ingredients that is served either fresh or cooked in Indonesian, southern Indian, and Malaysian cuisines. It is usually served as an accompaniment to rice and/or as a side dish. There are several kinds of sambal, but the one most commonly used is sambal olek, the basic ingredients of which are chiles, salt, and brown sugar. Sambal is available at Asian or Indian specialty food stores and at some online sources.

SUGARCANE

Sapodilla Also called ciku or sapota, the sapodilla is a fruit native to the tropical Americas and is widely grown in parts of Africa, the West Indies, and Southeast Asia as well. The fruit is round or oval in shape, varies in size, and can weigh anywhere from 6 to 12 ounces. When ready to be picked, the sapodilla turns a sandy brown color and looks like a large potato. After it is picked and left to ripen off of the tree, the fruits' thin skins will yield to pressure, and the flesh inside will be yellow- to pinkish-brown, very juicy, and sweet. Fresh sapodillas are available during the autumn months; out of season you can find the fruit in cans at Asian and Latin American specialty food stores. They make a great addition to fruit salads and smoothies.

Sapota (see Sapodilla)

Seaweed A Japanese essential, seaweed comes in many shapes and forms and is often used as a thickener or to enhance flavors of your dish. The three commonly used seaweeds are wakame, nori, and kombu. All three have flavors of the ocean. Wakame is primarily used in making soups like miso. It is dark green and very high in protein, with a very pleasant flavor and an almost slippery texture. It is sold in dried form and must be soaked in water before using. Nori is dried seaweed that is pressed into paper-thin sheets. The sheets are used to make sushi rolls and to accent sashimi, and they're also often julienned and added to soups or used as toppings. Nori is black in color, and has a slightly chewy texture. Kombu is primary used to make stock, such as dashi, the base for miso soup. Kombu comes in large sheets. All three seaweeds can be found in plastic bags at Asian specialty food stores or some online sources.

Semolina Semolina is a durum wheat flour that is more coarsely ground than other wheat flours. It looks similar to couscous. Semolina is used for making puddings and gnocchi, as well as all of our favorite pastas. Semolina flour is available at most Italian markets, specialty food stores, and at some online sources.

Serrano Peppers (see Chiles)

Sesame These ancient seeds date back to Babylonia, where they were used in preparing breads. Today, every region of the world uses sesame in some form: the seeds come in different varieties—the unhulled seeds, which are either black or golden brown and white, and the hulled seeds, which are the most popular and used in cooking.

When toasted, sesame seeds acquire a delicious nutty, crunchy taste, making them perfect accents when sprinkled on biscuits and breads, and even over ice cream instead of chopped nuts. Black sesame seeds are used in Japanese and Chinese cooking, and golden sesame seeds garnish and flavor the traditional Turkish bread called simit, sold by street vendors. In Africa, sesame seeds are called benne seeds, and benne wafers—cookies made with a good amount of sesame—are delicious treats in the U.S., after having traveled to the south by way of African slaves. Sesame seeds are available in the spice section of almost any supermarket.

Sesame Oil or Gingelly Oil This ancient oil has been consumed for centuries—the amber-colored oil is extensively used in Chinese, Korean, and Japanese cooking, imparting intense sesame flavor from seeds that have been hulled and toasted prior to pressing. The lighter version is used in India for cooking and medicinal purposes. There it is known as gingelly oil or til oil. The amber-colored version of sesame oil can be found at Asian specialty food stores. Gingelly oil can be found at Indian specialty food stores.

Shaddock or Pomelo Shaddock is a yellow, pear-shaped fruit named for a 17th century British ship's captain. It is the largest of the citrus fruit family, and is native to Malaysia. It is believed to be an ancestor of the grapefruit. These giant, firm-fleshed fruits have less juice than a grapefruit and have a subtle, almost sweet-tangy flavor. They can be found fresh in season, during the autumn months.

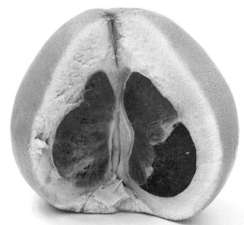

Shichimi Togarashi Sometimes called seven-flavors chile, this is a Japanese condiment. It is a spice blend made with a touch of chile along with sea salt, white poppy seeds, unhulled and black sesame seeds, flakes of nori, orange peel, and sansho (Sichuan peppercorns). As you can imagine, it is quite flavorful. It is often served as a condiment with rice or soup dishes. This intriguing spice can be found at Japanese and other specialty food stores.

Shiso or Perilla Leaves I love shiso leaves. They are warm and pleasant on the palate, with hints of cumin, cinnamon, and cloves. They are also beautifully shaped. The leaves are either green with a rough, crinkly edge, or purple and flat with a serrated edge. The green leaves are used with sashimi and sushi, while the purple ones are for pickling and coloring. Both kinds are delicious when chopped or julienned and added to steamed rice, salads, and soups. Shiso leaves are available at Asian specialty food stores and at some farmers markets.

Shrimp (Dried)  You'll see packages of tiny dried shrimp in Asian and Latin American specialty food stores. The shrimp should be pink. To prepare them for use in sambals, Chinese, and other Asian dishes, soak them in water for 5 to 10 minutes, pat dry with paper towels, and pound or grind them in a food processor. They're probably the ingredient you taste in Pad Thai that you can't quite put a name to. They are available at Asian specialty food stores.

Sichuan Peppercorns (see Pepper and Peppercorns)

Smoked Brie (see Brie)

Smoked Paprika or Pimentón (see Paprika)

Soba Noodles (see Asian Noodles)

Sorrel or Wild Rosella Sorrel is native to the Caribbean and is widely cultivated in Australia where it is known as wild rosella or hibiscus. The sorrel is scarlet red in color and has a crisp citrus flavor. It is not the same sorrel as the kind commonly used in salads. This sorrel is the kind used for making the many Caribbean specialty sorrel drinks, giving them a wonderful, rosy red hue. In Australia it's used for making tea and preserves. Sorrel can be found at some specialty food stores and online sources.

Soursop or Guanabana (see Cherimoya)

Soy Sauce Commonly used in Asian cuisine and sometimes referred to as thin or light soy sauce. Soy sauce is made from soybeans, roasted grains, and water and is naturally fermented and allowed to age. Today there is a slew of soy sauces of varying flavors and brands. All of these brownish liquids are salty and earthy-tasting and used as a seasoning or a condiment for meats, seafood, vegetables, and salads. Light soy sauce lacks the intense flavor and color of regular soy sauce because it comes from the first pressing of the soy beans. You can find soy sauce at your local supermarket.

Spring Roll Wrappers There are two varieties of spring roll wrappers. One variety is made from a combination of rice flour, wheat flour, and water, and can  be found in the frozen section of Asian markets. The other variety is dried; it is thinner and made from rice flour and water. (see Rice, Rice Paper)

Star Anise Native to China and Vietnam, these beautiful dried star-shaped fruits are from the Chinese magnolia tree. The tree is an evergreen that also grows in Japan, India, and in certain parts of the Philippines. Star anise shouldn't be confused with aniseed. Although they share a similar anise flavor, star anise is much more pungent, and suggests a combination of cloves and licorice. An essential ingredient in five spice powder, star anise is also used in many South Asian cuisines, especially with roasted meats. Whole, it also adds flavor to stewed and poached fruits (pears poached with star anise are an especially delicious combination); ground it adds unique flavor to pies and many other desserts. Star anise can be found in jars in the spice section of almost any supermarket and at specialty food stores.

Star Fruit Call it star fruit, five-finger fruit, or carambola, this exotic fruit grows on trees that can grow 12 feet tall and display clusters of small, lilac-colored flowers. Each fruit has five pronounced vertical ribs, so that when cut horizontally, each slice resembles a star.  Star fruit is fleshy and can taste from sweet to sour. Portuguese traders first introduced the fruit to Africa and South America from their travels in India.

In fact, carambola is a Portuguese word meaning "food appetizer." This pretty fruit can be eaten raw, made into beverages, or used in preserves that particularly complement grilled fish. Star fruit is available year round at specialty food stores.

Sugarcane The canes are long, grass-like stalks that are squeezed by machines to extract their light golden, sweet, refreshing juice. Native to Asia but widely cultivated throughout the Caribbean and Australia, sugarcane juice is a popular street drink. Many street vendors sell pieces of the stalk for chewing as a juicy snack, and the fibrous white stalk within the hard brown outer casing is often cut into sections and used as tasty, decorative skewers for barbecuing and frying everything from shrimp to chicken. Some online sources offer sugarcane stalks cleaned, cut, and ready for use at your next barbecue. Look for whole or chopped sugarcane stalks at Latin American and Indian specialty food stores and at some online sources.

Sumac Sumac is native to Iran and is also cultivated in Sicily, Turkey, and several regions in the Middle East. Sumac berries are harvested when their outer flesh is crimson. They are then sun-dried and ground into a powder. Sumac has a delicious, fruity, lemon-like tang and a light aroma of unripe limes. It's the main ingredient in a much-used Middle Eastern spice blend called *zathar*, which also includes sesame seeds and thyme. The famous Lebanese salad called fattoush (page 138), made with fresh herbs and pita bread, isn't really complete without the magic of sumac. It is available at specialty food stores.

Tahini or Sesame Paste Tahini is very popular in Middle Eastern countries. Simply, tahini is sesame seeds (see Sesame) that are ground into a thick paste. It is used as a dip for vegetables and other foods, as a spread, and is a must when making hummus (page 136). You can find tahini at almost any supermarket.

Tamarind Tamarind pods grow on large, shady trees. The fruit is hard and when unripe it looks green to light brown and tastes sour. When mature, the fruit turns into a dark brown, brittle pod. Inside the pod is a sticky, acidic-sweet pulp with hints of lemon containing many seeds. The pulp is eaten fresh, or used for making beverages, sauces, and marinades. When salt is added to tamarind, it is used for making chutneys and preserves, and is one of the mysterious ingredients in Worcestershire sauce. Tamarind is available in paste form, usually in small blocks, that must be diluted with water before using. In addition to the paste version, many West Indian and Asian markets also sell the whole pods, which are very sweet.

Tapioca Tasteless and starchy, tapioca is made from the root of the cassava plant and processed into small pearl-shaped spheres of different sizes, similar to sago pearls (see Sago Pearls). It is used mainly as a thickening agent, and is the basis of the ever-favorite tapioca pudding. You can find boxes of tapioca in almost any supermarket.

Taro If you've ever experienced a Hawaiian luau, chances are that part of your meal was poi. Poi is made of mashed taro, which is a tuber from a large-leaved tropical Asian plant. Most people don't think much of poi, but taro itself can be very versatile: it has a dense, nutty flavor and is quite good when deep-fried, roasted, or added to soups. The leaves can also be cooked and eaten. A good substitute for taro is sweet potatoes. Eating raw taro is not recommended as it can be toxic and harsh on the skin. Taro can be found at Hispanic or Indian specialty food stores.

Tea The word "tea" can have different meanings depending on which part of the world you're in. For example, in Guyana we referred to tea as our breakfast meal. Tea as most Americans know it is a beverage made by steeping tea leaves in hot water for a few minutes. All teas (white, green, black, and oolong) come from the same shrub (known as the Camellia tea shrub) which is native to southeast Asia, though it's now widely cultivated. White tea comes from the first buds of the Camellia plant—they are picked, steamed, and left to dry. The fuzzy white strands around the young leaf are what give this tea its white color. Green tea comes from the more mature leaves which blossom from the white buds. These leaves are picked, steamed, and dried. Well-known green teas include Gunpowder and Tencha. Black tea comes from leaves that have been fermented before being heated or dried—familiar black teas include Darjeeling, English breakfast, and Pekoe. Oolong tea has a flavor and color that is a mix of black and green tea, as it is produced from leaves that are only partially fermented. Flavored teas are made by simply adding various spices to plain tea—commonly added elements are cloves, cinnamon, jasmine, orange or lemon peel. My favorite is spiced masala chai.

Tejpat or Cassia Leaf, or Indian Bay Leaf
Tejpat leaves come from the cassia tree. They are sometimes called Indian bay leaves and are used in the cooking of northern India. These distinctive-looking leaves are slightly more slender than the more commonly used bay leaves, and have three noticeable veins. They have a unique, warm, musky aroma similar to allspice with warm citrus undertones. Tejpat leaves can be found at Indian specialty food stores.

Thai Basil (see Basil)

Thai Red Curry Paste (see Red Curry Paste)

Thai Red Pepper (see Chiles, Birdseye)

Tofu (see Bean Curd)

Tomatillo The tomatillo is a member of the tomato family, but the similarity stops there. Tomatillos are not actually tomatoes—they are smaller than most tomatoes, are light green in color, and come encased in a papery husk that must be removed before using. The flavor is sweet but tart and is divine in Mexican classics like salsas and moles, as well as in southwestern and Central American dishes. Tomatillos are available at some supermarkets and at Latin American specialty food stores.

Turmeric Turmeric is the rhizome of a tropical plant from the ginger family. It is used in Southeast Asian cooking, although it is native to India. The roots are quite pungent and bright yellow in color. There are two kinds of dried turmeric: Alleppy and Madras. Alleppy is the most commonly used, as its flavor is very close to fresh turmeric—it has a deep orange color and a floral flavor combining citrus and notes of ginger. Madras turmeric is generally used when color, not flavor, is called for. Ground turmeric is one of the essential ingredients in curry powder. For centuries, it has also been used in India for its medicinal properties. Turmeric is available in jars in the spice section of most supermarkets, at specialty food stores, and at some online sources.

Udon (see Asian Noodles)

Urfa Urfa, also known as Turkish pepper, grows in the cool climate of Turkey near the Syrian border. These chiles, which resemble red jalapeno chiles, have a sharp bite and are used in casseroles. Ground urfa can be found in plastic bags in Middle Eastern specialty stores or some online sources.

Vanilla A native of Mexico, the vanilla bean was used by both the Mayans and the Aztecs who used it to flavor a special drink prepared from water, cocoa beans, and chiles. Today, vanilla is cultivated in many countries: Madagascar, Indonesia, and Tahiti, among others. Some consider Mexican vanilla to be the most prized, but each country that produces it lends it a different flavor. Vanilla beans actually look like long, skinny, brown pods, and when they're harvested have neither fragrance nor flavor. These features only develop during the curing process. Most of us are familiar with vanilla and vanilla extract

when they are used in desserts, but contemporary chefs are discovering vanilla's affinity for enhancing everything from soups, sauces, shellfish, and more.

Vietnamese Mint, Laksa Leaf, or Rau-Ram Although it is called Vietnamese mint, this pungent, dark green leaf is not actually a member of the mint family, even though it strongly captures the essence and flavor of mint. It is a must for making the famous Vietnamese spring rolls (page 178), and in Thai, Malaysian, and Singaporean cuisines, particularly in soups. You can find fresh Vietnamese mint at Asian specialty food stores.

Wakame Seaweed or Curly Seaweed (see Seaweed)

Wasabi Wasabi is known as Japanese horseradish. Anyone who has had sushi knows that the little green paste pyramid at the edge of the plate packs a sinus-clearing punch. Wasabi is a knobby-looking green rhizome that grows in Japan near cold mountains. When collected, it is grated and dried into a beautiful jade-green powder. To make the paste you get on your sushi plate, it is mixed with water. Much of the wasabi we taste in the U.S. is not always completely authentic and is often colored for effect. For true, pure wasabi, it's worth it to mix your own using the powdered version. The leaves, flowers, stems, and freshly sliced wasabi rhizomes are all used to make a popular Japanese pickle called wasabi-zuke. Wasabi is available at Japanese, Asian, and other specialty food stores.

Water Chestnuts Water chestnuts are the edible tubers of the lily plant and are native to southeast Asia. They are brownish-black in color, making them look

almost like the hard-shelled chestnuts we like to roast in the winter. But these are very different: their skins are thin and papery and must be removed before using. In addition, any slight, tiny brown spots must be removed, or they will be fibrous and hard to chew. The flesh of the water chestnut is white and crunchy, and has a bland but slightly sweet taste. They're great sliced up and added to stir-fries (add them during the last 2 to 3 minutes of cooking so they stay crisp), and in salads and soups. Fresh water chestnuts are available at Asian and other specialty food stores. If you can't find fresh water chestnuts, the canned variety, either whole or sliced, is an adequate substitute.

Wattleseed Wattleseeds come from the Acacia tree, and while there are several kinds of Acacia, only a few yield edible seeds. The aborigines of Australia have relied on wattleseeds as a highly nutritious dietary staple for thousands of years. Processing the seeds to make them edible is an extremely labor-intensive job, which makes these seeds ten times more expensive than nutmeg. Wattleseeds have a unique and delicious flavor: they blend hints of chocolate, hazelnuts, mocha, and a coffee-like taste. The aroma is also slightly coffee-like. These wonderful, exotic seeds are primarily used for making desserts, cakes, and damper—the national bread of Australia. You can find wattleseeds at specialty food stores and online.

Wild Rosella (see Sorrel)

Wonton Wrappers These thin squares of dough are made with wheat flour, eggs, and water, and are used for enclosing a variety of fillings. They can be boiled and dropped into soup, or deep-fried and served as appetizers. Some cooks like to use wonton wrappers as a

ANNATTO SEEDS

CORIANDER SEEDS

WHITE PEPPERCORNS

INDIAN LONG PEPPER

STAR ANISE

SICHUAN PEPPERCORNS

ALLSPICE BERRIES

GREEN CARDAMOM

"shortcut" when making ravioli: instead of making homemade dough, the squares are stuffed with the desired filling and sealed closed, boiled like regular ravioli, and then sauced. They're usually in packages in the refrigerated sections of Asian markets.

Yellow Split Pea Flour (see Dhal)

Yucca and Yucca Flour (see Cassava)

Yuzu This yellow-to-orange skinned citrus fruit is relatively rare and highly prized. It is cultivated in Japan, but native to China. In Japan, the fragrant rind, as well as its acidic, tart flesh, are used in soups, desserts, teas, and aromatic sauces. Yuzu can be found at Asian and other specialty food markets.

Zedoary or White Turmeric Zedoary is native to Indonesia and is very popular in most southeast Asian cuisines and in European cooking. It is also known as white turmeric; in Thailand it is called *khamin khao*. In India, Indonesia, and Thailand, fresh zedoary is used in soups, salads, and curry dishes, and for making pickles. Fresh zedoary tastes like a combination of young ginger and green mango. The dried version is less acidic and a bit musky, with a hint of camphor. Zedoary is sometimes

confused with kenchur, which is also used as a substitute for ginger. It is available at southeast Asian, Indian, and other specialty food stores.

Zhoug This fiery spice blend is used extensively in Yemenite cooking. It can be made into a wet rub for fish or kebabs by adding fresh chiles, or made into a dry rub by adding dried spices. It can also be used as a condiment in sandwiches and pita bread, as well as on falafel and kebabs. Zhoug is made with cumin, black pepper, lots of chiles, and cloves. Zhoug can be found at specialty stores, or you can make your own blend following the recipe on page 139.

ONLINE SOURCES

If you have difficulty finding some of the ingredients mentioned in my recipes, these specialty stores and websites may be able to help.

Exotic Fresh Fruits & Vegetables

www.melissas.com
1-800-588-0151

Wild Game and Specialty Meats

www.exoticmeats.com
1-800-680-4375

www.lobels.com
1-877-783-4512

Ethnic Foods of the World

www.nirmalaskitchen.com
1-800-522-8505

www.cortibros.biz
1-800-509-3663

www.cubanfoodmarket.com
1-877-999-9945

www.williams-sonoma.com
1-877-812-6235

www.tienda.com
1-800-710-4304

www.wholefoods.com

www.wildoats.com

store.amigofoods.com

www.mexgrocer.com

www.amazon.com

INDEX

A

B

babaganoush, Algerian roasted garlic-chile, 101

balachan (trassi), 263

bamboo shoots, 263

banana(s):
blossom, 263
in South American passion fruit smoothie, 81
Xian five-spice, rolls, 201

banana leaves, 263
for plantain and pumpkin dukanoo, 56

barberries, 263–64

barfi (spiced carrot pudding), 215

basil, 264
in fragrant flower salad with passion fruit vinaigrette, 25
in Ju's curry noodle soup, 166
rice salad, floating market, 168

bay leaves, 264
for Turkish lamb kebabs, 121

beans:
black and white, Felix's Chilean pork soup with, 86
see also Chinese long beans

bean sauce, Hunan spicy fish with gingered black, 199

bean sprouts:
in classic Vietnamese spring rolls with spicy peanut sauce, 178–79
in Mr. Chu's pho, 181

beef:
Sichuan peppercorn-sesame, 195
soup (Mr. Chu's pho), 181
stew, Jasmine's, with kopan masala, 214
see also steak

bell peppers, in John's Greek village salad, 125

berries, luscious mango lassi with rosewater and, 148
see also specific berries

besan flour, 264

betel leaf, 264

bilimbi, 264

bitter melon, 264–65

blackberries, in Andean mora berry cheesecake, 94–95

blood orange(s), 265
Ayurvedic papaya and, salad, 153

Boston lettuce:
in Ayurvedic papaya and blood orange salad, 153
in fattoush salad with sumac, 138

breadcrumbs:
in Aunt Camille's spice-crusted rack of lamb with mashed ginger-lime sweet potatoes, 254–56
in North African spiced lamb burgers, 106
in pork cutlet with gingered snow peas, 226–27
in zucchini pancakes, 123

breadfruit, 265

Brie, 265
melts, pear and smoked, 251

brown sugar:
in Bahamian ginger beer, 40
in plantain and pumpkin spiced dukanoo, 56
-rum sauce, Aunty Daisy's Guinness Stout muffins with, 29–30
in spiced carrot pudding, 215
in tamarind chutney, 151

bush tomatoes (akudjura), 265
and asparagus frittata, 237

butter:
in Aunty Daisy's Guinness Stout muffins with brown sugar-rum sauce, 29–30
ghee, 277
in pear and smoked Brie melts, 251
in spiced carrot pudding, 215
tea, Tibetan, 209
in Trinni shark and bake sandwiches, 48–49

buttermilk:
jerk fried chicken, Clifford's, 45–47
in Rosalita's arepas con queso, 82

C

cabbage:
Chinese, 270
in Maya's Tibetan momos, 210

candlenuts (kemiri), 265

capers, 266
in John's Greek village salad, 125
and shallot sauce, tuna in grape leaves with, 127

F

G